WISBECH GRAMN

Name	Form	Date
T. Scott	L6S	Sep 78
Graham Stewart	L6S	
N R C Barnett	B6W	13/9/77
James Clayton	5W	11/9/78

Descriptive
Economics

Descriptive Economics

C. D. HARBURY

Professor of Economics
The City University, London

Fourth Edition

Pitman Publishing

Fourth edition 1972

SIR ISAAC PITMAN AND SONS LTD.
Pitman House, Parker Street, Kingsway, London, WC2B 5PB
P.O. Box 46038, Portal Street, Nairobi, Kenya

SIR ISAAC PITMAN (AUST.) PTY. LTD.
Pitman House, 158 Bouverie Street, Carlton, Victoria 3053, Australia

PITMAN PUBLISHING COMPANY S.A. LTD.
P.O. Box 11231, Johannesburg, S. Africa

PITMAN PUBLISHING CORPORATION
6 East 43rd Street, New York, N.Y. 10017, U.S.A.

SIR ISAAC PITMAN (CANADA) LTD.
495 Wellington Street West, Toronto, 135, Canada

THE COPP CLARK PUBLISHING COMPANY
517 Wellington Street West, Toronto, 135, Canada

ISBN: 0 273 36034 5

Text set in 9/10pt. Monotype Times New Roman, printed by letterpress, and bound in Great Britain at The Pitman Press, Bath

62—(B. 864: 48)

Contents

Preface

MOST teachers of economics would endorse the view that there is no one proper and generally accepted way of approach which should be adopted for all types of student. Some favour an immediate immersion into economic analysis, others a more gradual advance into theory tempered with an understanding of the economic problems of the modern world, but probably nearly all would agree that the approach needs to be varied for different levels of student.

There are, moreover, certain classes of student whose background knowledge of the main facts of economic life is so rudimentary that the full significance of economic theory cannot really be appreciated. Notable here are pupils in grammar and other secondary schools whose difficulty in understanding the abstract concepts which are the tools of economic analysis is quite generally recognized. The syllabuses of most of the examining bodies at the Ordinary level of the General Certificate of Education, and much, too, of that at the Advanced level, now call principally for a knowledge of the general structure and activities of the British economy. Experience suggests that it is too much to expect many students to appreciate, for example, the marginal productivity theory of distribution when they are barely aware of the occupational distribution of the employed population and of the activities of trade unions, or to understand the theory of the incidence of taxation unless they have previously learned what the principal kinds of taxes are.

For students of this type descriptions of the economy do exist, but nearly all are very limited in scope, and many of the remainder incorporate also substantial amounts of economic theory. Some of these texts are, of course, quite excellent and of undoubted value to certain grades of student, but equally unsuitable for those for whom this book is intended.

This book is offered, then, to first-year students of economics who are in need of a comprehensive and yet straightforward description of the British economy. Apart from an introductory chapter designed to explain in the simplest possible terms the nature of the main economic forces at work, the bulk of the book is unadorned by formal theory, though facts and institutions are described and relationships put the way they are because of the existence of underlying and implicit theoretical justification. It sketches the solid framework of the British economic system, emphasizing the main dimensions of the economy, in production and consumption, distribution and finance. It is designed to acquaint the reader with such matters as the main characteristics of the population, the chief forms of industrial organization, the importance of different types of economic activity and the structure of several leading industries, the activities of trade unions and of the Government, the distribution of income and wealth, the nature and functions of the principal financial institutions, and Britain's position in international trade. It has been designed, from the outset, either to be used by itself as an introduction to the subject, with the intention of being followed in due course by an advance into theory, or, for students who intend to adopt a mixed approach, to be used as a companion volume to one of the standard theoretical textbooks of which, it is to be noticed, some of the better ones have tended in recent years to be virtually devoid of descriptive material. It is offered in particular to candidates for the Ordinary level examination in economics for the General Certificate of Education of most examining bodies, and to those taking Advanced level papers also where the syllabus covers descriptive economics. It will also prove useful to candidates for examinations in economics of the Royal Society of Arts and other professional bodies, to adult education classes taking economics for the first time, and to intending university entrants who desire to provide themselves with a background description of the British economy before embarking upon the full rigours of economic analysis. Finally, it may, I believe, be especially valuable as an introduction for overseas students who, after an education in a completely different economic and social background, may find themselves faced with the need to study the economic organization and problems of Great Britain for a British degree course.

The book is thus, explicitly, an elementary one. It is largely founded upon statistical material, official and otherwise, though the use of tables of statistics has been almost completely eschewed in favour of a liberal scattering of charts, maps and graphs which, I believe, bring out with generally greater clarity the chief orders of magnitude, which are all that it is necessary to grasp.

Each chapter is supplied with exercises to which considerable importance is attached. They are designed to acquaint the student with some of the more familiar and easily accessible sources of economic statistics such as *The Times Business News*, *The Financial Times*, *The Economist*, etc., to foster the intelligent use of data, and occasionally to encourage the collection of original material of a simple kind. They provide, in addition, supplementary information on the most recent of trends, which cannot be dealt with in the book itself. They may be supplemented by further questions in my *Workbook in Introductory Economics* (Pergamon Press, 1970). Overseas students will also be able to substitute data from their own countries for many of the exercises.

Five years have passed since the third edition of this book. It has therefore become necessary to revise it radically to take account of all the changes that time has wrought on the structure of the British economy. The revisions are extensive, as any reader of the last edition will notice, and no attempt can be made to list them here. The basic nature and form of the book remain unchanged, but it may now be said to outline the characteristics of the British economy at the beginning of the 1970s.

Adequate acknowledgement of all sources is, for obvious reasons, an impossible task, and I have thought it best to avoid cluttering the text with footnotes and the charts with notes and sources which, while detracting from the essential simplicity of the treatment, would also mean very little at this stage to the type of reader for whom the book is designed. I am, none the less, overwhelmingly indebted to the numerous authors of books and articles whose findings have been incorporated, and I hope that for this reason they will accept this composite acknowledgement of gratitude. Only in the case of two of the diagrams which I have more or less directly borrowed can I make specific acknowledgement—in particular to the Controller of H.M. Stationery Office for permission to reproduce the chart of Fig. 4.8, which is taken from the Report of the Monopolies and Restrictive Practices Commission on the Supply of Electric Lamps (H.C. Paper 287, 1950–1), and to Professor P. Sargant Florence for the data for Fig. 3.2.

The number of my colleagues whose help I have been fortunate enough to receive continues to grow. I should particularly like to record that without the encouragement and advice of Professor A. Beacham, then of the University College of Wales, Aberystwyth, the first edition would never have been written. And had I not been fortunate enough to be able to draw upon the first-hand experience of teaching economics for the G.C.E. of Mr. R. Szreter, now of the University of Birmingham School of Education, the book would have contained the many deficiencies and obscurities which he pointed out. For those that still remain, the responsibility, of course, is mine.

The City University, London   C. D. HARBURY
September, 1971

CHAPTER 1

Introduction

THE reader of this book is about to view a panorama of the economic life of Britain in the second half of the twentieth century. He will see such things as the number of people who live in the country, how many of them go out to work, what sort of jobs they do, how they are paid, the amounts of the different types of goods and services that are produced, the way in which their production is organized and goods made available in the shops. He will see the chief regions in which industries are located, the number and size of firms in different industries, the principal financial institutions and their purposes, the nature of trade unions, the extent of unemployment, the main activities of the government and the chief taxes which it collects, and the sort of goods that are imported and exported and the countries with which this exchange is carried on.

By the time he has reached the last page, the reader should be in a position to answer most of the important questions about the British economy, which begin with the words: what? where? which? how many? how much? in what ways?—in fact every type of question except the majority of those which begin simply with how? or why? and which require an understanding of economic theory. Now, this is indeed a serious limitation, but it is an inevitable one which must be faced. Anyone who wants to learn the answers to questions about *how* the economic system works will have to go further in his study than this book will take him, and it is the author's hope that the knowledge he acquires will stimulate sufficient interest for him to wish to do so.[1] The question whether the advance into economic theory, which will help to answer the hows and the whys about the economic system, should be attempted simultaneously, or whether it is better to establish a solid background of factual material first, is not one to which a general answer can be given. As indicated in the Preface, the best way to approach the study of economics almost certainly differs for

[1] The reader might like to look at the author's own recent *An Introduction to Economic Behaviour* (Fontana/Collins, 1971), which will take him through the first steps in theory.

1

various kinds of student, and one can do no more than suggest that the expert advice of teacher or tutor be sought in each individual case.

For the reader who elects to concentrate first, then, on the descriptive side of economics before embarking upon theory, it is not possible to give all the answers to the specific hows and whys about every part of the economy in which he happens to be interested. However, it is possible, and indeed essential, to mention briefly the main economic forces which are at work, and to provide some very general explanation why the pattern which he is about to examine exists—why resources are employed in the particular uses that they are, and why the particular selection of goods and services produced happens to be that selection rather than any other.

SCARCITY

First of all, it is necessary to emphasize that labour, machinery, land and all the other resources needed for production, usually called "factors of production," are limited in supply, and that since the resources are limited, the goods and services which can be produced must, of necessity, be limited as well. This scarcity of goods in general does not, of course, imply that it would not be possible to produce as much of any individual item that is desired, but it does imply that there are not enough of all of them to give everyone as much of everything as he would like. It involves, above all, a problem of choice—of deciding how much of each commodity shall be produced, and the pattern of production prevailing at any time depends on the result of these decisions.

TYPES OF ECONOMIC SYSTEM

The nature of economics is to concern itself with the question of choice, and in this connexion it is useful to distinguish between three ways in which economic decisions can be taken.

The first is of major importance in some primitive societies, where virtually all production is undertaken within a self-sufficient family or tribal unit, and where tradition usually dictates how much hunting, fishing, cooking and other tasks shall be carried on and who shall do them. These societies are generally referred to as *subsistence* economies. They are characterized also by the absence of exchange between the individual families or tribes. They are, in consequence, barely relevant to a consideration of advanced economies in the modern world.

The second method of deciding how much of each and every good and service shall be produced is to leave it to the State to plan the allocation of all resources from a central office. Such economies are referred to as being centrally *planned*, or *command* economies. In a large industrial country there is fairly obviously a limit to the extent to which detailed central planning and allocation of resources can be made. The Soviet Union and other communist countries, however, may be said typically to make a great many economic decisions in this way.

The third possible method of deciding how resources should be allocated is of particular interest to us. For, in Britain, there are relatively few centralized governmental decisions in peacetime about what should be produced. That does not mean, of course, that it is a matter of pure chance what goods and services result. Indeed, if you think about the fact that when you go shopping you find, pretty well, what you want at prices which you expect to pay, it must be obvious that the system is not completely random. When you reflect further that the articles you purchase have been produced by persons with whom you have almost certainly had absolutely no direct contact, the whole business seems, perhaps, rather remarkable, and it deserves further explanation. Broadly speaking we can attribute it to the fact that the greater part of production is by firms which are owned and controlled by private individuals aiming to make profits. And it is the existence of this profit motive, together with the preferences of consumers, working through what is known as the price mechanism which determines the pattern of production. Systems in which economic decisions are made in this way are usually called *market* (or exchange) economies, and the way in which they function may be explained by the following simple illustration.

THE PRICE MECHANISM

Imagine, first, that all the firms in Britain were busily engaged in producing as much clothing as they could manage, and nothing else. Clearly such a situation is inconceivable for two basic reasons: one, that there would be more clothing than was required; and two, because there would be absolutely no supply of all the other goods that are wanted—food, drink, fuel, household goods and so forth.

The effects of this surplus of clothing and deficiency of everything else are not difficult to imagine. Individuals will not be willing to spend all their money on clothes, and in order to try and sell them the price will have to be lowered, while they will offer large sums of money for the other goods which they want but which are not at present being supplied. Furthermore, since all the clothing cannot be sold, and the price has fallen, the firms making clothing will find that their profits have fallen, and some of them may now even be making losses. What is more natural than that they should turn to produce those other things which are in great demand, and in which lines they see the possibility of making profits again? Moreover, in a sense, we can say that the new pattern of production reflects the preferences of consumers for less clothing and for more other goods, since by offering more money for these other goods they have made such production profitable and so induced producers in less profitable businesses to turn to them.

Even when the new pattern of production is established there is no reason why it should remain permanently fixed, for, if anything should happen to make one sort of good more profitable to produce than it was before, as for example, a change in people's tastes from eating marmalade for breakfast to eating lemon curd, then this will cause the demand for marmalade to fall and that for lemon curd to rise, so that producers will find that they can sell the latter good at a higher price while the price of the former has to be lowered. Provided that nothing has happened to alter the costs of producing either good, this means that the production of lemon curd is now more profitable and the production of marmalade less profitable. Some firms, therefore, may be induced to change over from the production of marmalade to that of lemon curd until the extra amount of curd now coming on to the market forces down the price, and profits are about the same in the two lines, so that no further incentive to change exists. In the end we shall once again find that consumers' preferences have guided production, through their effect on prices and profits, to a more satisfactory assortment of the goods which they want.

Although the working of the price mechanism, as described above, appears to solve the problem of choice and to allocate scarce productive resources in an efficient and satisfactory way, we must be careful not to jump to the conclusion that it is necessarily the best way of doing so. For one thing there are political considerations to be taken into account. Living in a society which is based on the freedom for individuals to make profits is different in many ways from living in one in which economic decisions are made by the government. While, as private individuals, we may have distinct views about which system we prefer, it is no part of the job of the professional economist to pronounce on what is right or wrong in this matter. Moreover, both planning and pricing systems fail in some ways to allocate resources efficiently. Under central planning, there is no certainty that the planners will select that combination of goods and services which best reflects the desires of the community as a whole. An economy working under a completely free price mechanism is similarly deficient in some respects. We shall return to consider the reasons for this shortly. Before doing so we shall have to probe just a little more into the nature of the forces which appear to drive production in a market economy, since, if price movements direct output, we ought to know what lies behind price movements.

THE MARKET

In economics, prices are thought of as being determined in a market. It is therefore important to explain that this term has a much wider meaning here than in everyday language. Any commodity which is bought and sold is considered as having a "market" in which the transaction is completed. It includes not only places like local vegetable and other street markets which exist in certain definite places, but the market for each good is, rather, any area within which buyers and sellers are in touch with one another. Consider, then, the individuals who enter a market wishing to do business. They naturally group themselves into two distinct categories, potential buyers and potential sellers. We are interested in buyers and sellers from the point of view of price determination, and it is at once clear that both the amounts which buyers are prepared to buy, or *demand*, and the amounts which sellers are prepared to offer, or *supply*, are related to the market price of a commodity. Let us look then, at the nature of this demand and supply as it might exist in a typical market, for instance, that for tinned peaches.

Demand

From the point of view of potential purchasers, the demand for a commodity bears a particular relationship to its price. It is not likely to be for a fixed quantity regardless of price but should be thought of rather as a *schedule* of amounts that would be bought, in a given period of time, at different prices. Such a demand schedule can be conveniently set out as two columns in a table as in the following example (which makes use of hypothetical figures).

Demand Schedule for Tinned Peaches

Price p	Number of Tins demanded per week
10	900
15	500
20	250
25	100
30	75

It is important to stress that the whole schedule of demand at different prices is *not* meant to represent quantities purchased at different times either in the past or in the future. It is rather a statement of the amounts which would be bought per unit of time if market price happens to be at different levels. In the case of the demand for tinned peaches which we are considering here, it is convenient to think of the quantities which might be bought *per week*.

We must now make an important observation about the nature of the demand for a commodity. For although it is certainly true that the amount purchased is liable to be influenced by factors other than the price of an article, if, for the moment, we deliberately ignore these it is characteristic of the demand for a commodity that people are prepared to buy larger quantities the lower the price. In the hypothetical demand schedule for tinned peaches, this is the case. At prices rising from 10p to 30p per tin the quantities which would be bought decline from 900 to 75. Two reasons may be offered for this. The first relates simply to the total number of purchasers entering the market. At a price of, say, £1 a tin only an addict or a very rich man will buy tins of peaches. But as the price drops nearer to that of other substitute foods and within the range of more and more people with lower incomes, so the quantities purchased may be expected to rise.

The second reason why demand tends to increase as price falls relates not to the total number of persons buying the good, but to the quantities bought by each individual purchaser. We can fairly reasonably assume that if someone buys something it is because he wants it, that is to say it gives him some satisfaction. Moreover, it is also reasonable to believe that the amount of satisfaction he derives from having *additional* units of a good tends to fall off the more of them he has. We do not have to be able to measure the abstract quantity of satisfaction to be able to see this. Assuming that I like tinned peaches, for instance, when I only have a single tin a week I enjoy them a lot. A second tin also gives me much pleasure, but perhaps a trifle less, the third tin certainly less, the fourth tin less still, and by about the tenth tin per week I am hardly enjoying them at all. Now the extent to which satisfaction falls off as consumption in a given period increases must clearly differ both from one good to another, and for different individuals. But a person cannot, in general, be expected to pay more for a commodity than what he considers it is worth to him. Hence, if the price is low he will tend to buy more than if the price is high.

We can summarize the arguments of the last two paragraphs in the following way. The difference in demand of 825 tins at prices of 30p and 10p in our example is most likely to be made up partly of more people buying tinned peaches, and partly of existing purchasers buying extra tins when they are cheap.

Supply

While the demand schedule represents the quantities that would be bought at different prices, we can also distinguish a supply schedule which represents a parallel relationship between price and the quantities which potential sellers are willing to offer for sale. A typical supply schedule, also hypothetical, might be as follows.

Supply Schedule for Tinned Peaches

Price p	Numbers of tins supplied per week
10	50
15	200
20	250
25	275
30	300

It may be observed that this schedule contrasts sharply with that of demand, in that it shows the amount supplied increasing with a rising price and dropping with a price fall. It is convenient to think of the reasons for this in terms of the changing amounts supplied by an individual supplier. For simplicity he may be identified as a manufacturer whose firm is engaged in putting peaches into tins. We may assume, then, that he would be prepared, in general, to produce a larger output if he were offered a higher price for his product. It is true, as we shall see, that this depends upon his costs of production, and that it is not always necessarily the case, but, it is more than likely that if he attempts to produce a higher output from his existing factory and machinery there will come a point at which it costs him more to do so. He will bother to do this only if the price is high enough to warrant it. He will, for instance, have to work in more cramped surroundings, and bottlenecks may start to interfere with the flow of production as some equipment reaches maximum capacity. He may also find that the prices of the resources which are used in production are themselves being forced up by the increased demand for them. For these and other reasons costs of production will tend to rise, and the supplier will only bother to expand output if the price is high enough to warrant it.

PRICE DETERMINATION

The supply and demand for tinned peaches have both been stated to be related to price. This being the case it is apparent that price can act in such a way as to balance supply and demand. Indeed, the purpose of this discussion is precisely to demonstrate that the activities of buyers and sellers tend to drive price to a level at which supply and demand are balanced. In our example it can be seen that the price at which such a balance exists is 20p. At this price consumers are prepared to buy 250 tins, which is exactly the same amount as suppliers are prepared to offer for sale. If the market price is in fact 20p there will be no disappointed buyers or sellers. Compare the situation with any other price. At 30p a tin, for instance, suppliers would be offering 300 tins, while only 75 would be bought. There would be an excess of supply over demand. What would happen to this excess supply? In conditions of free competition the disappointed producers with unsold stocks would be forced to cut their price in order to dispose of them. And it would only be when the price had fallen to 20p that supply and demand would be balanced.

Conversely, suppose the price were only 10p per tin. It would now be among consumers that we should find disappointment, since they would be prepared to buy 900 at that price, but producers would only be prepared to supply 50. The latter would soon find that they would get much more than 10p a tin if consumers were free to bid for them. In other words there would now be excess demand, forcing prices up. And, again, it would only be if prices rose to 20p that supply and demand would be balanced.

The previous paragraphs describe the working of the price mechanism. The argument is quite self-contained, but it may be alternatively represented in the form of a graph as shown below, which may help some readers to understand it. The axes of the diagram represent the

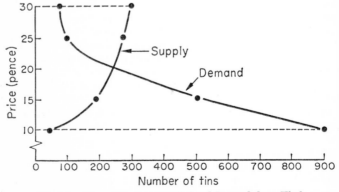

Fig. 1.1.   **Tins of Peaches Supplied and Demanded per Week**

price and quantity of tins supplied and demanded. The demand schedule appears as a demand curve, and the supply schedule as a supply curve. The price at which demand and supply are balanced is where the two curves cut. This is technically known as the "equilibrium" price. At higher prices the amount producers offer for sale exceeds the amount consumers are prepared to buy, and price tends to fall. At prices below the equilibrium price, the quantities demanded exceed those producers are prepared to supply, and price tends to rise.

THE RESPONSIVENESS OF DEMAND AND SUPPLY TO PRICE

We cannot take the analysis of price much further here. But it is useful to make the point that the demand–price and supply–price relationships which we have called the demand and supply schedules differ for different commodities. For some goods, changes in price evoke much larger changes in quantities supplied and/or demanded than for others. From the demand side one can say that, in general, a given change in price tends to have a greater effect on the quantity demanded the more substitutes there are for a good. For example, one might well expect larger variations in demand for tinned peaches, toffees or espresso coffee machines than for toothbrushes, sugar or vacuum cleaners. Moreover, the demand for a particular make or brand of commodity, such as a vacuum cleaner, tends to respond rather more to price changes than for the whole class of commodities, for the same reason of the availability of substitutes. It is also true that articles on which consumers spend only a small part of their incomes are inclined to be insensitive to price changes. It should be noted too that the demand for most goods is inclined to respond more to a change in price the longer the time you give it to do so, as the news spreads and habits are broken. If kippers became more expensive, relative to other things than they are now, people would probably still continue to buy nearly as many for a while, but would switch perhaps to smoked haddock or maybe smoked plaice(?) as time passed.

On the supply side, responsiveness to price changes is closely related to costs of production. If, for instance, costs do not rise much as output expands one can expect a greater increase in supply with a given price increase than if they do. And, again, responsiveness will tend to be greater the longer the time one allows for a firm to adjust itself to changing circumstances, and for new producers to enter or leave the industry. If we look for a moment behind the bare costs to the factors determining them, we might observe that this is very much a question of the techniques of production used in a particular industry, and of how easily extra resources can be attracted to increase output. Moreover, it is worth drawing attention to the fact that some industries are typified by conditions of *falling* costs associated with rising output, at any rate up to a point. In the production of motor cars, for instance, the average cost per unit tends to fall as production increases. It is on average much cheaper to produce 100,000 cars per annum than a mere 1,000. In such industries, where mass production techniques are employed, there are usually heavy initial costs of setting up factories equipped with high productivity machinery. Once these are installed, the cost per unit falls, since the initial outlay for equipment does not have to be increased as output expands. These *overhead* costs are fixed regardless of how much is actually produced, and are simply spread (or averaged) over larger or smaller quantities.

CHANGES IN SUPPLY AND DEMAND

The responsiveness of supply and demand to price changes for different commodities can be said to determine the extent to which market price will be affected if anything happens to change either one or other of them. It means, for instance, that a material drop in the supply of petrol is likely to induce significant increases in price in view of the difficulty of running vehicles on other fuel, even though it would be likely to cause some decline in demand as people economized in using their cars. A similar drop in the supply of pears, on the other hand, would probably have a smaller effect on price as people switched to buying more apples and other fruit instead. Conversely, a sudden increase in demand for a good, the supply of which can be readily increased without a substantial rise in costs, would not push up price as much as if the extra supply was only obtainable at much greater expense.

This raises the whole question of what causes changes in supply and demand themselves. Clearly this is a matter upon which generalization is not easy as it differs from good to good and from one time to another. It may, however, be useful to think of changes in the demand for a commodity as deriving from either changes in such things as people's incomes, tastes and fashions, as well as the size of the population and prices of other goods. Changes in supply, on the other hand, tend to arise from changes in costs of production which, in turn, follow such things as the development of new processes and techniques, and any changes in the prices of the resources used in production.

THE PRICE MECHANISM AND ECONOMIC EFFICIENCY

The price mechanism has been shown to involve a system for allocating scarce resources among competing uses, in which the relative values placed by consumers on different commodities and their relative costs of production play a part. As it is sometimes put, the price mechanism helps to answer the question of what shall be produced. Moreover, since people who value things highly tend to be prepared to pay for them, the system helps answer the question for whom are goods and services produced. We might also add that labour, machinery, land and all the other resources used in production, themselves have prices which have to be paid for using them, and which are also determined by supply and demand. And since business firms which produce commodities generally tend to try and keep their costs down by using the cheapest efficient combinations of resources, the pricing system also helps to solve the question of how to produce the goods in the economy. We may now end this chapter by returning to consider the question of how well the price mechanism does its job.

In trying to answer this question we would do well to remember that there are inescapable political and moral issues bound up with the evaluation of any economic system on which we can at best do no more than offer an opinion. We may, however, quite legitimately, observe that the prices which people are prepared to pay for goods and services in the market must surely bear some sort of relationship to the values that they place on them. With regard, for instance, to the sort of change in tastes, mentioned earlier in the chapter, from marmalade in favour of lemon curd, it would seem that, if the price mechanism brings about a shift of resources from marmalade to lemon curd production, there is at least something to be said for it. But, as previously indicated, this cannot be taken to mean that the pattern of resource allocation under a completely free pricing system is necessarily ideal or even better than under any other, for there are certain universally recognized deficiencies to be considered.

In the first place, it is essential for the system to be judged efficient that, when relative prices change, as for instance with a change in tastes, there should not be any artificial barriers which prevent production changes following suit. In terms of the demand and supply analysis which we have been using, if there is an excess of demand over supply at the ruling market price, then firms in the industry should be able and willing to expand output, or, if not, then other firms should be free to enter the industry and do so instead. This indeed is the function of *competition*. If the market contains so many producers that no single one, by itself, is large enough to exert an influence on price, and there is freedom of entry into the industry and a general awareness of demand and supply conditions throughout the market then competition is said to be *perfect*, and these results should follow. ("Perfect," it may be noted, is not used here in the sense of excellent. It merely refers to the fact that there is an extremely high degree of competition.) If the market for a product is, in some way, restricted, competition is said to be *imperfect*. In actual fact it is well known that in some industries there are only a few firms which, because of their size, are able to sell at a relatively high price by restricting production, and at the same time there are obstacles to entry, like the existence of patent rights, which restrict the entry of new firms.

Again, the pattern of prices ruling in the market depends partly upon the amounts of various goods which people are prepared to buy at different prices. But we cannot assume that everybody necessarily knows enough about all the goods and services available to be able to plan expenditure wisely. Disappointments follow some purchases simply because we do not fully appreciate all the characteristics of an article—how well some household appliance will work, or how suitable some fabric is for a particular purpose, for example. This may be due to sheer ignorance, misleading advertising or any other cause. There are certainly some goods and services, too, which benefit the community as a whole, like roads and prisons, and which would hardly be provided on an adequate scale if they depended on being sold to individual consumers. Moreover, the pattern of prices in the market depends on the goods which consumers decide that they need. But needs alone are not enough. It is amounts actually spent which are critical. In so far as the influence which each individual exerts upon prices is related to the amount which he personally has available to spend, the resulting pattern of prices depends also upon the distribution of income and wealth among individuals. It is true that the income a man receives is itself influenced by demand and supply considerations. One reason why an architect earns more than a bus conductor, for instance, is because the former's scarce special skill is more highly valued by society than the latter's. But unless we are prepared to say that we think the distribution of income is satisfactory, we cannot conclude that the pattern of prices ruling in the market reflects best the wishes of the community as a whole.

Finally, it is necessary to take account of the fact that the price mechanism takes time to bring about changes in the allocation of resources appropriate to changing economic and social conditions. There are, too, occasions and circumstances when the process itself takes so long that considerable dissatisfaction can result. In this connexion by far the most important deficiency is the apparent inability of a freely operating price mechanism to ensure anything like continuous full employment of a nation's resources. Clearly, if there are substantial resources lying idle for long periods, a lot more interest is likely to be shown in getting the idle ones busy than in allocating those at work. The forces which determine the size of the total output of the economy are rather different from those of an individual industry and they only began to be understood properly in the 1930s. Suffice it here to say that total output depends on the total amount of spending that consumers and businessmen do, and there is no reason for believing that a completely free pricing mechanism will happen to ensure the proper amount of it. Sometimes spending may be deficient and lead to unemployment. At other times the total may be excessive and lead to inflation—a tendency for the general level of prices to rise.

THE MIXED ECONOMY

We have now seen some of the advantages and disadvantages which the price mechanism possesses. A comparison of it and of a system of central planning would be, to say the least, interesting. We are, however, certainly not in a position at this stage to judge the respective merits of the two systems. Fortunately, too, we do not have to make a clear choice. It is hardly surprising perhaps to be told that Britain is really best regarded as a mixed economy and contains elements of both pricing and of planning. The price mechanism operates quite strongly in major areas of the economy, while, in peacetime, relatively little detailed central planning of production takes place. However, the government certainly does interfere with the flow of activity in many ways to try and make the price mechanism work more effectively, especially in order to influence the level of total spending and therefore the size of national output and to control inflation. Again, taxes are raised and the proceeds spent, not according to the wishes of consumers as expressed in market prices, but according to decisions reached in Parliament. Special action is taken, too, from time to time, by the government to encourage production in particular industries, such as those which produce goods for export, or in different regions, and for many other reasons, which will be encountered throughout the book.

This brief and solitary excursion into the theory of price formation and resource allocation has been made to give the reader some notion of the general reasons why the pattern of economic activity in Britain happens to be that which is described in the following pages, to which we may now turn.

The order of treatment adopted is by no means the only one which could have been chosen, and I shall not even try to claim it is the best possible. It seems to suit the material very satisfactorily, and it should in any case be followed rigidly by the reader, since he will find that many chapters assume a background of knowledge acquired in earlier ones.

EXERCISES

As explained in the Preface, considerable importance is attached to the exercises, which are designed, among other things, to acquaint the reader with some of the more familiar sources of data on economic matters indicated below.

1. *The Times* (*T.*). The Business News section is especially useful for financial data.

2. *The Financial Times* (*F.T.*) covers much the same ground as *The Times* but in greater detail.

3. *The Economist* (*E.*) often contains useful statistical material on recent trends.

4. *Economic Trends* (*E.T.*), a monthly publication of the Central Statistical Office, contains a number of valuable series, some in chart form.

5. *Annual Abstract of Statistics* (*A.S.*) is of inestimable value. It covers a tremendous amount of subject matter but requires very careful use.

6. *Britain, An Official Handbook* (*B.*) is prepared annually by the Central Office of Information, and is a most valuable reference book.

7. *The British Economy, Key Statistics* (*K.S.*) is published periodically by Times Newspapers Ltd. for the London and Cambridge Economics Service. It is exceptionally useful as a source for long-run trends.

8. *Monthly Digest of Statistics* (*M.D.S.*) supplements the *Annual Abstract of Statistics* for the most recent trends.

9. *Financial Statistics* (*F.S.*) is published monthly by the Central Statistical Office and contains statistics on money, banking, foreign exchange, the government's accounts and other financial institutions.

10. *Bank of England Quarterly Bulletin* (*B.E.*) is similar to *Financial Statistics* but more limited in coverage in some respects.

11. *Whitaker's Almanack* (*W.A.*) contains a large amount of relevant material and is published annually, usually towards the end of the year.

12. *The Statesman's Yearbook* (*S.Y.*) may also be useful if available.

13. *Progress Reports* issued monthly by the Information Division of the Treasury contain helpful commentaries on current trends. They can also be obtained from the Central Office of Information.

(*N.B.* Items 4, 5, 6, 8 and 9 are available through Her Majesty's Stationery Office.)

Parenthetical reference to one or more sources, indicated by the initials shown above, is given at the end of each exercise, but it will soon be found that a slight modification of the details asked for may, in many instances, enable the question to be attempted from a source other than the one recommended, if that is not available. (This may be particularly useful for overseas students, who want to relate the exercises to data for their own countries.) One or two other sources also are occasionally suggested. Finally, because information on different topics dealt with in the book is available for different geographical areas, it is only necessary to remind the reader that the title "United Kingdom" includes the territory of Great Britain and Northern Ireland, while the name "Great Britain" refers to the three countries, England, Scotland and Wales.

CHAPTER 2

Population

THE economic world in which we live is more than a little influenced by the number of us who are in it. The more people there are, the more mouths there are to feed, but at the same time the more hands there are to do work. It is sensible, therefore, to commence our survey of the economic life of this country by taking stock of its population. We are fortunate in that every ten years since 1801 (with the exception of 1941 when the war prevented it) the population has been counted in a full National Census, the last being taken in 1971. The Census is carried out by distributing to every house in Britain a form containing a number of questions addressed to the head of the household. These questions have varied considerably in the past, but today they include details of the age, sex, marital status, education and occupation of the individuals who are living there. The amassing and arranging of all this material, of course, takes a long time, and it is usually several years before all the information is published in a number of large volumes. Population details, therefore, are always a little bit out of date, but the speed at which any changes take place is normally so slow that this does not matter very much.

This vast amount of information available is very valuable, for it means that we can ascertain not only how many men and women there are in the country, but also how many there are of different ages, where they live and how they earn their living.

The Growth of the British Population

In 1801, when the first Census was taken, the total population of this country was roughly twelve million. Since then it has grown at an astonishing rate. As Fig. 2.1 shows, it had doubled itself in sixty years, and by 1861 there were over twenty-four million people. It had more than doubled itself again by 1951, when the population was over fifty million, and by 1971 it had mounted still further to about fifty-six million. It may seem puzzling at first that the number of persons living on this island should have multiplied so slowly as to reach only ten million after many thousands of years, and yet should increase at such a startling speed in a mere century and a half. A moment's reflection, however, reveals one simple reason—the more people there are the easier it is for the population to increase by a large amount. When there were only a small number of people, a doubling of them made only a small number more, while a doubling of ten million, as we have seen, raised the population by ten million.

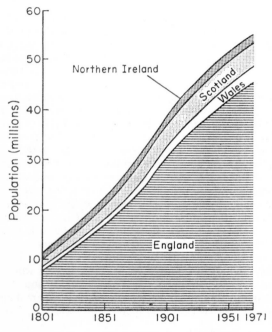

Fig. 2.1. Population of the U.K., 1801–1971

But this is only a mathematical reason, and while it helps to account for the great increases in the nineteenth and twentieth centuries, it is not a sufficient explanation; for a population of ten thousand persons which doubles itself every second generation will reach ten million in five to six hundred years, whereas we know that it took very much longer to reach this figure. Clearly we must seek some further reason which will explain why the population did not double itself in such a short period, and at the same time why the rate of increase was stepped up so rapidly about two hundred years ago.

One key to the problem is found in the decrease in the *death rate* (that is, the number of persons who die each year per thousand of the population)—and particularly in the infant mortality rate—which accompanied the great advances in industrial and agricultural techniques beginning about the middle of the eighteenth century. Before then, approximately seven out of every ten children born died before reaching the age of five, while today only one baby in twenty-five fails to live through those crucial years. Now, migration apart, the population will increase in any year if the number of births exceeds the number of deaths. But the fall in the infant mortality rate meant more than simply an immediate rise in numbers. For as more babies survived, so more of them grew up to have children of their own. The population, in consequence, continued to rise, and the rate of increase was stepped up. The fall in the death rate was probably due at first to more food and better living conditions, reinforced later by medical advances, new hospitals and improved sanitation.

It is also thought by some scholars that the earliest population increases were due more to a rise in births than to a decline in mortality. The available evidence is not strong enough to settle the controversy entirely, though it seems certain that birth rates did start rising in the eighteenth century as a result of social changes such as a fall in the age at marriage. In any event the increase in population was responsible for the concern expressed by Malthus in his famous *Essay on Population*, in 1798, that the population might become too large.

The Sex Ratio

Statistics of the size of the total population are very useful, but for many purposes they are insufficient, and we need also to know something about the relative numbers of men and women.

Taking the country as a whole, we are confronted with a considerable female predominance. There are about a million and a half more women than men, so that the former outnumber the latter by about 5 per cent. This is not the case for all age groups, however, and it is all the more surprising when it is realized that more boys are actually born than girls, and it is due to the fact that male death rates (including stillbirths) are higher, for almost all ages, than female.

Why women are able to survive better is not easy to determine. Biological factors seem to make them less susceptible to fatal diseases. But there are probably also social and economic reasons why they are less exposed to death. The most obvious case of men fighting wars and getting killed for their womenfolk was doubtless important in earlier times, though it can hardly be very applicable today. Any remaining influence arises more from the different nature of some of the work done by men and women, though this, too, is of much reduced significance. But it is still true that women are, by and large, employed in their own homes or in relatively safe jobs such as typists, teachers or fairly light factory workers. It is men, on the other hand, who are inclined to take the rather more dangerous jobs—such as in the docks and coal mines, as well as motor racing—where accident rates, and even industrial diseases, tend to be higher.

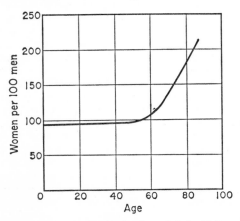

Fig. 2.2. **The Sex Ratio, Great Britain, 1969**
Number of Women per 100 Men

Somehow or other these factors combine to ensure that the male predominance in early life is reversed, though recent reductions in the number of stillbirths and the infant mortality rate have put back the age when it occurs. Women now begin to outnumber men in the late forties, but the difference only becomes really significant after the age of 70, when for every hundred men there are about a hundred and fifty women.

Marriage

Another matter of some importance is that of marriage. For the earlier men and women get married and the more of them do so, the greater the probable number of babies that will be born. In the country as a whole roughly every other person is married, but that does not mean that one has only an even chance of getting married. For this figure includes both babies and children who are too young to marry, and old people who have been widowed or divorced, as well as all those who, in fact, do not marry at all. The majority of marriages, in fact, take place between people in their twenties, though it is perhaps remarkable that nearly half of all brides get married before their twenty-first birthday. A great many people also marry later, of course, and the proportion of married couples in the total population rises with age, and in the 35–44 age group nearly nine persons in every ten are married. The increase in widowhood and divorces in later life lowers the number of married persons below 50 per cent of all those over 65.

The figures which we have been using relate to the present day, but it is interesting to compare the situation with that of earlier years. For there has long existed a tendency, associated with rising living standards, for men and women to marry earlier in life. Since the First World War, for instance, the average age at marriage has fallen from 28 to 24 for bachelor bridegrooms, and from 26 to 22 for spinster brides. This trend has brought with it, too, an increase in the proportion of the total population who are married from about two-fifths to a half.

Size of Families

The consideration of the frequency and age at marriage leads conveniently to a most important feature of the population—the average size of the family. We cannot assume that children will adopt the same traditions of family size as followed by their fathers and mothers. As a matter of fact, one of the most important changes in the structure of the population in the past hundred years has been in the size of the average family. A special Family Census was taken shortly after the end of the last war; it examined the size of families of couples who married in 1925, assuming that, after twenty years of married life, they would have no more children. Fig. 2.3 compares these figures of the numbers of families of different sizes with those for couples who married about a century ago, in the eighteen-sixties and seventies, in the middle of the Victorian era of large families. The change is quite startling. Whereas every fourth Victorian family had at least nine children, only one in every forty in the generation of families of 1925–45 was as big as that. And, while two out of every three of the latter group of families had no more than two children, in every five Victorian families there was one which was as small as that.

The reasons for this tremendous fall in the size of families are extremely interesting even if they are not all very well understood. They are clearly associated with increasing knowledge and use of contraceptive techniques, themselves reflecting other changes—the growth of the middle classes, who tend to have fewer children, the emancipation of women, and a changed attitude towards family life and parental responsibility from that of the nineteenth century.

These arguments should not be carried too far. The period since 1945 has shown signs that the downward trend in family size has not

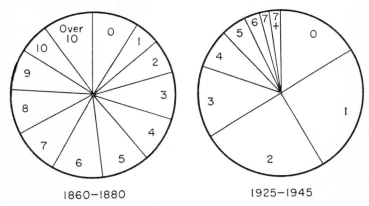

1860–1880   1925–1945

Fig. 2.3.   Size of Families: 1860–80 (England and Wales) and
1925–45 (Great Britain)
Number of Children per Family

only stopped but has even been slightly reversed. There has been nothing like a return to the Victorian family, of course, and one must be wary of reading too much into recent trends.

Shortly after the end of the last war, for instance, a natural increase in the number of births occurred, but, taken together with the trend towards earlier marriage mentioned above, it was impossible to know whether this would be offset by fewer children being born later on in married life. It is, however, now becoming fairly clear that this is not happening, and average family size is therefore thought to be rising slightly again.

It is worth adding a note to this discussion of family size about *households*. These are the units in which people live, and which therefore include all persons living together such as grandparents and friends. There are about 17 million private households in Britain and, during the century, their number has risen more rapidly than the population itself as a result of the decline in family size and other social forces. Changes in the number of households are of great relevance when questions of the availability of dwellings are under consideration.

Age Structure and Future Population Trends

Earlier in this chapter the increase in the population since the eighteenth century was discussed without mentioning whether the same trend is likely to persist. This is because we seem to have been passing through a rather difficult period and it is particularly hard to forecast what will occur. In the 1930s an actual decline in the population seemed reasonably close at hand, and this prompted the government to appoint a Royal Commission, in 1944, to examine the situation. By the mid-1950s, however, estimates of the future population had put the prospect of any decline back beyond 1980, and this view in turn soon gave way to forecasts of a fairly stationary population. Recent projections of current trends suggest rather that the population will continue to increase for the remainder of the century, and may even do so at an accelerating rate. Now, long distance forecasting of future population trends is a very complicated process, and past predictions have often been wrong. But it is useful to look a little more closely at the three main factors on which the size of the population depends—the birth rate, the death rate and the balance of migration movements.

1. MIGRATION

Emigration and immigration naturally have an effect on the size of the population. Throughout the nineteenth century migration was an important factor restraining the growth of Britain's population, since the range of opportunities, particularly in America, ensured that emigrants greatly outnumbered immigrants. Towards the end of the century immigration into Britain had also assumed sizable proportions, but in the sixty years after 1871 there was a *net* loss from migration of the order of 4 million. In the 1920s most foreign countries put up barriers to immigrants and the balance of movements between the Censuses of 1931 and 1961 was reversed to become one of a net gain of some half a million people. This figure, however, conceals the fact that, after the Second World War, Britain reassumed her traditional role as a country of emigration, chiefly to the Commonwealth (especially to Australia and Canada), and that this movement was offset in the late 1950s by increasing numbers of immigrants, again mainly from the Commonwealth (especially the West Indies, India and Pakistan). Net immigration in the 1960s began at a rate of about 150,000 per annum and prompted the government to pass the Commonwealth Immigration Acts, the first of which came in 1962, and which gave it power to restrict immigration from the Commonwealth. A sharp fall in the numbers of immigrants followed, and by the end of the nineteen sixties the balance of migration was a small net outflow from Britain.

2. THE DEATH RATE

The fall in the death rate, and particularly the infant mortality rate, has already been referred to as being partly responsible for the earlier great increase in population. In the present century, war years apart, death rates have continued to decline for all age groups. The improvement has been least for the over-fifties, where, therefore, the greatest future scope lies. But the number of years a baby born in 1970 can expect to live is, on average, 69 for a boy and 75 for a girl, compared with 49 and 52 at the beginning of the century.

3. THE BIRTH RATE

Migration apart, the main reason why uncertainty exists about forecasts of future population movements is associated with the birth rate. In the 1930s it had been running at only about half the nineteenth century level, and had given rise to predictions of a population decline, while it has since started to rise again in the period since the Second World War. Now, illegitimate births are about 9 per cent of the total, so that the number of babies born at any time depends principally upon three factors—the number of women of child-bearing age in the population, the proportion of them that marry and the number of children that each of them has.

The number of women of child-bearing age is fairly easy to predict for short periods ahead of 15 to 20 years, since it is largely determined by the number of girls under that age alive at the time. Hence, as family size declined after the Victorian era the numbers in the lower age groups also gradually fell. And, in particular, although the declining death rates helped to keep the population rising, the proportion of women in the critical child-bearing age group, 15–44, was declining. (See Fig. 2.4.) Any actual population decline was, moreover, additionally prevented by the offsetting tendencies, noted earlier, towards more and earlier marriages.

The difficulties of predicting completed family size have already been mentioned. The purpose of raising the subject again is merely to show how the past history of population growth affects inevitably also the prospects for future population size. Rapid increases in population in the nineteenth century produced large numbers of potential mothers 15 and more years hence. When the birth rate started to fall off, in contrast, there persisted a lingering decline in the numbers of women in the fertile age groups.

As far as the future population of the U.K. is concerned, therefore, we can say that reasonably accurate forecasts of the numbers of women aged 15–44 can be made for about 20 years ahead. But total population

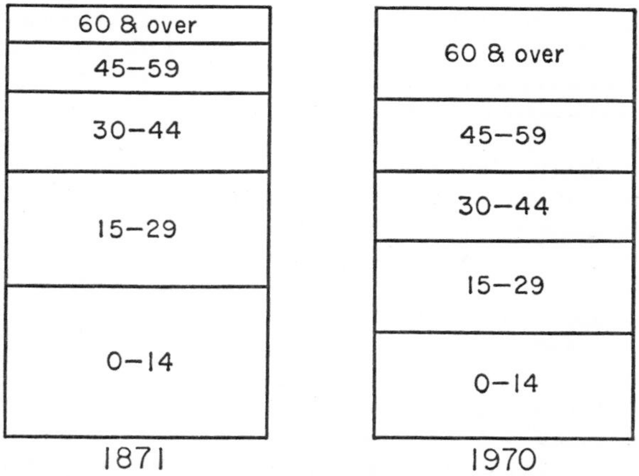

Fig. 2.4. **Age Distribution of Female Population in Great Britain, 1871 and 1970**

size can only be predicted if future family size habits are also known. Current estimates for the population of the U.K. at the end of the century are for some 66 million persons. But the frequency of revision of such estimates in recent years must lead us to treat them with caution.

Before leaving the subject of the age structure of the population, we may observe that while rising birth rates tend to increase the proportion of the population in lower age groups, falling death rates, on the other hand, tend to raise the proportions of older people. Referring again to Fig. 2.4, the contrast between 1871 and 1970 can be seen. At the earlier date only one woman in twelve was 60 years old or over, while in 1970 one in five was in that age group. This kind of consideration is most relevant to the question of providing pensions to people on retirement.

Geographical Distribution of the Population

The population of Britain is by no means evenly spread over the whole country. Turning back to Fig. 2.1, it is clear that England, Wales and Scotland have very unequal shares of the total population. If the population of each of these countries is related to its size, however, the inequality is even greater. For England has over four-fifths of the people and only just over half the land; Scotland has a third of the land, but only about a tenth of the people, and Wales has a tenth of the land but only a twentieth of the people. We can express these facts in another way, by saying that in England there are about nine hundred people per square mile, in Wales about three hundred and fifty, and in Scotland about one hundred and seventy-five.

The reasons for these very unequal densities of population are to be found in history. Differences in climatic conditions are partly responsible, but overwhelmingly the causes are economic. For all but a very select few of the population, where to live is decided for them by the whereabouts of the farms, factories, shops or offices at which they must work to earn their living. When Britain was an agricultural country, the population was fairly equally spread over the good farming land. With the growth of industry, however, the siting of factories became the predominant influence, and in order to understand the reasons for the present distribution of population, we must really look for the causes of the present distribution of industry. This will be dealt with in Chapter 4, and at the moment it is sufficient to recognize that, as industry grew in certain areas rather than in others, so the population of those regions increased.

The map opposite (Fig. 2.5) reveals the main features of the geographical distribution of the population, and shows the concentration around the principal centres of city life. At present something like four-fifths of the entire population live in urban areas and only one-fifth in the country. A good many even of the latter work in towns, and to emphasize the extent of urbanization it is worth recording that, in 1970, there were seventeen cities in Britain with more than a quarter of a million inhabitants, including at least three (London, Birmingham and Glasgow) with about a million or over.

But counting the city dwellers hides one important fact. Since the 1920s many of our largest cities have extended suburbs outwards so that they cover an area considerably larger than the actual city limits. In most of them one can go for twenty or thirty miles in the same direction without leaving the built-up area, and with no more sight of the country than an occasional park. These sprawling twentieth-century

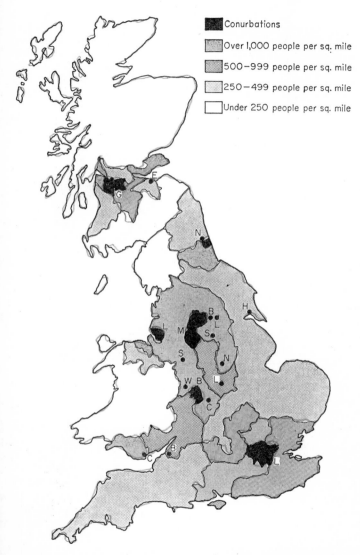

Legend:
- Conurbations
- Over 1,000 people per sq. mile
- 500—999 people per sq. mile
- 250—499 people per sq. mile
- Under 250 people per sq. mile

Fig. 2.5. **Density of Population per Square Mile, Great Britain, 1969**
Showing Conurbations and Towns with more than 250,000 Inhabitants

monsters have been given the equally monstrous name of conurbations. The Census distinguishes six of them in England (around Manchester, Birmingham, Leeds, Liverpool, Newcastle and London) and Clydeside in Scotland. Together they occupy less than 4 per cent of the land space in the country, yet they house more than a third of our people. Even more significant, perhaps, is that every sixth Englishman lives in the Greater London area and every third Scot is a Glaswegian. The Welsh also congregate in the south-east of the country and nearly two-thirds of them live in the adjoining counties of Glamorgan and Monmouth.

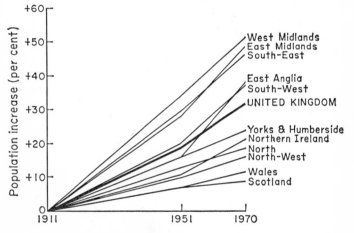

Fig. 2.6.   Regional Population Changes, U.K., 1911–70
Percentage Increases in Population

The background to this picture of an essentially urban society that modern Britain presents today is, of course, one of a prolonged rural exodus from the English villages, Scottish Highlands and Welsh hills into cities in the Midlands, the London region, the Clyde Valley in Scotland and elsewhere. But as rural depopulation has continued, the countryside has been gradually drying up and the towns have been growing by natural increase. Furthermore, behind the general trend there have also been important shifts in population between different urban areas themselves. In the main, such movements have been relative rather than absolute. Since the total population has been expanding, that is to say, there have not been many periods when major regions have suffered absolute declines in numbers, though the years between the two World Wars were exceptional in this respect in the case of Wales and Northumberland and Durham.

Fig. 2.6 brings out the main changes in the regional distribution of the population that have taken place since 1911. It shows that the greatest increases in population have occurred in the Midlands and South-east England, while Scotland, Wales, Northern England and Ireland have relative declines. These changes are the result of internal migration of workers and their families attracted by employment opportunities in the areas involved, and, as can be seen, the period after 1951 has not been materially different from that before that date in certain major respects. One difference which is not visible from the chart, however, should be mentioned. Since the Second World War it has been the medium-sized towns and the districts surrounding the large cities which have tended to grow most rapidly. This trend has been both helped and hindered by the Green Belt policy restricting urban spread. But, in an attempt to encourage some dispersal from the centres of heaviest concentration, the government passed the New Towns Act in 1946. By 1970 there were more than thirty new towns already in being or in course of establishment in Britain, with a total population of about three quarters of a million, the largest, at Basildon in Essex, having 100,000 inhabitants. All are designed as new, independent communities, containing industry as well as residential accommodation, and they have helped meet the overspill needs of cities like London, Birmingham and Glasgow.

The Working Population

We have investigated the size and geographical distribution of the population, and one last important question remains. In what ways do the people earn their living? But before answering, a distinction must be drawn between those who are "working", in the sense of being employed, working for themselves or as employers of others, and the rest of the community. For the size of this labour force is clearly of the greatest importance for the production of goods and services which everyone wants. Ideally it might seem best if there was nobody who did not contribute to the common pool by working, and the occupied population thus included every person in the country. But this is very far from being the case and only something like half of the total community are actually occupied.

How then do the remainder spend their time? Fig. 2.7 helps to provide the answer. First of all, about half are busy growing up. The school-leaving age ensures that the fourteen million boys and girls under 16 shall not undertake full-time work and they are therefore excluded from the labour force. Then, again, at the other end of the scale there is a similar, though smaller, group of those who are over 65. The major remaining group consists of housewives and other women who are busy keeping homes going. They are excluded from the occupied population, not because they do not work, but because they do not get paid a wage for doing it. True, they may be given a house-keeping allowance by their husbands but by no stretch of the imagination can they be thought of as being employed by them. Keeping house is an essential job, of course, and is often a full-time one, especially

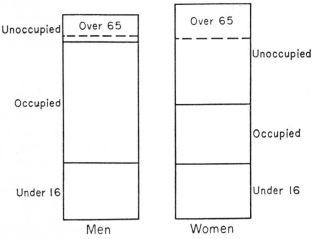

Fig. 2.7. **The Occupied Population, Great Britain, 1970**

when there are young children in the family, though one-third of the married women in Britain without children or with one child do in fact go out to work. It is, however, highly probable that some of the eight million married women of working age who stay at home could also if they wished, do outside work. We cannot tell how many of them there are. But only about half of the total number of women of working age are in the labour force, compared with 90 per cent of the men.

The rest of the non-working population are a mixed bunch and numeri-cally not very important. Some of these men and women of working age are idle rich, or even merely idle, and a few thousand more are in prison. But the majority fall into one of two groups of roughly equal size: those who stay on at school or are engaged in full-time education at universities or similar institutions, and those who are crippled or sick.

The occupied population, then, on whom the young and the old depend, comprises some twenty-five million persons. About two-thirds of them are men, and they are almost all between 15 and 65 years old. Nearly 90 per cent are employees, the remainder being employers and the self-employed.

Two important observations remain to be made. The first concerns the relative size of the working and dependent populations. For it is expected that the latter will become relatively larger in the next few years, leaving a relatively smaller population of working age to provide for them. There are two reasons for this, one relating to the old, and the other to the young. In the first place, the number of old persons will probably increase faster than the population of working age. This is really a consequence of the falling birth and death rates discussed earlier in the chapter, and as a result of which Britain acquired what has been called an ageing population, in which the proportion of those over 65 years has more than doubled in the last hundred years. It now stands at about 12 per cent, and will almost certainly increase somewhat for some years, until the upward trend in the birth rate since the Second World War has lasted long enough to check it.

It should be observed, however, that the young as well as the old are dependent on those of working age to provide for them. In so far as a rising birth rate helped to bring down the proportion of old people in the population, this cannot, initially, reduce also the proportion of all dependants. Moreover, the raising of the school-leaving age in 1972-3, and the tendency for more young people to undertake further education beyond the age of 16, prevent the size of the working population from increasing as fast as it otherwise would have done. The prospect, then, is one of little relief, as far as pensions are concerned, for some years, and of an increasing need for the provision of services required by the young—outstandingly, of course, education. And it is against this background of a declining proportion of persons of working age in the total population that current issues like postponing the age of retirement, and attracting married women back to work as their children grow up, must be seen.

The second observation concerns those who are physically fit and of working age, but who are not working because they cannot find jobs. These involuntary unemployed are included in the occupied population because, at the moment, we are interested in the proportion of the labour force in the various occupations and in the total number available for work. Since the end of the war the number of unemployed has

varied between about a quarter million and a million, representing about
1–3 per cent of the labour force. Before the war, however, unemployment was generally much higher and at one stage, in 1932, had risen
to over two and a half million, equivalent to one person in every five
in the entire working population. The proportion in some industries
and in certain districts was even higher. That so many people should
have been unable to find work was a grave condemnation of the
economic system. Most economists believe that the causes of this
breakdown are now understood and a recurrence can be prevented.
Certainly, unemployment has never been on the same scale since 1939,
and only time can prove them right or wrong. At the moment it is
another matter which concerns us.

The Problem of Classification

To find out how many people are employed in different jobs is a considerable problem. For if we were to count all the engine-drivers, the
fishmongers, the telephone operators, the wheelwrights, the dress
designers, the maltsters, the mechanics, the coppersmiths, the plumbers,
the market gardeners, and all the thousands of other specialists that
there are, we should very soon fill this book. In fact, the Census
Report itself includes such a book, and it makes very dull reading. What
we want is some method of grouping occupations into a small number
of categories which are easy to handle, and which bring out the most
important details.

There are two principal methods of classifying—

    1. Occupational Grouping—that is, grouping according to the
type of job that the individual performs.
    2. Industrial Grouping—that is, grouping according to the industry
in which the individual works.

Each of these classifications has its uses, and the one used may
affect the grouping of some workers. For example, a bus driver would
be both occupationally and industrially grouped as a driver in the
transport industry. But a lorry driver employed by a firm of chemical
manufacturers would only occupationally be classified as a driver;
under an industrial grouping he would be placed under the chemical
industry.

1. OCCUPATIONAL GROUPING

Let us start by examining the occupational grouping, since that is the
one which is probably more important to the individual. Fig. 2.8 (p. 32)
distinguishes the principal types of occupations. The English have

been called a nation of shopkeepers, but although approximately one-tenth of the working population is engaged in the business of selling (including here commercial travellers, sellers of insurance policies, stocks and shares, etc., as well as the actual shopkeepers), in fact, production workers are considerably more numerous and about a quarter of the labour force work in factories. Clerical workers are the next largest single category representing one in eight of the economically active. There are two other substantial groupings, each of which includes a fairly wide range of occupations. These are the service and recreation workers, and the professional and technical group. The former are distinguished by the fact that they provide some kind of rather personal service for our use or enjoyment. They include, for instance, firemen, hairdressers, maids, police and sweeps, but the largest single sub-category are the hotel and restaurant workers of whom there are close to a million in Britain. The professional and technical group also embraces many skills. It includes, not only architects, doctors, teachers and similar professions, but such others as draughtsmen, journalists and nurses. The other categories shown in Fig. 2.8—unskilled labourers and storekeepers, transport workers, builders, farm workers, administrators and managers, miners, and the armed forces—comprise the remaining third of the working population.

It is interesting to inquire how this distribution of occupations halfway through the twentieth century compares with earlier times; for the occupations of the people are a mirror of the economic state of the country. Without going into details concerning individual jobs, two outstanding features may be indicated. First, employment in agriculture has become of decreasing importance in Britain for the past two centuries, and today the proportion of the population working on farms is one of the smallest of any country in the world. Secondly, as agriculture declined the number of factory workers rose until, in this century, they too began to decline and the number of ancillary workers crept up. By the middle of the twentieth century there were more workers in the combined groups of clerks, personal servants, shopkeepers and the professions than in the factories.

2. INDUSTRIAL GROUPING

The grouping of workers by the industry in which they are employed rather than by the jobs they do is shown for the main industries in Fig. 2.9. Two principal differences between this and Fig. 2.8 should be mentioned. First, there is the disappearance of the clerks and the unskilled workers from the new classification, since there are, of course, no clerical or unskilled workers' industries. Clerks and labourers are employed by almost all industries and are, accordingly, spread among them. Secondly, there are the new "industries" of national and local government service which employ about one in twenty workers, and public utilities (gas, water and electricity) of about the same size.

The revised classification again points to the outstanding importance of manufacturing industry, which accounts for the employment of about

Fig. 2.8. **Occupational Grouping of the Working Population in Great Britain, 1966**

one-third of the working population. Second place is taken by the financial and professional group which occupies one in every seven of the labour force, and third by the distributive trades (retail and whole-sale shopkeeping) which account for one in ten.

One disadvantage of this broad industrial grouping is that it does not bring out a number of medium-sized but clearly defined industries. It is important to know, for example, not only how many workers are

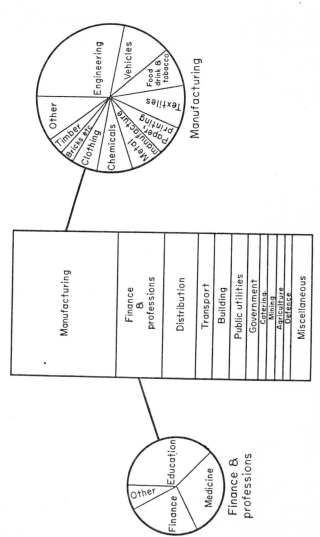

Fig. 2.9. **Industrial Grouping of Working Population, U.K., 1970**

employed in manufacture generally, but also how many are in the engineering industry, the textile industry, and so on. This is particularly the case with two of the main groups—manufacturing industry and the professions—the principal subdivisions of which are separately shown in the illustration.

1. *Manufacturing Industry*. The dominant position of the broad engineering group (including shipbuilding) is at once apparent, for it employs about one in every four factory workers. The vehicle, food and textile industries are next largest, each employing roughly one factory hand in ten, while paper and printing, metal manufacture (mainly iron and steel), chemicals, clothing, bricks, china and glass, and timber industries are sufficiently important to be separately distinguished.

2. *Finance and the Professions*. Roughly three and a half million persons are in this category, and it is here that we find many really interesting jobs. Education, medicine and finance account for 90 per cent of them, the last of these including insurance and banking.

Women's Occupations

Some idea of the work that women do has been suggested earlier in the chapter, but the information given by the Census on the division of occupations allows us to be more specific.

Outstandingly popular among women is office work. There are more than two million female typists and clerks in the country—twice as many as there are men. As far as industries are concerned, the manufacture of clothing is one of the leaders, for about three-quarters of the workers there are women. There is also a female majority in several branches of the textile industry, in the distributive trades and in school teaching, as well as in certain sub-groups such as chocolate manufacture, pottery and other light industries. But men are really rarest in a number of smaller occupational groups like nursing and office cleaning, and among cooks, waitresses and telephone operators.

The Rest of the World

Although we live on an island, we should avoid insularity, and it would be inappropriate to end this chapter without venturing abroad. Britain has a population of over fifty million, but the world contains three and a half thousand million people, over half of whom live in Asia. And a total population increase larger than the entire United Kingdom population is currently added to the world each year. Hence we must not lose perspective, for less than twenty out of every thousand human beings are British. It is rather like comparing Snowdon with Mount Everest. Seen close up the Welsh mountain appears large enough, but compared with the highest mountain in the world it dwindles to the size of a large hill.

EXERCISES

(For key to symbols indicating sources, *see* p. 14.)

1. Draw a chart showing the number of men and women in the total population of Britain in 1931 and at the last Census. Has the ratio of men to women changed in these years? (*W.A.*, *A.S.*, *B.*)

2. Find out how many children there were in your grandparents' family, and in your parents' family, and estimate how many you would like to have yourself. Assemble the information for the whole class, and calculate the average family size for all three generations.

3. On a rough skeleton map of Great Britain underline all towns with a population of over 100,000. What proportion of the total population lives in these cities? (*W.A.*, or the handbook of one of the national motoring organizations.)

4. What is the population of your home town? What was it twenty years ago, and a hundred years ago? Has it increased more or less than the total population, and can you explain why?

5. Find the number of persons engaged in manufacturing and the total in civil employment for the following years—
  1924, 1937, 1948, 1960 and the latest year available. Express the former as percentages of the latter. (*K.S.*, *A.S.*)

6. Prepare a simple form to be used in a small population census for the households in which all the members of the class live. Request information concerning age, sex, occupation and industry in which employed, for each member of the household. Tabulate your results and, wherever possible, compare with the national averages. (*A.S.*, *W.A.*)

7. Find out the number of married women in the labour force last year and express this number as a percentage of—
  (*a*) the total female labour force,
  (*b*) the total female population,
  (*c*) the total female population of working age.
Make the same calculations for ten years ago and compare your results. (*A.S.*)

8. Prepare a chart similar to that of Fig. 2.4, showing the age distribution of the population for 1981, as estimated by the Registrar General. How do the relative sizes of the working and dependent populations compare with those for 1970 and for the last year for which statistics are available? (*A.S.*)

9. List the numbers engaged in employment in the following categories last year and in the previous year. Calculate the percentage increases or decreases in each case.

> Agriculture and fisheries
> Mining and quarrying
> Manufacturing
> Construction
> National Government Service (*A.S.*, *W.A.* or *M.D.S.*)

CHAPTER 3

Industrial Organization

THE standard of living in any country depends to a very large extent on the amount and variety of goods produced and on the efficiency with which this production is carried on. We must, accordingly, devote some attention to the structure of our industry, looking especially at such details as the size of firms, the location of industry and the characteristics of a few of the most important industries.

In order properly to understand this structure, however, we must first set the stage by examining the legal and institutional framework within which this activity takes place. For there is little doubt that the character of production in this country has been much influenced by the background of institutions which has grown up with it and, in particular, by the forms of business organization. Briefly, we may distinguish two principal groups of these—

1. *Private enterprise*, by which is meant all business organizations, such as firms, which are owned and controlled by private individuals who take the responsibility for decisions and attempt to make a profit.

2. *Public enterprise*, by which is meant all organizations within industry which are owned or controlled by the State, which endeavours to operate them in the general public interest.

PRIVATE ENTERPRISE

The private firm has always been the most important form of business organization in this country. Here it is necessary to distinguish between a number of different types—

1. The One-man Business

The oldest and the simplest form of business organization is the one-man concern. The distinguishing feature of this type of enterprise is not that all the work is necessarily done by one man, though this may quite frequently be the case, but that the whole business is owned by one individual. The one-man firm is no longer of outstanding importance in British industry, but examples are still quite common in some trades such as farming and shopkeeping. We shall have something more to say about this type of individual enterprise when we come to examine the retail trade (*see* Chapter 6).

2. Partnerships

More common than the one-man concern, though still of relative insignificance in the whole of industry, is the Partnership. Whenever the size of a firm becomes too large for one individual to be able to supply all the capital needed to keep it going, the alternative of entering into partnership with a number of other persons, each of whom would contribute a share of the capital and take out a proportionate share of the profits, becomes an obvious solution. Under the law any number of persons up to twenty (or more in certain cases) may become partners in a business which may be set up either for a definite or for an indefinite period of time. Each of the partners has the right to take a share in the running of the business and each, acting independently, may bind all his partners to abide by any agreements he has made with outside persons. The risk of being in partnership with a person or persons who prove to be unreliable, unscrupulous or even merely inefficient is consequently particularly great, since the individual partners are all legally liable to meet the total debts of the partnership even if they have been incurred by the activities of another partner and not by themselves. There is no limit to this liability, which extends to the whole of the firm's debts, regardless of the amount of capital which the individual partners have originally contributed. Thus, for example, in a two-man partnership, where one partner supplies £5,000 of the original capital and the other only £500, if the partnership incurs net debts to the extent of £3,000 and the first partner becomes bankrupt and unable to meet any of the debt, the partner who put down only £500 in the first place may have to meet the whole of the £3,000, even if it means selling his own house and any other property in order to do so. The great risk involved in this kind of enterprise has quite naturally led to its dwindling in importance in this country. Today, partnerships exist only in relatively small numbers, generally where one or two members of a family are in business together and mutual confidence is strong. The local butcher's shop, run by father and son, is typical of this compact family partnership arrangement. It is also common among members of certain professions, such as doctors and solicitors.

Mention should also be made of one exception to the rule that all partners are liable to the full extent of the partnership debts. There are a few so-called Limited Partnerships, where any partners who do not take part in the running of the business are only liable to the extent of the capital they have put into it. Limited partnerships, however, are not a common form of business organization in this country since the advantage of limited liability is available to a far more attractive institution—the joint-stock company.

3. Joint-stock Companies

Public prejudice against the joint-stock form of organization in the eighteenth and nineteenth centuries was strongly influenced by the abuses of company promoters at the time of the South Sea Bubble, and it was not until 1855 that the great privilege of limited liability was made generally available. Today joint-stock companies are the most important form of business enterprise in Britain. Such companies must include the word "Limited" (or "Ltd.") in their name so that outsiders may know that the liability to meet the debts of the company is limited for every individual owner of the business (known as a *shareholder*) to the extent of the amount of capital that he or she has contributed or promised to contribute. The advantages of this privilege are very substantial and include—

(*a*) *Large amounts of capital* become much easier to raise. This follows from the reduced risk to the individual investor, who knows from the beginning what is the maximum amount of money he can lose, should the worst come to the worst. He will no longer be so afraid of venturing into business with other people whose names he may not even know; in fact, in many large companies there are thousands, and even hundreds of thousands, of shareholders, the vast majority of whom contribute only a minute proportion of the total capital of the business. Were it not for the privilege of limited liability it would be impossible to raise anything like so much money for one concern. The widow with a small inheritance and little business acumen, for instance, rarely dares to risk going into partnership with another person. She may, however, be quite prepared to acquire a small shareholding in one or more joint-stock companies without having to take any part in the management, secure in the knowledge that, even if the firm should go bankrupt, she would be liable only to the extent of her participation in the ownership of the capital.

(*b*) *Transfer of ownership* can take place with a minimum of formality. Since the reduced risk calls for a less urgent need for each shareholder to know the others intimately, it is a matter of comparative indifference who actually owns the capital of the firm. It consequently becomes possible for any shareholder to sell his share in the business to anyone else. This gives him the additional security, which is absent in a partnership, that if he is in urgent need of money he can always sell out immediately. The great importance of this transferability of shares in joint-stock companies has also given rise to the appearance of a very specialized market place where these shares may be bought and sold, called the Stock Exchange, about which we shall have more to say in a later chapter (*see below*, pp. 252-5).

The advantages which limited liability gives to the individual company are, as we have seen, considerable, but they are matched to some extent by an increased risk to others, especially companies and individuals who do business with it, and minority shareholders whose interests may be lost sight of in very large companies. There is also a risk that unscrupulous company promoters may fraudulently try to raise funds from the public for their own ends. In attempting to safeguard the community from these risks, the State has introduced a number of regulations concerning the management and publication of information about joint-stock companies in a succession of Companies Acts. These rules have changed over the years, but they also vary according to the type of company. There are two principal types to be distinguished: Public Companies and Private Companies.

The difference in privileges and restrictions of the two types will become clear as we proceed. It is useful, at this stage, however, to make the general observation that public companies are greatly outnumbered by private ones, but tend to be very much larger. There are approximately half a million companies in existence, but only a mere 3 per cent are public companies. On the other hand, the great majority of large businesses in Britain are organized as public companies. Some indication of their relative importance may be gleaned from the fact that over half of the total gross profits earned by all companies operating in the fields of manufacturing, building and distribution in recent years went to roughly two thousand of the largest public companies.

PUBLIC COMPANIES

The most important legal requirements for the formation of a company are—

1. The promoters of the company must draw up what might be called its "constitution." This takes the form of two documents which must be submitted to the Registrar of Companies in London for approval.

   (*a*) *The Memorandum of Association*, which must set out the name of the proposed company, where the registered office will be situated, and the amount of authorized capital, and must give some details of the objects of the company. This latter provision, originally intended to restrict the scope of the company's future activities, is now largely a nominal one, as present-day Memoranda give such very broad and general limits to the objects of the company that it is rarely precluded from entering into any kind of business at all.

(b) *The Articles of Association*, a document which relates to the internal constitution of the company, and gives such details as the rights of shareholders, the frequency of the company meetings, the methods of appointing company officers, and so on.

When these two documents have been submitted and certain other relatively minor requirements have been met, the Registrar may issue a *Certificate of Incorporation*, which grants the company the right of limited liability and, if it is a private company, authorizes it to commence business.

2. If shares are to be offered for sale to the public, the company must also file with the Registrar of Companies a *Prospectus*, giving all the financial details of the company, including its assets and liabilities, and its expectations of earning power. If a public company can raise its capital without appealing to the public, a *Statement in lieu of Prospectus* is filed. In the case of a public company, the Registrar of Companies requires to be assured of the success of the issue before he grants a trading certificate.

3. The above conditions, which must be fulfilled, are once-and-for-all measures in that, once it has complied with them, the company can carry on indefinitely. After incorporation, the most important general provision concerning public companies undoubtedly relates to the *publication of accounts*. For at the end of each financial year every public company is under an obligation to publish, and to file with the Registrar of Companies, a copy of its audited Balance Sheet and related documents which, taken together, enable a member of the public to obtain some idea of the financial operations of the company over the period. This provision is a vital one both for shareholders and prospective shareholders, and also for other firms who may wish to do business, perhaps on a large scale, with the company in question and who, by virtue of the limitation of liability which the company enjoys, might otherwise not be prepared to take the risk.

BUSINESS ACCOUNTS

The two main accounts which are prepared by companies are the Balance Sheet and the Profit and Loss Account.

1. *The Balance Sheet.* A business operates by virtue of the fact that it has various resources, or *assets*, at its disposal, and the balance sheet consists of a statement of the value of these on a particular day when the account is drawn up, together with all the *liabilities*, or financial claims on these assets. It is usual to distinguish between two kinds of assets. In the first place there are the *fixed* assets, like land, buildings, machinery and equipment belonging to the company, which are essential to the operation of the business. Secondly, there are the *current* assets, which are, so to speak, the results of the business operations, and which are regularly being changed into and out of cash. They include, in particular, stocks of raw materials and unsold stocks of finished products, debts due to the company from traders who have purchased its products, and cash itself. There is usually also a rather different type of asset called "goodwill," which is classed as fixed. While often difficult to put a value on, this is a financial estimate of the benefit deriving from a firm's reputation.

The balance sheet of a hypothetical company is shown below—

"Rubby Shops Ltd."

Balance Sheet as at 31st December, 19..

	£			£
Capital and Liabilities		*Assets*		
Issued Capital		Fixed Assets		
Ordinary shares . .	x	Land, buildings . .	x
Preference shares .	x	Machinery, equipment .	x
		Goodwill . . .	x
Loan from X.Y.Z. Bank	x		
Ltd.		Current Assets	
Current Liabilities		Stocks of raw materials .	x
Sundry creditors . .	x	Stocks of finished products	x
		Cash at bank . . .	x
	—		—
	£x		£x
	=		=

The liabilities of a business are the financial claims on the assets and, since all the assets must be owned by someone, the total liabilities must be the same as the total assets. On this side of the account, too, a twofold classification is usual. Here the main basis of division is between liabilities to proprietors, or owners proper, and liabilities to other creditors. The latter include, for instance, debts owed to raw material suppliers who have not yet been paid, together with other trade creditors, as well as to those, such as a bank, which have made loans to the business. A company is owned, however, by its share-holders, and the proprietary interest is represented by the Share Capital which they contributed.

A single balance sheet gives a picture of the financial state of a business at the time that it is taken. To appreciate better the company's prospects, however, it is necessary to compare a run of balance sheets over two or more years and to observe the progress that has occurred in the growth or depletion of its assets. Furthermore, a company's state may most usefully be studied with the help of the Profit and Loss Account.

2. *The Profit and Loss Account.*   Whereas a balance sheet relates to the position at a particular *point of time*, the profit and loss account is a record of a company's operations over a stated *period of time*, such as a year. As its name implies, this is a statement of the residual profit or loss incurred by the company in the period, and is derived by taking all the revenue earned by the firm and subtracting all the costs incurred in earning it. The extent of detail about costs shown in the published profit and loss account is naturally limited. Behind the summary figures given, we may distinguish between manufacturing costs, selling costs (including advertising and distribution, etc.), the costs of administration, and financial costs (such as bank loans). An example of a simple profit and loss account is given below. It is useful, especially from the viewpoint of managerial control of a business to consider separately the *Prime* costs (sometimes called variable or direct), which tend to vary directly with production, and *Overhead* costs (sometimes called fixed or indirect), which are less closely related to the exact volume of output.

Profit and Loss Account for the year ending 31st December, 19..

Expenditure	£	Income	£
Manufacturing costs (prime and overhead)	x	Revenue from sales . x	
Selling costs (distribution, etc.) .	x		
Administrative costs (salaries, office, etc.)	x		
Financial costs (interest) . .	x		
Depreciation . . • .	x		
Taxation	x		
Net profit, after tax, for year .	x		
	£x		£x

Examples of variable cost items are wages of operatives, raw material used and fuel consumed; while overheads, on the other hand, include managers' remuneration, office expenses, rent, repairs, the cost of research and development, etc.

The revenue side of the account may be subdivided according to the principal interests of the company, and before subtracting the costs mentioned above in order to ascertain the net profits for the period, it is usual to make a deduction for the *depreciation* of the assets of the business which are subject to physical wear and tear and tend also to become obsolete. Depreciation allowances are therefore provided in an attempt to measure the loss which is occurring. It is sometimes convenient to think of these provisions as building up sums which could replace assets at the end of their lives. This does not imply, of course, that all assets either will or should be replaced. And, in periods of changing prices and in face of uncertainty about the eventual life of an asset, it should not be expected that exactly appropriate sums are provided. In practice, the choice is between one of a number of alternative conventional formulae for allocating depreciation. A further deduction must then be made in respect of any tax due to the government, and the final residual represents profits available for distribution.

As with a single balance sheet, the profit and loss account for one year's operations may not afford a very good guide to a company's financial state. This is particularly true if a company has, for instance, been expanding its factory space or installing a lot of expensive equipment. Expenditure of this nature can pull down the profit for a particular year, but with new long-lasting assets it can imply higher profits in the future. Taken together a series of balance sheets and profit and loss accounts afford a much more useful picture. However, even these may be misleading for a number of reasons. The valuation of balance sheet assets and liabilities, for instance, may not be adequate. All assets are just not continually offered for sale on the market, and balance sheet assessments inevitably involve some rather arbitrary judgments about their value. Matters like this can be of great importance if comparisons between companies in different lines of business are attempted, by calculating their respective profits as a percentage of capital employed. Moreover, one should beware of assuming that conditions which gave rise to the satisfactory performance of a company in the past will continue unchanged in the future.

Finally, published accounts may not always contain as much detail as one would like to have for some purposes, but changes in the law in recent years have improved the position of shareholders by calling for the publication of further information about the company's affairs.

The Companies Act of 1967, for instance, added the requirement to publish figures of annual sales turnover, in cases where it exceeds £50,000, and the average number of employees, if in excess of 100, and certain other details.

PRIVATE COMPANIES

As we have seen, the great majority of companies are not public but private, and are relatively small in size. A private company is required to file its Memorandum and Articles, but in order to qualify for certain privileges, such as the freedom from the obligation to issue a Prospectus, the number of shareholders must not exceed fifty, and shares cannot be offered for sale to the general public.

Until fairly recent legislation, some private companies were allowed the highly valued exemption from publishing their accounts. However, this privilege was finally withdrawn in 1967, though, as mentioned above, small companies (below stipulated sizes) are excused the obligation to disclose information on sales turnover, employment, and certain other matters.

TYPES OF SHAREHOLDERS

A joint-stock company is a form of business organization in which a number of persons invest their money with the object of making a profit. The way in which profits are distributed among them, in the form of *dividends* on shares, and the extent to which they have a say in the control of the firm's operations, depend principally on the type of shares which they hold. There are two main groups—

1. *Preference Shares.* Holders of preference shares, as their name implies, have the right to share in the profits before other shareholders. As a rule, the dividend which they receive is fixed in advance as a percentage of the capital invested. Butlins Ltd., for example, have a 6 per cent preference share, and Pye of Cambridge Ltd., a $5\frac{1}{2}$ per cent preference share. Holders of these shares, therefore, receive dividends of £6 and £5.50 respectively, for every £100 worth of shares which they possess. So long as the company makes sufficient profits to meet the dividends of the preference shareholders, they all receive their dividends in full. Of course, if the company makes no profits at all, then there are no dividends paid (the dividend is then said to be "passed"), but even if the company has a phenomenally profitable year, preference shareholders get no more than their fixed rate of dividend.

Sometimes there may be more than one group of preference shares in the same company. Courtaulds Ltd., for example, have a group of

5 per cent first preference shares and another group of 6 per cent second preference shares. In this case, the 5 per cent preference shareholders are entitled to their dividend before the second preference shareholders, should the profits be insufficient to meet the dividends on both groups of shares. It should be noted that in return for this loss of priority for receiving dividends the second preference shareholders are offered a higher rate of dividend.

It is presumed, unless stated to the contrary, that preference shares are *cumulative*, i.e. when a dividend is passed, the preference shareholders are entitled to have the deficiency made up to them in a later year when profits may have risen. Usually, however, the cumulative right is evidenced by the name given to the shares. Courtaulds' shares are in fact called first and second cumulative preference shares.

Occasionally, a special type of preference share is issued by a company, granting the holder a fixed rate of dividend, but also giving him a small share of any additional profits. This type of share is called a participating preference share, and the fixed rate of dividend on it is usually less than on the ordinary preference share. An example of this is the Trianco Group Ltd.'s 6 per cent cumulative participating preference shares which entitle the holders to share in any surplus profits over and above their 6 per cent in any years when sufficient profits are made.

Preference shareholders generally have little say in the management of the firm, since their dividend is less dependent on the amount of profits than that of the other group of shareholders. Whether or not they are entitled to vote in the annual general meeting of the company is laid down in the Articles of Association but, as a rule, they have a vote only if their dividend has been passed or not met in full.

2. *Ordinary Shares.* Holders of ordinary shares (known also as *equities*) are distinguished from preference shareholders by the fact that their rate of dividend is neither fixed nor stipulated in advance, but depends entirely on the amount of profits made from year to year. If the business consistently makes a loss, then no shareholders receive a dividend, but if only a small profit is made, then the ordinary shareholders are not entitled to anything until all the preference dividends have been paid in full.

This residual nature of the dividend on ordinary shares may cause it to fluctuate considerably from year to year. The smaller the proportion of the capital of the business that is in the form of ordinary shares the higher is said to be its *gearing* ratio, and the more likely this is to be true. Consider the two businesses H.I.G. Co. Ltd. and L.O.W. Co. Ltd., in the example below. Both have the same profits available for distribution in each of two years and the same total of issued capital, but they have different gearing ratios. H.I.G. Ltd. is highly geared with 80 per cent of its capital in the form of 5 per cent preference shares and, when profits are doubled in a good year from £5,000 to £10,000, it would be possible to raise the dividend on ordinary shares sixfold from 5 to 30 per cent, after meeting the obligations to preference shareholders. L.O.W. Ltd., on the other hand, is low-geared with only 20 per cent

		£
H.I.G. Co. Ltd. Share capital	5 per cent Preference shares	80,000
	Ordinary shares	20,000
		100,000

	Allocation of Profits		Dividend Rate per cent	
	Year 1	Year 2	Year 1	Year 2
	£	£	%	%
Needed for Dividend on fixed-interest stock . . .	4,000	4,000	5	5
Available for Dividend on Ordinary shares . . .	1,000	6,000	5	30
Total . .	5,000	10,000		

		£
L.O.W. Co. Ltd. Share capital	5 per cent Preference shares	20,000
	Ordinary shares	80,000
		100,000

	Allocation of Profits		Dividend Rate per cent	
	Year 1	Year 2	Year 1	Year 2
	£	£	%	%
Needed for Dividend on fixed-interest stock . . .	1,000	1,000	5	5
Available for Dividend on Ordinary shares . . .	4,000	9,000	5	$11\frac{1}{4}$
Total . .	5,000	10,000		

of its capital in 5 per cent preference shares, and the same doubling of profits would only permit a rise from 5 to 11¼ per cent for the ordinary shareholders.

It should not be thought that the rates of dividend on ordinary shares necessarily fluctuate as much as this example suggests. For

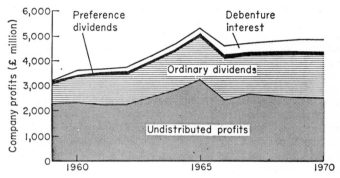

Fig. 3.1. **Company Profits, U.K., 1959–70**
Allocation of Income after Taxation

purposes of illustration extremely different gearing ratios have been used. It also does not follow that merely because large profits are available for distribution they will always be distributed. There are good reasons why a portion should often be retained in the business to provide a reserve in case profits should fall in the future, to replace machinery and other capital equipment, and to enable the company to expand its activities—for example, by installing new or bigger premises.

Fig. 3.1 shows the way in which company profits have, in fact, been allocated in this country during recent years. It should be noted that the relative stability exhibited there is largely the result of lumping together figures for all companies and thereby concealing variations from year to year in the profits (and dividends) of individual companies. Close inspection of the chart shows also that the share of company profits paid out, as distinct from being retained in the business, tended to increase especially towards the end of the period. This is partly the result of changes in the taxation treatment by the government of company income which, in the past, tended to discriminate in favour of undistributed profits (*see below*, page 198).

Before leaving the subject of ordinary shares, it should be pointed out that the rates of dividend declared on them are percentages calculated on the nominal value of the shares and do not represent the rates of profit which all shareholders receive on their capital. They may be the profit rates received by any original shareholders, who bought the shares when they were first issued. It depends upon the price which the person who became a shareholder actually paid for the shares. Tate & Lyle Ltd., for example, paid a dividend in 1970/71 of 10 per cent on each of their £1 ordinary shares. Thus, a person who possessed 100 of them received £10. It is, however, unlikely that many shareholders paid exactly £100 for 100 shares, so for them the rate of profit is not 10 per cent but something else. In mid-1971 for instance, the market price of one of these shares was in the neighbourhood of £1·50, so that someone buying shares then would have paid not £100 but about £150 for them. For him, the dividend represents the relationship between the £10 received and the £150 invested, which is not 10 per cent, but more like $6\frac{2}{3}$ per cent. It is usual to call this relationship between the dividend and the market value of the share the *yield* of $6\frac{2}{3}$ per cent to distinguish it from the dividend of 10 per cent.

DEBENTURES

Some part of a company's trading capital may be issued in the form of debentures. Debenture holders are sometimes confused with preference shareholders, with whom they have some common features, but a debenture is essentially different from a share of any kind, and may most properly be regarded as a rather special kind of IOU which the company gives to a person in return for a loan. The rate of interest on debentures is fixed in advance, such as the United Biscuit Company's 8 per cent debentures, holders of which have the prior right to receive this interest before any dividends are paid on preference or ordinary shares. In the event of the company going into liquidation (i.e. being wound up), again debenture holders, as creditors of the company, have the first claim (together with any other trade creditors) to return of their capital, and for this purpose their holdings may be additionally secured by a guarantee on any specific asset belonging to the company. Thus, when issuing the debentures, the company may pledge that a building or any other piece of equipment shall be attached to them so that, on winding up, that asset may be sold and the proceeds used exclusively for the repayment of the debt to the debenture holders. Other forms of loan capital include loan stock, which is less often secured by the company's assets. Sometimes the stock is *convertible*, which gives the holder a future right to convert it into ordinary shares.

DISTRIBUTION OF SHARE OWNERSHIP

The ownership of the shares in joint-stock companies is a matter of some interest, though the information on it is not complete. The bulk of ordinary shares are probably owned directly by individuals, though so-called "institutional" investors, such as insurance companies (*see below*, pp. 243 ff.) are substantial shareholders. Independent estimates suggest, however, that small (if increasing) numbers of persons own stocks and shares (probably no more than 5 per cent of the total population), but a very high proportion of the value of privately owned shares is concentrated in the hands of an even smaller number of large shareholders.

The importance of the distribution of ownership of ordinary shares is related to the control of the general policy of individual companies which is decided at company meetings. For "industrial democracy" is based upon the principle of one vote for every voting share held, and whoever can raise a majority of votes at meetings can therefore control them. There is no general rule concerning the proportion of total shares which must be held to give a controlling interest, as this varies from case to case. Certainly it must be rare, except in very small companies, that as much as 50 per cent is necessary. It may well be a good deal lower than that, especially if the company is a big one with a widely diffused share ownership. The absence of the majority of small shareholders from company meetings, not to mention the behaviour of those who do attend, may reduce the proportion of votes needed for effective control to a mere 10 per cent or even less in some cases.

It would be an over-simplification to think of the control of a company as being always associated with a single individual, as there is often a small group of shareholders who exercise control by acting collectively. In fact, it has been suggested that such a group is unlikely to act consistently together if it exceeds twenty persons, and a study of control in a sample of joint-stock companies from this point of view has been made. One of the results of the investigation is to reveal the very wide variation between different companies in the extent to which control may be in the hands of a small group. Fig. 3.2 shows for a select number of large companies covered by the inquiry how the largest twenty shareholders own such very different proportions of the voting rights in individual companies—from over 90 per cent of the voting rights in Consolidated Tin Smelters Ltd. to a mere 4 per cent in the United Molasses Co. Ltd. As stated earlier, some shareholders in these companies may not be persons, but institutions or other companies. Where one company holds shares in another this may lead to concentration of a rather different kind, and is discussed in Chapter 4 below.

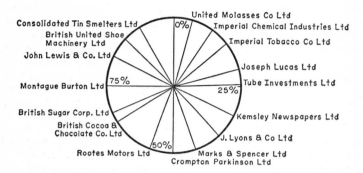

Fig. 3.2. **Ownership and Control in Selected British Companies, 1951**
Percentage of Total Voting Rights Held by the Largest 20 Shareholders
(The percentage is measured separately for each company, clockwise from
the "12 o'clock" origin)

MANAGEMENT

Everyday decisions concerning the management of the business are not taken by the shareholders, few of whom are, in any case, in possession of sufficient information to be able to do so, but are the concern of the *Board of Directors*. Directors are officials of the company, nominally appointed by the shareholders at the annual general meeting to run the company, though they may often be (and in the case of public companies are required by law to be) shareholders as well. In fact, the directors themselves in some quite large companies own a controlling interest and even a majority of the voting shares.

In practice, the degree of control that the shareholders exercise over their directors depends very much on the particular circumstances of the companies, but quite frequently it is extremely slight. This is especially the case where the distribution of shares is very wide and there are no really large shareholders, and it is largely the result of the small attendance at company meetings. Absentee shareholders have the right to appoint "proxies," or agents, to vote for them at the meeting, but as the directors are in by far the best position to secure proxies, they themselves are often armed with an overwhelming number of votes and can control the decisions of the meeting.

The directors elect one of their number to be Chairman and titular head of the company, and another (sometimes the same person) to be Managing Director, who is personally responsible to the Board of Directors for the running of the company. The Managing Director is nearly always a full-time appointment, and it is usually he who appoints the staff—Works Manager, Sales Manager and the other heads of department, each of whom is responsible through him to the Board. The other directors meet only infrequently, and many of them may be directors of several other companies at the same time.

4. Other Types of Private Business

A number of other relatively minor forms of business enterprise are to be found in Britain. Some of these are variants of the joint-stock company and include companies incorporated by Royal Charter, such as the Hudson's Bay Company.

A more important group are known as Co-operative Societies, the capital of which is provided, not by shareholders, but by the customers of the business who also receive the dividends. These are most important in the retail trade, and consideration of them will be deferred to Chapter 6.

PUBLIC ENTERPRISE

That part of the economy which is run by the State and is not in the hands of private individuals comes under the heading of public enterprise. The idea that the State should be directly responsible for some economic activity is certainly not a new one, though the scope of this activity has tended, on the whole, to increase during the present century. Public enterprise really consists of two rather different parts. First there are the activities which are run more or less directly by the government, or which are subject to parliamentary control and dependent financially upon the Treasury, like the Civil Service, the armed forces, schools, hospitals and so on. The second range of activities are known as the nationalized industries. They can most clearly be distinguished from the first group by the fact that they are, in contrast, organized in such a way as to enjoy a relatively high degree of freedom from control by Parliament and of financial independence. They tend also to produce goods and services for sale.

The present size of the public sector, as measured by the number of persons working there, lies somewhere between a fifth and a quarter of the labour force, while private enterprise employs the remaining 75 to 80 per cent. The activities under the direct control of the government are, however, dealt with in Chapter 8, and the discussion here is confined to the nationalized industries. The latter are responsible for the employment of roughly 8 per cent of the total working population. This figure may be compared with one of about 2 per cent at the beginning of the century, though the major part of the increase occurred in the period 1945–51, the first occasion that a Labour government had held a working majority in the House of Commons. The State had, however, taken over a number of activities previously performed

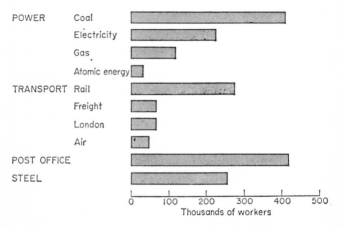

Fig. 3.3. Public Enterprise in Britain, 1970
Employment in the Major Nationalized Industries

by private enterprise before this, and though the Labour Party has tended to favour nationalization a good deal more strongly than the Conservatives or Liberals, there has not always been major political disagreement between them over the nationalization which has taken place. From 1951–64 and since 1970 a succession of Conservative governments did make arrangements for the return to private hands of certain sectors of public enterprise, but no wholesale programme of denationalization was undertaken. Nor did the Labour government (1964–70) extend the public sector significantly, except for renationalizing the steel industry.

Fig. 3.3. shows the extent of employment in the largest nationalized industries, and brings out their very different sizes. The Post Office is the largest employer of labour of the nationalized industries, but power

and transport together employ about two-thirds of the total. Other
public undertakings, like the B.B.C., the Forestry Commission and the
Bank of England are too small to be worth representing graphically on
the chart.

The precise forms of nationalization adopted for each industry have
not been identical in all details, and some of the more important will
be examined later. Certain features common to most, however, may
first be noticed.

1. COMPENSATION

The former owners of industries which have been taken into public
ownership have been compensated by a payment from the government.
The value of the businesses has generally been determined by the
market price of their shares at a prescribed date some time before the
decision to nationalize was put into effect. Owners have normally
been compensated by the issue of government securities bearing a fixed
rate of interest guaranteed by the Treasury rather than by cash.

2. THE PUBLIC CORPORATION

The most common procedure for nationalization adopted in this
country in the present century involves the setting up of a public
corporation to manage each industry. The form and functions of these
bodies differ somewhat from case to case, but in all of them there is a
close resemblance to the boards of directors of joint-stock companies.
The Chairmen and members of the corporations are all appointed by
the appropriate Minister (e.g. Minister for the Environment, Secretary
of State for Trade and Industry) but they are otherwise free from
day-to-day interference in the management of their affairs. Moreover,
none of the employees of the corporations is a Civil Servant. The
major appointments are generally made for a fixed period of years,
and matters of wages and conditions of service for the staff are determined independently from those in the Civil Service.

Until recently the Post Office was in a rather special category, being
run as a government department. But the essentially commercial
character of most of its operations has now been recognized, and it was
turned into a Public Corporation, similar to those of the other nationalized industries, in 1969.

3. THE CONTROL OF NATIONALIZED INDUSTRIES

Since public corporations are to a certain extent independent bodies,
which do not have to face a shareholders' meeting every year, it is

clearly important that they should have to submit to some control from outside. This they do in three main ways.

In the first place, each nationalized industry is subject to a considerable measure of control from the appropriate Minister. As already mentioned, he appoints the members of the boards of the corporations. The Minister is also generally given overriding powers of direction and a particular responsibility where such questions as development programmes and research are involved. Ministerial powers over specific matters are written into the individual Acts of nationalization.

While Ministers are not responsible to Parliament for the day-to-day administration of the nationalized industries, Parliamentary control can be exercised through the normal procedures. Particularly important in this connexion are debates on the annual reports of the corporations, and the work of the House of Commons Select Committee on the Nationalized Industries, which was formed in 1957 especially to examine their reports and accounts.

Finally, provision is usually made in each industry for the establishment of Consumers' or Advisory Councils. These are intended as vehicles for the consuming public to voice their satisfaction or dissatisfaction with the way in which things are run. The Councils are representative of the major classes of consumers, e.g. the Domestic Coal Consumers' Council and the Industrial Coal Consumers' Council. They are also sometimes appointed for different regions, as the twelve Consultative Councils for gas for each of the regional Gas Boards in England and Wales, and a similar number for electricity.

4. FINANCIAL OBLIGATIONS

It is in the nature of the nationalized industries in Britain that most of them are in part commercial undertakings, which have, in addition, certain social obligations which can interfere with commercial success. Such obligations arise, for instance, from a desirability accepted by many people to provide electricity, mail or transport services to rural areas at less than their full cost, or from the monopolistic positions which some of them hold.

The Acts establishing the nationalized industries charged them with general responsibility for efficient operation and called for the publication of an annual report and accounts. But the financial obligations imposed on the nationalized industries have changed significantly over the years as a result of an increasing awareness of the commercial side of their operations and of a desire to compare their performance with that of companies in the private sector of the economy.

Capital for development, for example, is provided by the Treasury and used to carry a fixed rate of interest for all the public corporations. But, though this is still generally true, recognition of the risks involved in overseas airline operation and in the activities of the nationalized steel industry, led to the introduction of a form of equity capital for them with, effectively, a variable dividend payable from year to year with fluctuating profits.

The original financial obligations laid on the industries were not very precisely set out in the Acts establishing the corporations and varied also somewhat from one industry to another (as, indeed, has actual performance), but they called in general for a policy for each industry to break even over an average of good and bad years. A substantial change in policy by the government, however, followed the publication of two White Papers in 1961 and 1967. The first of these led to the setting of a target rate of return on capital for each nationalized industry. The targets were arrived at after consideration of the social obligations of each industry and its past financial history. They varied from $12\frac{1}{2}$ per cent for the Electricity Boards to the same break-even formula for coal.

The 1967 White Paper was more concerned with *new* investment than with the average rate of return on capital employed. The main innovation at this time was the introduction of a so-called "test discount rate". The exact meaning of this term is beyond the scope of this book. The test discount rate is, however, supposed to be an approximate measure of the real cost of using capital in the public sector of the economy. It can be changed from time to time, reflecting changes in the cost of raising capital. Effectively, nationalized industries are required to estimate the profitability of any new investment project by comparing its expected rate of return with that which might be earned if the capital were used in the private sector. This does not mean that social obligations are completely ignored. The nationalized industries may include estimates of certain social benefits when making calculations of profitability using the test discount rate. In addition, in the case of the railways, the principle of distinguishing between services which could be judged solely by their commercial viability and others which could only be justified on social grounds was introduced by the Transport Act of 1968. This was followed by a "hiving off" policy—offering purely commercial parts of nationalized industries for sale to private enterprise to operate at a profit—after 1970. Thos. Cook and Son, the travel agents, nationalized in the course of the 1947 Transport Act as a subsidiary of the railway companies, was one of these.

The Major Nationalized Industries

1. POWER

There are four industries to be considered, coal, electricity, and atomic energy.

(a) *Coal*. The first major industry to be taken into public ownership in the wave of nationalization that followed the Second World War was coal. Indeed, the transfer, in 1947, of the 750 separate undertakings with a total capital of over £400 million and then employing about three-quarters of a million workers can be said to have been a major step in the nationalization of industry.

Members of the National Coal Board are appointed by the Secretary of State for Trade and Industry, who retains also a general power of direction over it. The Board has charge of the whole of the coalfields of Britain, and although it maintains a highly centralized organization it has, of necessity, to exercise control of its 300 odd collieries by grouping them into some eighteen areas. The N.C.B. has made both profits and losses in its years of operation, and it was set the objective of breaking even from 1961.

(b) *Electricity*. The key position which the supply of electricity holds in the economy of the country led to some State control as far back as the nineteenth century. The first major Act of nationalization, however, dates from 1926. This was when the Central Electricity Board was established, not to take over the generation of electricity, which was left in the hands of private owners and local authorities, but to construct and operate a national system of electricity transmission over the whole country. The National Grid, which was set up, now comprises about 6,000 route miles of electricity network, linking the most important generating and distributing stations and ensuring that, within limits, any area is adequately supplied with electricity even if its local generating plant is out of action or unable to fill its requirements.

Some twenty years later public ownership was carried a stage further when, by an Act of 1947, electricity generation as well as the National Grid was taken over by a new body—the British Electricity Authority (subsequently renamed the Central Electricity Authority). At the same time fourteen separate Area Electricity Boards were set up to organize the distribution of electricity in the different regions of the country. Each of these is separately required to publish an annual report and statement of accounts. Apart from certain rearrangements in Scotland, where electricity supply is controlled by two bodies—the North of

Scotland Hydro-Electric Board and the South of Scotland Electricity Board—the industry continued to operate in this manner for a decade.

The organization of the industry was criticized, however, by a committee appointed by the government (the Herbert Committee) in 1956, mainly on the grounds that too much power lay in the hands of the Central Authority. In order to meet some of these objections, certain measures for decentralization were introduced by an Electricity Act in the following year. The Area Boards were given greater independence and the Central Electricity Authority was dissolved. Its place was taken by two new bodies. Bulk generation and the responsibility for the Grid were given to a Central Electricity Generating Board, while an Electricity Council, which included in its members the chairmen of the twelve Area Boards in England and Wales, was given the task of generally promoting efficiency and co-ordination within the industry. The Council is also charged with making financial arrangements for capital needed for development and acts in an advisory capacity to the Secretary of State for Trade and Industry.

(c) *Gas.* The supply of gas for domestic and industrial purposes before nationalization was in the hands of some thousand private companies and local authorities. The distinguishing feature of the Gas Act of 1948, which brought about the transfer to public ownership, was that, at its inception, the structure laid down for the industry was in essence one of decentralization. It is true that a central body, the Gas Council, was set up as with the other public corporations, but the main responsibility for the supply of gas was entrusted to twelve almost autonomous Area Gas Boards from the outset.

The Gas Council is composed of the twelve chairmen of the Area Boards together with a full-time chairman and deputy. Its powers have been increased in recent years, though its control over the Area Boards remains slight. Since 1965 the Gas Council has become a trading as well as a co-ordinating body—joining the oil companies in the search for natural gas as well as buying and distributing it.

(d) *Atomic energy.* Nuclear energy provided about 12 per cent of Britain's fuel supplies in 1970, and the proportion is likely to increase substantially in the next few years. The public corporation responsible is the United Kingdom Atomic Energy Authority (A.E.A.) though its functions extend to other fields, such as desalination and atmospheric pollution, as well as to the defence aspects of nuclear energy. The A.E.A. was set up in 1954 and operates five stations producing electricity, including Calder Hall and Windscale. There are also other nuclear power stations which are owned by the various electricity authorities, but the A.E.A. itself is responsible for research and development in nuclear energy.

2. TRANSPORT

Most forms of inland transport, the second important industry to be nationalized after 1945, had already been subject to public control for a long time. The railways had always had to comply with a variety of State regulations and had even been run by the government for the duration of both the First and Second World Wars. And the traffic problems of London as early as 1933 had led to the creation of the largest public corporation established before 1939—the London Passenger Transport Board—in order to provide a properly co-ordinated system of transport there.

The transport industry that was nationalized by the Act of 1947, however, was by far the most complicated that had ever been transferred to a public corporation, and it also employed close on 900,000 workers. Disagreement between the principal political parties at the time was, moreover, strong and both the organization of the industry and the sections of it remaining in the public field have since been subject to more than one radical change.

The Act of 1947 made provision for a central body, the British Transport Commission, appointed by the Minister of Transport, and six Executives responsible for the management of the railways, road haulage, docks and inland waterways, road passenger transport, hotels, and London transport. All of these, with the exception of the London Transport Executive, were subsequently abolished by the Transport Act of 1953. At the same time the road haulage industry was largely denationalized, the plans for gradual acquisition of road passenger transport undertakings were abandoned, and the railways and remaining activities of the industry were taken directly under the control of an enlarged British Transport Commission, with specific requirements for the decentralization of railway management.

These arrangements continued until 1960 when the government, prompted by the serious financial plight of the railways, appointed a special Advisory Group to report on the organization of the Transport Commission. The main conclusion reached by the government after receiving its report was that the activities of the Commission were so large and diverse that it was virtually impossible to run them as a single undertaking. A new structure was, therefore, introduced by the Transport Act of 1962 which abolished the British Transport Commission and provided for decentralization and the replacement of the Commission by separate authorities: the British Railways Board, the London Transport Board, the British Docks Board, the Inland Waterways Authority, and individual boards to run British Road Services and each of the other subsidiary activities of the nationalized transport industry. The policy of distributing the functions of the British Transport Commission among independent bodies was continued by the 1968 Transport Act. The British Railways Board was reduced in size, and concentrated its activities on main line inter-city transport. At the same time, it was decided to award grants to British Rail for socially desirable unremunerative operations, so that it could cease making losses and be expected to pay its way.

The 1968 Act set up certain new bodies, among them a National Freight Corporation, which was given the task of integrating long-distance freight haulage by road and rail. Freightliners Ltd., a subsidiary of both the National Freight Corporation and of British Rail, was set up to market and control these services. Local Passenger Transport Authorities, with members appointed in the main by the local authorities concerned, were also established to co-ordinate all public transport within their areas. The Authorities appoint Executives to take over municipal bus undertakings, to run services themselves, and to arrange others as necessary with British Rail and other operators. The 1968 Act set up also a National Bus Company to take over nationalized bus services in England and Wales, outside London and the municipal undertakings. It operates more than 20,000 vehicles over the country.

Civil airlines. The British Overseas Airways Corporation (B.O.A.C.) and British European Airways (B.E.A.) were the last pre-war and the first post-war public corporations. They were established to develop a national civil airline service in circumstances which inevitably involve important political issues and impinge on international relations. B.O.A.C. is engaged in long-distance civil air transport and is in competition with other national airlines as a result of which its earnings may vary substantially from year to year. As mentioned earlier, the dividend which it must pay to the Treasury for the use of its capital is allowed to vary with its current profitability. B.E.A. runs services within the United Kingdom and Europe. Until 1961 it was given a statutory monopoly position in Britain, but since then it has had to face increasing competition from independent companies, such as British United Airways, on many domestic routes and in other services, including package holidays on the Continent.

3. THE POST OFFICE

As previously mentioned, the Post Office was run directly by a government department until 1969, when it was turned into a public corporation. It is, however, in fact the oldest of Britain's state undertakings, preceding the advent of the penny post in 1840 by nearly two hundred years. The Post Office accounts usually show an overall surplus, but this conceals the fact that the revenue from postal services has generally been large enough to cover the losses on telecommunications, especially telegrams.

4. STEEL

The last of the industries transferred to public ownership by the post-war Labour government was steel. Without doubt it was the most controversial of its nationalization measures. Delays were caused by the Conservative majority in the House of Lords, and the Iron and Steel Corporation of Britain did not come into being until 1951. The new corporation was, however, fated to have a short life, and by 1953 the succeeding Conservative government had brought in a Second Steel Act to denationalize the industry, and by the time a new Labour government committed to renationalization had been elected in 1964, all but one company had been sold back to private owners. The 1967 Iron and Steel Act then transferred the assets of thirteen major steel companies to a new British Steel Corporation, which is responsible for about 90 per cent of the total output of crude steel in Britain, leaving some 200 smaller businesses in the private sector.

Public Control of Private Enterprise

Apart from the fields in which the State has assumed direct responsibility for particular industries the government undertakes, in quite a number of ways, to exercise some lesser control over private enterprise, with a view to influencing the direction of its activities. These may, quite conveniently, be considered under two heads—

1. GENERAL PLANNING MACHINERY

Britain is not a country where detailed central planning of the allocation of resources plays a major role as it does in some others. As we have seen, something like three-quarters of the economy is in the hands of private enterprise and even the public sector is, to a considerable extent, decentralized. But increasing support has been forthcoming in recent years for some central exchange of information about individual industries which are interdependent, as well as for the formulation of some kind of national economic plan for growth, within the existing industrial framework.

In 1962, the government set up the National Economic Development Council (soon referred to as "Neddy") comprising representatives of public and private enterprise and of organized labour. It is served by a National Economic Development Office (N.E.D.O.). The Council was given the task of examining the economic performance of the economy and considering ways of increasing its rate of economic growth. A number of more specialized Economic Development Committees were also established for individual industries (known as "little neddies") to assist in considering problems and obstacles to growth on a smaller scale.

The change in government after the election in 1964 was followed by a movement to strengthen the economic planning machinery, and a new government department was created to formulate a long term economic plan for Britain with the help of a reconstituted N.E.D.C. In 1965, the Department of Economic Affairs published a National Plan aimed at producing about 25 per cent more in 1970 than in 1964 (an annual average growth rate of about 3.8 per cent). The plan was not, however, repeated, and in 1970 the Department of Economic Affairs was itself disbanded and its activities reverted to the Treasury, which set up a special National Economy Group to look after the country's overall economic strategy. The Treasury is, therefore, the government department responsible for forecasting future economic trends, and for formulating policies designed to achieve the main economic objectives at which the nation is aiming—in particular those relating to the rate of economic growth, the general level of prices, unemployment and the balance of payments (see below pp. 274–7). The Treasury remains in charge also of the traditional tasks of taxation and the control of public expenditure.

One aspect of economic policy which has been particularly important in recent years concerns movements in the general level of prices and incomes, and successive governments have attempted to exercise control over them in one way or another. Various means have been employed, including those known as monetary policy and fiscal policy, which will be discussed later in the book after we have dealt with the banking system and the government's own income and expenditure with which they are concerned. At this stage, we may note attempts by governments to exert some direct influence over income and price increases by the establishment of new machinery. In 1957, a Council on Prices, Productivity and Incomes was set up, consisting of three independent members to consider these matters. The Council produced four reports, but was not particularly successful and was replaced by a National Incomes Commission (N.I.C.) shortly after the formation of N.E.D.C. The new Commission was given the job of expressing a public view on pay claims in the hope that this might induce employers and employees to limit increases, but it was, in its turn, replaced after the change of government in 1964 by a National Board for Prices and Incomes. This last body consisted of members from both sides of industry and was charged with formulating, in consultation with N.E.D.C., both an *incomes policy* and a *prices policy*—setting some national target for income and price increases and pronouncing on specific cases of price and income changes referred to it by the government. The new Conservative government, elected in 1970, then wound up the National Board for Prices and Incomes, but announced its intention to set up a new Office of Manpower Economics to give it advice on the pay of certain public service groups. The future of any national prices and/or incomes policy for Britain is, therefore, at the time of writing, uncertain.

New machinery for economic planning at the *regional* level was introduced into Britain in 1965 with the establishment of two bodies for each of the major regions into which the country was divided. The Regional Economic Planning Boards consist of representatives of each of the main government departments in the region, and are given the tasks of co-ordinating their work and of drafting regional economic plans. They are assisted by Regional Economic Planning Councils, whose members are, in contrast, part-timers chosen for the range of interests and experience which they represent, including industry, commerce, local government and the universities. The Councils' job is mainly an advisory one, touching on both the formulation and implementation at regional level of economic plans.

2. MEASURES RELATED TO SPECIFIC PROBLEMS

State intervention in the private sector to deal with specific matters takes many forms and is carried out by various government departments. Thus, measures have been taken to influence such things as agricultural marketing, road transport vehicle licensing, the conditions of sale of goods and services, research and development, housing and industrial building, the settlement of wage rates, hours of work and industrial disputes, monopolies and restrictive practices, exports, imports, banking, rents and many other aspects of economic life. These measures have few, if any, common features and it is more suitable to defer consideration of them until we come to discuss the particular aspect of the economy which each concerns.

EXERCISES

(For key to symbols indicating sources, *see* p. 14.)

1. Go through the company reports which appear in the back pages of the past two issues of *The Economist* or *The Financial Times* and make three lists—
    1. Those firms which made *more* profit than last year.

2. Those firms which made *less* profit than last year.

3. Those firms which made losses.

Now do the same thing for exactly one year ago and compare the proportions of the total in each group.

2. Rank the major nationalized industries according to the size of the surplus or deficit each made last year. Then re-rank according to the percentage increase in surplus (or reduction of deficit) over the previous year. (*W.A.*)

3. Draw a graph, on the lines of Fig. 3.1, showing the allocation of gross company income into the following categories for the last ten years.

(i) Dividends and interest, (ii) Taxation and profits due abroad, (iii) Undistributed income after taxation. (*A.S.*)

4. Find out the names of the chairmen and, where possible, their salaries, of the following public corporations—

British European Airways
Electricity Council
British Overseas Airways Corporation
British Railways Board
Atomic Energy Authority
National Coal Board
Gas Council
British Steel Corporation.   (*W.A.*)

5. From the Trade and Professional section of *Kelly's Directory* for the district in which you live, find the proportion of the total number of businesses which are joint-stock companies in the following trades—

Coal merchants	Hotels
Furniture manufacturers	Laundries
Breweries	Paint manufacturers
Gown manufacturers	Builders

Would your results have been very different if you had been able to calculate the proportions on the basis of the value of total sales?

6. From the list of London share prices in *The Financial Times*, select any six companies which have issued preference shares, and list them in order of the fixed rate of interest which they pay. Now make a note of the price of the shares (i.e. the price you would have to pay to buy now), and calculate the yield you would receive if you bought £100 worth of them. (*Hint:* Divide £100 by the price of the shares. This gives you the number of shares which you will be able to buy. Now using the guaranteed rate of dividend work out how much you would earn each year on your investment. This is the yield of the share.) List them again in order of yield. Can you suggest any reasons why the order may not be the same?

7. Obtain copies of the latest annual reports of the Area Gas and Electricity Boards which operate in the district in which you live. Compare—

(i) The sizes of the two Boards.
(ii) The numbers employed.
(iii) Total income and total profit.
(iv) The change in output compared with the previous year.
(v) The change in prices charged compared with the previous year.

8. Find out the number of new companies registered in Britain last year, and the total number of companies in existence. Calculate the former as a percentage of the latter. (*W.A.*).

CHAPTER 4

The Pattern of British Industry

THE fundamental purpose of all economic activity is production. For prosperity depends, in the last resort, upon the quantity and quality of goods and services that are produced. The institutional framework within which this activity is carried on is, as we have seen, a complicated one. But there is a further aspect of complexity that we must face. This has come about as a result of specialization.

Specialization

There are two principal types of specialization. First, there is specialization between individuals. Our discussion of the occupational distribution of the population has already told us something of this. We have seen that some of us are clerks, others plumbers, electrical engineers, unskilled labourers and so on, with the result that it is very rare to find that any single article of consumption is produced entirely by one individual. Production is today a complex process because it is the result of co-operation between large numbers of individuals each doing a very small part of the job. Consider, for example, the production of a simple article like a reel of cotton. Who has "produced" it? Clearly, so many people have had a hand in it that it would be difficult to mention them all. In the factory where it is made there is the girl who operates the machine which spins the thread, but there are also the supervisors who watch that she works properly, the buyer who orders the raw cotton, the mechanic who keeps the machine working efficiently and the cleaner who keeps the place fit to work in, to mention a few.

It is this specialization, or division of labour as it is sometimes called, which accounts for our relatively high standard of living. For it is not difficult to appreciate that as every person concentrates on a single task, not only does he save time by not having to change from job to job, but he also develops greater efficiency in the one he stays at. Our society is far removed from the days of cave men, when it was really possible to say that one man did make a primitive hatchet. He simply looked for a pointed stone, which he sharpened by rubbing it against a hard rock, and fastened it to a stout stick with a length of strong grass. He and he alone made the hatchet. Specialization among individuals was almost non-existent.

The second type of specialization in our industrialized society today is between firms. This is, perhaps, slightly less complex, largely by virtue of the fact that there are, of necessity, fewer firms than individuals in the country. It is none the less as important as specialization between individuals in maintaining the efficiency of production. Our cotton-reel factory is dependent upon many other firms in different industries: on the planters who grow the cotton, on the factories that produce the spinning machines, the office equipment and everything else that the factory uses and, of course, on the farmers who grow the food without which the workers would starve. The degree of dependence on other firms naturally increases the smaller is the firm in question but, even in highly integrated large-scale industries, it is still very great. The finished product of one firm is often the raw material of another. (It is then referred to as an *intermediate* product.)

A very useful way of keeping the importance of this specialization in mind is to classify all productive activity under one of three basic heads: primary, secondary and tertiary production.

Primary production consists of all that economic activity which is a first step in the productive process; that is, the harvesting of the natural resources of the world, especially agricultural crops and minerals, which provide the foodstuffs and basic raw materials upon which other production depends. By and large, the producers who come under this head are in agriculture and mining. The cotton growers in our previous example of the reel of cotton are primary producers. So, too, are coal miners and wheat farmers, fishermen and oil prospectors. For coal, wheat, fish and oil are all instances of raw materials secured from nature rather than by any form of manufacture.

Secondary production is concerned with the later stages in the production of finished goods. Any industry which does not produce a raw material, but which uses a raw material to manufacture its own product is an example of secondary production. Thus the gasworks, which uses the raw material coal, the flour mill which uses wheat to make flour, the fish cannery which uses the fish, and the oil refinery which makes petrol from mineral oil, are all instances of secondary production. They *use* raw materials or foodstuffs in order to *manufacture* their products, but they do not actually produce the raw material themselves.

Tertiary production, which becomes particularly important in advanced industrial countries, concerns not so much the actual production of goods at all, but the provision of *services* which make it easier for other producers to get on with their jobs. Thus the transport industry provides a tertiary service; so do shopkeepers, clerks and professional workers. None of them is directly concerned with the actual production of a commodity, either at the primary or secondary level, though their activities greatly increase the efficiency of the country's economy.

The placing of individual workers into any one of the three categories is not always a straightforward matter, and arbitrary decisions have often to be taken, but Fig. 4.1 has been drawn up to show the general

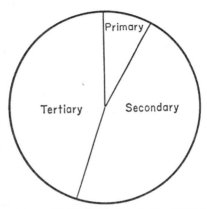

Fig. 4.1. **Types of Industrial Activity in Great Britain, 1971**
Percentage of Total Labour Force Engaged in Primary,
Secondary and Tertiary Production

pattern of production in this country. As is seen, secondary production, which comprises all manufacturing business, accounts for about one-half of total production, while primary production, comprising here only agriculture and mining, is much less important and is responsible for less than one-tenth. Tertiary services, on the other hand, are very nearly as important as secondary production; they include workers in transport, distribution, commerce, government and the professions, and cover the remainder of economic activity. This fact, i.e. that secondary and tertiary production account for such a high proportion of total production, is one indication of the advanced state of industrial organization in this country. This is clearly brought out if we compare the situation today with that of the past. Even one hundred years ago the proportion of the labour force engaged in primary production was about 25 per cent. Were reliable figures available for, say, three hundred years ago, the contrast would be much more striking. At that time agriculture was almost the only important industry, and the proportion of the labour force engaged in primary production was correspondingly higher. Manufacturing business was still rare and in those days, before railways and cars, transport was difficult and the numbers in government service and the professions were much fewer. Employment in secondary production was the first to grow with the Industrial Revolution. Later, tertiary activities expanded, and in recent years have even gained some ground from secondary production. It is, of course, the great increase in the degree of specialization which is largely responsible.

In this chapter we are concerned, in the main, with primary and secondary industries. Some mention is made of a number of tertiary activities, but one of the most important of these—distribution—is of sufficient interest to merit a chapter to itself.

The Structure of British Industry

Our knowledge of the distribution of the labour force (*see* Chapter 2, Fig. 2.9 and accompanying text) has already given us some idea of the importance of different industries in the economy of Great Britain. This general picture may now be expanded and clarified further. For the government makes a habit of collecting information relating to each industry and publishing it in a Census of Production. We are able to use these statistics to verify our knowledge of the industrial groupings. The Census figures are also a better guide to the relative significance of different industries, since they are concerned not only with numbers of workers but also with the value of output. Although the results measured in either way are not very different, the latter method is safer because some industries can employ comparatively few workers and yet produce a relatively valuable product, and vice versa. The chemical industry, for instance, is one such, and employs about 6 per cent of the manufacturing labour force, while the net value of the chemicals it produces is more like 10 per cent of total manufacturing output. The clothing industry, on the other hand, also employs about 6 per cent of the labour force in manufacturing industry, while the net value of its output is only 3 to 4 per cent of the total.

Fig. 4.2 is based on the Census of Production and shows the relative importance of the chief industrial groups according to the value of their net outputs. Again, we find engineering in the leading position, with an output nearly a quarter of the total value of manufacturing production. Some distance behind are food (including drink and tobacco), vehicles, chemicals, paper and printing, textiles, metal manufacture (largely iron and steel) and other industries as shown.

The Census is not nearly so comprehensive in its coverage of non-manufacturing industry, which is, therefore, not shown in the chart. But the value of output of the building industry is about half-way in

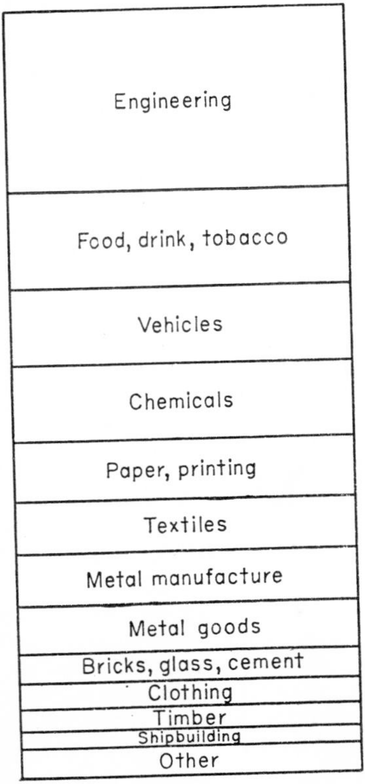

Engineering

Food, drink, tobacco

Vehicles

Chemicals

Paper, printing

Textiles

Metal manufacture

Metal goods

Bricks, glass, cement

Clothing

Timber

Shipbuilding

Other

Fig. 4.2.   **Manufacturing Industry, U.K., 1968**
Relative Importance of Different Industries by Value of Output

size between engineering and food, drink and tobacco, while mining would come between clothing and bricks, glass and cement.

Industrial Change

It is difficult to stress too strongly that the structure of industry is always changing. It is especially important to do so in this book because we are constantly looking at the economy at a particular time, taking a snapshot of it, as it were, using an instantaneous exposure to arrest movement. Some idea of the changes which have been taking place can be obtained by comparing the situation at different times. Fig. 4.3 does this for 1958 and 1970, with 1963 as an intermediate year as well, though it must be noted that, because of the length of time between the two dates only broad orders of magnitude should be distinguished. The diagram is drawn up on the basis of the level of output in each industry, after making allowance for changes in the value of money. The figure also shows the average increase for all industries, and we can use this to help distinguish three broad groups—

Rapidly expanding industries, where output rose considerably more rapidly than the average.

Expanding industries, where output rose at much the same rate as the average.

Declining industries, where output rose considerably less than the average, or not at all.

1. *Rapidly Expanding Industries.* The two major industries in this group have been the pace setters of the economy since 1958 and in both of them output rose significantly faster than the average for all manu- facturing industry. They are chemicals and engineering, and there is no great sense in trying to make comparisons between them. They both comprise groups of industries within which it would be possible to distinguish sub-groups which grew more rapidly and less rapidly.

2. *Expanding Industries.* The second group of industries comprises a wider range—bricks, glass and cement, paper and printing, vehicles, food, drink and tobacco, textiles, metal manufacture, metal goods and clothing—all of which expanded, but at a significantly slower rate than that of the pace setters which we have just noticed—chemicals and engineering. Although there is in fact quite a difference in the rate at which the fastest and slowest industries in this group have been growing there is no point in going into the fine detail of distinguishing between them, since, again, each comprises sub-groups which themselves grew at different rates. For example, expansion of output in the man-made fibres section of the textile industry more than offset a decline in cotton textiles.

3. *Declining Industries.* There are two major industries which can quite clearly be seen to have lost ground since 1958. They are mining (mainly coal) and shipbuilding. In this group it may be worth while

pointing out that output in these industries in 1970 was actually lower than in 1958. Thus, they were not merely declining relatively to the national economy, but they were absolutely less important too.

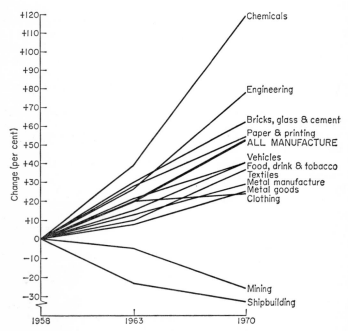

Fig. 4.3.   **Industrial Change, U.K., 1958–70**
Percentage Change in Industrial Production

The Location of Industry

We should not need to be told that industry is not evenly spread over the whole of the country. Our knowledge of the geographical distribution of the population (*see* Chapter 2) should enable us to deduce that fact. For, without identifying cause and effect, it is obvious that a district which is densely populated will have a larger proportion of industry in it than a sparsely populated area. In fact, the map in Fig. 2.5 (p. 25) showing the density of population is also a good guide to the location of industry.

But there is more to be said in explanation of the location of industry. For different regions tend to specialize in different industries, and we find that some, like textiles, are very highly concentrated in relatively few districts while others, like building, are more evenly spread over the country.

The reasons why certain districts specialize in particular industries are very interesting, but they are usually also complex and could form the subject of profound study. Such a study would probably involve a great deal of historical research, for most of the older industries, such as cotton textiles or shipbuilding, are today found in Lancashire or on the Clyde, largely because these industries have been there for so many years that it would require a tremendous upheaval to shift them, and even new firms probably find themselves almost automatically attracted there. Generally, we can say that any particular industry was originally set up in an area because, at some time or other, it was probably a most suitable place in that the cost of producing there was at least as low as anywhere else.

It may have been the need to be near a source of power that was the dominating influence. Witness, for instance, the location alongside rivers and streams of the cotton-spinning mills in the eighteenth and early nineteenth centuries. For, before the advent of the steam engine, water was the only important source of power for the factories. With greatly improved transport and the widespread distribution of electric power, this restriction no longer prevails, but heavy industries, like iron and steel, using a great deal of coal and coke which is fairly expensive to transport, still tend to be found near to the coalfields.

Closely related to the availability of power as a factor in location is the need to be near to the supply of a bulky raw material which is being processed. An example of this is to be found in the chemical industry, where an important section producing alkali (used in the manufacture of soap, rayon, glass and many other products) is quite highly concentrated in Cheshire, near to the supplies of brine, limestone and coal which it uses. This attraction of the raw material helps to explain a gradual change in the location of the iron and steel industry away from the coalfields and nearer to the iron-ore supplies. For, as the richer ore deposits are worked out, the industry has to turn to deposits of a lower grade, such as those in Lincolnshire and Northamptonshire. Lower-grade ore, however, means that much more of it has to be used to produce the same amount of steel, and it would be wasteful to transport the bulky ore a long way to the furnaces.

Then again, it may be that the need for a ready supply of labour has been the dominating factor. This was an important influence in the location of new factories after the Second World War. For, though unemployed labour may often have been forced in the past to move to a district where employment was available, it has become increasingly difficult to induce people to leave their homes and move to a totally different part of the country. This is especially the case when the labour required must be skilled in a particular way. Thus we should not expect to find many precision-instrument factories in the Scottish Highlands since, apart from anything else, there are no skilled engineers there, and it is not easy to persuade skilled ones to move there.

Finally, the main influence in location may have been the desire to be near to the market where the finished product is sold. This has the greatest bearing when the raw materials used are not very bulky, since the cost of transporting them may well outweigh the advantage of being near to a market. The majority of industries do not, in fact, use very bulky raw materials, and proximity to the market is probably the most important factor influencing the location of many new factories. It is almost always true that to be near to a big market is to be near to a big town and thus, at the same time, to have the added advantage of a plentiful supply of labour. These two factors, nearness to markets and labour, are the main reasons why industry has tended to concentrate itself in and around our main cities. Whenever a new factory is built in a town it tends to attract people to come there to seek employment, and this in itself makes both the market and labour supply bigger, and may thus further increase the town's attractiveness.

Location of Industry in Great Britain

There are two ways of looking at the location of industry in Great Britain. One is to concentrate attention on each industry in turn and examine the extent to which it is spread over the different regions in the country. This method is frequently employed, and we shall use it in our discussion of certain major industries in the next chapter. The alternative which, if it is very thoroughly done, gives the same general picture, is to look rather at the different districts and see how far each has specialized in particular industries. To do this really adequately would require a separate book, but we can get a good first approximation by dividing the country into the eleven standard geographical regions used by the Department of Employment, and examining the extent of concentration of particular industries in each.

This is done in Fig. 4.4 which is based on the number of workers employed in each industry, and which should be read alongside the adjoining map of Fig. 4.5. Each of the eleven areas has a column to itself, each space in which corresponds to an industrial group. Where this space is marked with a cross, the percentage of the total area labour force in that industry is greater than the percentage of the labour force in that industry for the country as a whole. Thus, wherever a cross appears, the region is to some extent specializing in that particular industry. Wherever there is a blank space, on the other hand, the region is not specializing in that industry although, of course, it may well be producing a certain amount of the goods in question. There may be two possible reasons for the non-specialization. One is that

	South-East	East Anglia	South-West	West Midlands	East Midlands	Yorks. and Humber.	North-West	Northern	Wales	Scotland	N. Ireland
Manufacturing											
Chemicals							×	×			
Metal manufacture				×	×	×		×	×		
Engineering	×			×	×		×	×			
Shipbuilding			×				×	×		×	×
Vehicles			×	×	×		×				
Metal goods				×	×						
Bricks, glass, cement				×			×	×			
Textiles						×	×	×		×	×
Clothing					×	×	×	×	×		
Food, drink, tobacco		×	×				×	×		×	×
Timber, furniture	×	×					×				
Paper, printing	×						×				
Non-Manufacturing											
Agriculture		×	×		×					×	×
Mining					×	×		×	×	×	
Building			×					×	×	×	×
Gas, water, electricity											
Transport	×						×				
Distribution	×		×							×	
Commerce	×										
Government	×		×								×
Professions	×	×	×						×	×	
Miscellaneous	×	×	×								

Fig. 4.4. **Regional Specialization, U.K., 1970**

("X" signifies that a region has more than the national average percentage of its labour force working in a particular industry.)

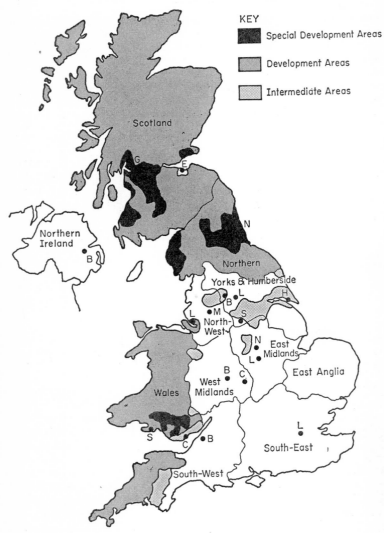

Fig. 4.5. **Standard Regions, U.K., 1970**

the particular industry is one which happens to be concentrated in other areas. In that case, of course, there must be a cross against some other region or regions. The other explanation is that it is an industry in which no district is specializing for the simple reason that it is fairly evenly spread over the country. Thus there are no crosses against gas, water and electricity, which are not highly concentrated in any regions.

SOUTH-EAST ENGLAND

This region includes the Greater London area and, having by far the largest population of any region, employs over a third of the entire labour force in the country. It is not surprising to find, therefore, that the South-East takes first, second or third place by size of employment in agriculture and in every industrial group except mining, steel and textiles. The influence of London is seen in the predominant specialization in the non-manufacturing sectors—especially in commerce, the professions, government, distribution and transport. Nearly all the head offices of banks, insurance companies and other financial institutions are in the City. The main government departments are also in London, which is the pivot of the nation's railway network, and the chief shopping centre in the country. The region is an important producer of foodstuffs, chemicals, clothing, vehicles and light engineering goods, but it specializes (in the sense of employing more than the national average percentage of its labour force) in printing and publishing, furniture and shipbuilding, the last of these being helped by the inclusion within its boundaries of the ports of London and Southampton.

EAST ANGLIA

This is the foremost agricultural region in England and Wales, and about 8 per cent of its labour force is employed on the land. The food processing (canning and freezing) in which its specializes is dependent both on its farm produce and fish, and on the proximity of the London market. The region contains important footwear factories, and just qualifies for specialization in the timber and furniture group. In the non-manufacturing sector, it has more than the national average of workers in building and the professions, as well as in the miscellaneous group of services, explained partly by the presence of the hotels of its tourist resorts on the coast.

SOUTH-WEST ENGLAND

The South-West resembles in several respects East Anglia—containing the important tourist counties of Devon and Cornwall, and specializing in agriculture and food processing, but also in shipbuilding. The industrial centre of the region is at Bristol where vehicles (mainly aircraft), tobacco and other industries flourish. Like East Anglia again, the South-West is predominantly non-manufacturing, with above average employment in the professions, government service and distribution.

WEST MIDLANDS

The degree of concentration in manufacturing industry in the West Midlands is higher than in any other region in Britain. Over half the workers there are employed in factories making a very wide range of products. The region specializes in engineering, vehicles, iron and steel, metal goods and the bricks–cement group which includes the potteries of Staffordshire. Together, these industries account for about a third of total employment. Much of the heavy industry is in the so-called "Black Country" around Birmingham and Wolverhampton, which constitutes one of the major industrial centres in Britain.

EAST MIDLANDS

Not very much more than half the size of the West Midlands, judged by its labour force, nor quite so heavily dependent on manufacturing industry, the East Midlands nevertheless specializes also in iron and steel, engineering and vehicles—largely in its chief cities, Nottingham, Leicester, Derby and Northampton. The region is well known for its hosiery, footwear and clothing factories, and possesses a sizeable agricultural sector. Also within the boundaries of the East Midlands are the coalfields of Derbyshire and Northamptonshire, and nearly 20 per cent of the country's coal-mining labour is employed there.

YORKSHIRE AND HUMBERSIDE

The principal specializations of this region are the two groups of industries, coal and iron and steel, and clothing and textiles. It is the largest employer of coal-mining labour of any region, and clothing and textiles occupy over 10 per cent of the labour force, reflecting the fact that the bulk of British wool and worsted production takes place in the West Riding in and around Bradford, Huddersfield, Halifax and Leeds. Specialization in metal goods is substantially due to the Sheffield cutlery trades, and the region is an important producer of glass and timber. A quarter of the British labour force in the manufacture of chocolate and sugar confectionery occurs in York and elsewhere within the region's boundaries, which also contain the major fishing ports of Hull and Grimsby on which food processing and other industries are based.

NORTH-WEST ENGLAND

The densely populated North-West England includes both the Manchester and Liverpool conurbations and is the largest of all the standard regions after the South-East. Predominantly industrial, it takes in the Lancashire cotton textile industry and, together with clothing, this group occupies about 10 per cent of its labour force. The North-West is the leading producer of glass, and the second largest employer in chemicals, paper and printing, timber, and the food, drink and tobacco groups. Liverpool and the Chorley–Leyland areas substantially account for the vehicle specialization, much of which consists of commercial motors. Engineering has been increasing in importance—the numbers employed exceed those in clothing and textiles—and electrical and textile machinery stand out. Shipbuilding is mainly done at Barrow and on the Mersey. The North-West is the only region outside the South-East to have more than the national average employment in transport, and part of this is to be explained by the existence within its boundaries of the Manchester Ship Canal.

NORTHERN ENGLAND

The population of this region is largely concentrated around Tyneside, and is particularly dependent on traditional heavy industry, though this has been diminishing in recent years. Its main specialisms are coal, iron and steel, chemicals and shipbuilding. Together, they account for the employment of nearly a fifth of all workers and about a third of all men. Engineering has grown in importance as a policy of diversification has been pursued, and the region now just qualifies as being specialized in engineering, which employs over 10 per cent of its labour force.

WALES

Wales is largely mountainous and sparsely populated, though the proportion employed in agriculture is below the national average. This is somewhat misleading, however, as the country has a relatively large number of small self-employed farmers, who do not technically count as employees. The population is heavily concentrated in the area of the South Wales coalfield, and 6 per cent of the labour force is in coal mining, though the proportion has fallen substantially in recent years with the decline of the coal industry. The other main Welsh specialization is in iron and steel (including tinplate), which accounts for 10 per cent of total employment, but the range of its manufacturing industry has been widening recently to include, for instance, light engineering and clothing factories. The country also employs more than the national average number of workers in building, government and the professions.

SCOTLAND

Scotland is a large area, over half the size of England and Wales together, though much of it, like Wales, is sparsely populated and mountainous, with little industry of any kind. There is, accordingly, a relatively high proportion of the labour force in agriculture and food processing as well as in distribution. The majority of the population, and hence the industry, is situated in the central lowlands, where specialization is in coal, textiles, centred principally on Paisley, and shipbuilding, for which the Clyde is world-famous. Scotland also has more than the national average proportions of building and professional workers.

NORTHERN IRELAND

Northern Ireland is a small region with a labour force of not many more than half a million, for all of whom it has, nevertheless, had some difficulty in finding jobs. One in every eight employees is in clothing and textiles—especially the long-established linen and the newer synthetics. Agriculture and food, drink and tobacco are also important, as is the Belfast shipyard, the largest in the United Kingdom. A wide range of other manufacturing industries is also being introduced into the country, which employs more than the national average percentage of workers in building and in government service.

Changes in Location

Our previous discussion of regional specialization failed to reveal one other aspect of the location of industry. For the years since 1918 have seen a considerable redeployment of industry over different parts of the country. In this connexion the decades between the two World Wars were outstanding and witnessed a striking growth in the relative importance of Southern England and the Midlands at the expense of Northern England, South Wales, and Scotland.

To account for these changes two main reasons may be offered. In the first place there was the tendency for industrialists to move southwards when erecting new factories, attracted by the growing market of Greater London. Moreover, the development of electricity as a source of power released them from the need to be near to the coalfields. The second explanation is the one that carries more weight. As we saw earlier, all our industries have not been expanding at the same rate and, in fact, some have even been declining. Most of the new and expanding industries such as engineering, motor cars and electrical goods were those in which the South and the Midlands were specializing, while the staple industries of the nineteenth century, especially textiles, coal and shipbuilding, were declining in importance and were largely concentrated in the North of England, and in Scotland and South Wales.

GOVERNMENT POLICY

The decline in these areas caused serious local unemployment and it was not long before the government began to take steps to try to arrest the movement. The first was taken in 1934, when certain of these "Special Areas" were scheduled as being depressed and Commissioners were appointed to try and attract new industry into them. Post-war Distribution of Industry Acts reinforced this policy, giving powers to the government including that of building factories for letting in the areas (renamed Development Areas) and making loans and grants to encourage individual firms to go there.

In a negative way, too, the government's control over factory location was materially strengthened as a result of the Town and Country Planning Act, 1947, by which new factories require planning permission from the local authority and, for those of 5,000 sq. ft. or more (3,000 sq. ft. in the Midlands and South-East), the granting of an Industrial Development Certificate by the State. The government has, therefore, been in a position to influence the location of new plants by the withholding or granting of permission for particular sites. One may well imagine that the decisions to build extensions to productive capacity in areas of relatively excessive unemployment in Merseyside, Scotland and South Wales, made by leading car manufacturers and others in recent years, have been affected by this sort of consideration.

Several extensions to the policy designed to reduce the imbalance in regional development have been grafted on to this foundation. The Local Employment Acts of 1960 and 1963 increased the government's power to give help where it was needed, and the Industrial Development Act of 1966 allowed the government to substitute cash grants instead of the tax allowances for firms located in the Development Areas and substantially increased the total value of financial inducements made. In 1965 new controls were introduced over office building in the Midlands and the South-East. In 1967 firms in the Development Areas were offered a Regional Employment Premium related to the number of workers on their books—a measure which seems to hit more directly at the problem of unemployment than that of making capital grants for new buildings and plant, which might be more likely to make capital-intensive rather than labour-intensive investment relatively more attractive.

As might be expected, the strength of the policy measures adopted in recent years substantially aided the Development Areas (though at a considerable cost), and relieved their plight as was seen in the reduction of their unemployment levels relative to those of the prosperous regions (*see below* Chapter 7, pp. 177–8). A side effect of the success, however was the appearance of so-called "grey" or "intermediate" areas, such as parts of Lancashire and Yorkshire, which were neither prosperous nor so depressed as to qualify for Development Area status. The Hunt Committee was appointed to look into their problem and, after its report in 1969, the Local Employment Act of 1970 was passed designating them Intermediate Areas, able to qualify for some of the assistance available for the Development Areas proper. The latter, as defined in 1970, contain something like a fifth of the working population, and contain Special Development Areas with particularly acute problems (*see* map on page 74). The whole question of regional planning is, moreover, watched over by the Regional Planning Boards and Councils referred to earlier (*see above* page 62).

Industrial Concentration

One of the outstanding features of industrial development in the past hundred years has been the growth in the size of firms and the extent to which industry has become concentrated in a relatively few large concerns. The days when the majority of goods were produced in a great number of small factories have disappeared, and the typical unit in many industries today is the gigantic corporation. There are many reasons for this development, but two of the most important will suffice—

1. Over a wide section of industry, production in large units is more efficient than in small. Mass production has come about where it is both easier and cheaper to produce large quantities of standardized products in a big factory than many slightly different ones in a number of small factories. This is, indeed, no more than an aspect of the specialization among firms and among individuals that we noticed at the beginning of this chapter. For as firms grow they are able to employ specialist personnel and equipment which is not worth while at a low level of output. Henry Ford achieved success by realizing this and mass-producing millions of motor cars, all exactly like one another. Today all the cheapest cars come from big factories. A modern counterpart is that automation is just not worth while unless the scale of output is large enough.

2. Under private enterprise, if any firm comes to dominate the industry in any particular line of business, it is able to do things which the existence of effective competition from other firms might prevent, such as raising its prices to the consumer, restricting output to maintain demand for its product, or stifling any technical inventions which might make its product obsolete.

In the discussion which follows, therefore, we are able to attribute the growth of large-scale organization in industry to the desire for more efficient production and for greater market control, though it may not always be clear just how far each motive is responsible in any particular case.

THE SIZE OF MANUFACTURING ESTABLISHMENTS

In attempting to assess the importance of large- and small-scale production in present-day Britain, it is wise to start by looking at the size of the individual factories, workshops, plants, etc., which are

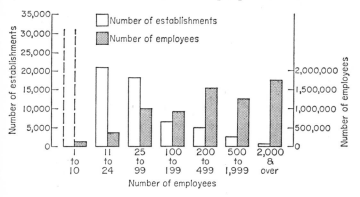

Fig. 4.6.   **Size of Manufacturing Establishments, Great Britain, 1963**
Establishments Classified by Numbers of Employees

officially and collectively known as establishments. For although, from the point of view of control, the firm is the unit one should start with, the organization of industry into establishments tells us something rather more basic, and may even help to distinguish between the two motives for expansion which have been mentioned. Thus a single firm may well own more than one establishment and may, in fact, have expanded its activities in this way in order to try to dominate the market but it is, on the whole, unlikely to allow production to increase in any one establishment if this is more costly than producing the same amount in a number of small ones.

Fig. 4.6 is based on information published by the government in the Census of Production and, although it is certainly incomplete in it recording of very small establishments, it reveals that they are by far the most numerous. Of the total of over 80,000 manufacturing establishments covered in the Census, nearly two-thirds employ less than 2: workers, while more than 80 per cent employ fewer than 100.

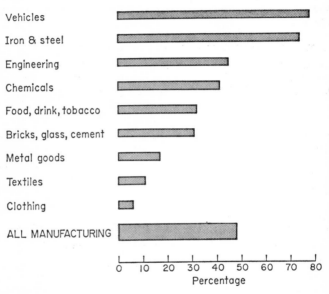

Fig. 4.7. **Employment in Establishments with 1,000 or More Workers, Great Britain, 1963**
Percentage of Total Employment in Establishments with 10 or more Workers

This way of looking at the structure of industry conceals the more important fact that large-scale production is dominant in manufacture the 2,700 establishments employing more than 500 workers each which represent approximately 2 per cent of the total, are so big that altogether they employ something like 50 per cent of the manufacturing labour force. Furthermore, the 430 largest establishments of all, each of which has more than two thousand workers on its payroll, account for over a fifth of total employment in manufacturing.

Large-scale production is, of course, much more common in some industries than in others. Some idea of this is given in Fig. 4.7 which shows the percentage of total employment in establishments with 1,000 or more employees. We find that the two prime large-scale industries are vehicles and iron and steel, where these large establishments are responsible for over 70 per cent of their relevant labour forces, while in engineering and chemicals they account for more than 40 per cent. At the other end of the scale we should notice, in particular, the clothing and textile trades, where concentration in large plants is least common.

THE SIZE OF BUSINESS ENTERPRISES

The concentration of industry in large establishments is, as we have just seen, very considerable. But, as we also know, an individual company or firm may well own more than one establishment and, in order to see the full extent to which *control* is concentrated, it is necessary to widen our idea of a business. Individual firms are frequently not independent of each other and the unit of control may thus be considerably larger than the firm, and the degree of concentration so much the greater. We may then proceed directly to consider the ways in which such a link between firms may be made effective. It is useful to consider these under two heads—amalgamations between firms, and inter-firm co-operation.

1. AMALGAMATIONS BETWEEN FIRMS

Amalgamations, or mergers as they are commonly called, between two or more companies are a direct means of establishing larger units of control of business enterprise. The precise form of the amalgamation differs from case to case. It may be that a small firm is merged into a larger in such a way as to lose its identity completely, or, alternatively, the arrangement may involve a minimum of company reorganization. A frequent method makes use of what are known as *holding companies.* Under this system the principal company, which is known as the *parent*, becomes a holding company by buying enough shares in another company to give it a controlling interest. The second company then becomes the *subsidiary* company of the parent. This sort of control is often gained by making what is called a *take-over bid.* This consists of an offer to purchase, made to ordinary (voting) shareholders in the company it is desired to acquire. The offer can take the form of cash or shares in the prospective parent. If enough acceptances are received to give control, the company taken over becomes a subsidiary.

The acquisition of subsidiaries in this manner became quite a common affair in the 1950s and accelerated in the 1960s. The majority of such acquisitions take place quietly, but a few are attended by a good deal of publicity, especially if they involve well-known companies and a lengthy struggle with rising offer terms or international relations. Chrysler's acquisition of Rootes Motors is a case in point. The frustrated attempt by one giant company, Imperial Chemical Industries (I.C.I.), to take over another, Courtaulds, is a second. The degree of concentration that may be achieved by the use of holding companies is, in principle, almost limitless. For there is nothing to stop a subsidiary company from itself acquiring a controlling interest in another company or companies, which then become subsidiaries of the subsidiary. These, too, in their turn may control subsidiaries of their own, and a pyramid of companies may be built up, such as that of the Sears Group (*see* Fig. 4.8), all of which may be ultimately governed by the main parent holding company. Sears Holdings Ltd. heads a group, under the chairmanship of Mr. Charles Clore, which is one of the largest fifty companies in Britain, with a sales turnover of more than £250 million, employing over 60,000 workers, and which itself extends control over more than a hundred subsidiaries and through five pyramidal tiers. And there are even larger groups in existence, such as Shell, B.P., I.C.I., Unilever, Imperial Tobacco, British Leyland, Courtaulds, Dunlop and Marks and Spencers.

The motives which cause companies to grow by merger are frequently complex, but it is useful to distinguish between the amalgamations between companies producing a similar range of products and those which extend over different stages in the production process. The former type of merger, between similar kinds of business, is often called *horizontal* integration, and examples are those between Triang and Meccano, Dixon's and Bennett's photographic retail chain stores, and, within the Sears group, between Dolcis, Manfield, Lilley and Skinners and other shoe shops. Integration between firms at different stages in the production process, on the other hand, is referred to as *vertical* integration. This may extend backwards to earlier stages, such as the Dunlop ownership of tropical rubber plantations, or Ford's acquisition of Brigg's Motor Bodies. Alternatively, the direction of integration may be forwards to later stages, as evidenced by Distillers' take-over of United Glass Ltd., or the acquisition by many brewery companies of public houses which enable them to sell their beer direct to the public.

Some mergers and take-overs do not appear on the surface to have

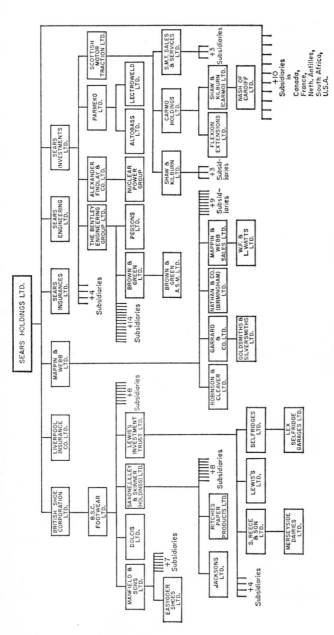

Fig. 4.8. Company Structure: The Sears Group, 1970

elements of either vertical or horizontal integration but this may conceal less obvious matters, such as a means of disposing of by-products or utilization of expertise in a related field, which may help to explain such otherwise unlikely combinations as, in the Unilever group, detergent, margarine and ice-cream manufacture and fish-retailing. But it is useful to distinguish also a third type of integration whose primary effect is of *diversification* in contrast to the other two. The Imperial Tobacco Company, for instance, moved into quite new fields with the purchase of Anselm Holdings, producing plastic mouldings for the motor industry, rather remote not only from its main cigarette production, but also from its other developments such as potato crisps. The Sears group, too, as Fig. 4.8 shows, exhibits considerably diversified interests, with groupings in engineering, motor distribution, and the gold and silversmith trade, backing its main line in shoes. Diversification, as an end in itself, may be expected as a company seeks opportunities for the employment of managerial skills and other spare resources, especially in activities which seem likely to expand more rapidly than its existing ones. It has undoubtedly shown signs of flourishing in the period since 1950, though the majority of enterprises continue to be relatively specialized.

In the Census of Production of 1963, 53 industry groups were distinguished in manufacturing and an attempt to quantify diversification can be made. It showed that near to 80 per cent of enterprises with more than 100 workers confined their activities to a single industry group and were to that extent specialized. At the same time diversification among some of the largest enterprises was considerable. Of 210 enterprises employing more than 5,000 workers, for instance, 52 were engaged in at least seven industry groups. The precise measure of diversification, it should be realized, depends upon the number of industry groups and the way in which they are defined. The narrower the definition of an industry, the greater the degree of diversification which will be recorded. Hence, not too much significance should be attached to the figures themselves. But it is worth noticing that the extent of diversification tends to vary considerably from one industry to another. There are notable differences, for example, between enterprises whose main interests include chemicals, iron and steel, radio and telecommunications and aircraft, which are inclined to be more highly diversified, and those at the other extreme, including clothing, footwear, furniture, and chocolates and sweets, which are not.

The relative importance of large businesses in British industry is not easily measured, but some light can be thrown on the matter by the results of the Census of Production taken in 1963. These give the

shares in manufacturing production accounted for by business enterprises, where the term enterprise is used to mean one or more companies
under common ownership or control.

Fig. 4.9 presents a general picture of the situation which is not

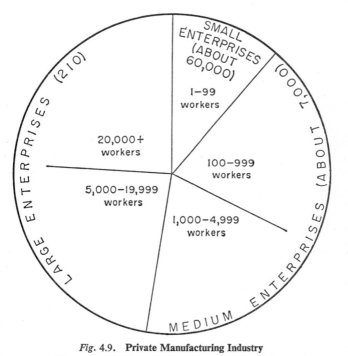

Fig. 4.9. **Private Manufacturing Industry**
Share of Total Net Output produced by Enterprises
of Different Size, U.K., 1963

comparable with that of Fig. 4.6, which relates to establishments, but
almost certainly indicates a higher degree of concentration in the
largest units. Although more than 60,000 enterprises were distinguished,
the 210 largest, each employing five thousand workers or over, produced
almost half of total private manufacturing output. And among them
were 38 giants, with at least twenty thousand employees each, and
producing almost 25 per cent of total production.

The degree of concentration in individual industries, of course, varies as much when we take enterprises as our unit as when we take establishments. And, though the measure of concentration in an industry, like the measure of diversification discussed above, is liable to be influenced by the way in which the industry is defined, some idea of the variation is given in Figs. 4.10 and 4.11 for selected industries.

The first diagram (Fig. 4.10) shows the share of the largest five enterprises in total sales by the industry. Thus, while there are highly concentrated industries, such as cigarettes, gramophone records and wallpaper, there are others, like machine tools and sections of the clothing and textile industries, where the share of the biggest firms is very low. The figures used for the preparation of this section of the diagram are affected by the number of enterprises in each group as well as by the size of the largest of them, and an alternative approach is given in Fig. 4.11 for certain other industry groupings. This is not confined to the largest businesses, but shows the relative importance of large, medium and small enterprises in total output. The general picture, however, is not affected by the change and remains one of wide diversity. To take extremes as examples, more than three-quarters of aircraft, motor vehicle and radio output occurs in enterprises employing at least 5,000 workers, while in clothing and leather less than a quarter of total production comes from those very large firms.

Finally, it is necessary to indicate that the extent of industrial concentration in large enterprises existing now is almost certainly greater than it was some years ago. Comparable statistics over a long period are not easy to find, but at the Census of Production in 1935 there were only about half as many enterprises employing 5,000 or more workers as there were in 1958, and their share in total employment was also about half as great. The period between the Censuses of Production of 1958 and 1963 also shows a significant rise in the share of total manufacturing output by large firms with 5,000 or more employees.

Somewhat different evidence for the fact that this trend almost certainly continued in the 1960s may be seen from the fact that the 28 biggest companies owned 30 per cent of the total assets of large manufacturing businesses in 1961, whereas by 1968 they owned 50 per cent of the total assets of the survivors of these large companies.

This increasing size has, no doubt, been partly due to the natural tendency for firms to combine and grow, but it was undoubtedly helped by the establishment, in 1966, of the Industrial Reorganization Corporation (I.R.C.) by the Labour government, in order to encourage

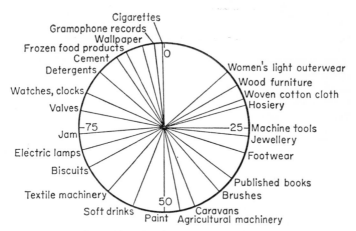

Fig. 4.10. Size of Business Enterprises, U.K., 1963

Percentage of Total Sales by the Five Enterprises with the Largest Sales

(The percentage is measured separately for each industry from the "12 o'clock" origin.)

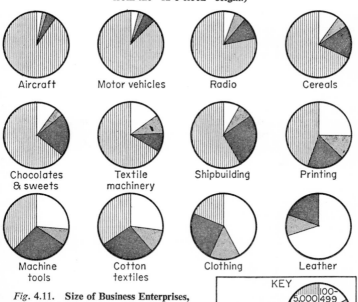

Fig. 4.11. Size of Business Enterprises, Selected Industries, U.K., 1963

Percentage of Net Output in Enterprises (with more than 100 Workers) of Different Sizes

mergers where firms are too small to reap large-scale economies and compete with international competition. The I.R.C. sponsored a fair number of such mergers, such as that between General Electric and English Electric companies, until it was abolished in 1971 (*see below*, page 95).

The growth in the relative importance of large firms should not, moreover, be taken to mean that concentration in the production of individual goods has necessarily increased to the same extent. This is mainly because of the observed tendency for businesses to diversify as they expand, spreading their interests over several industrial groupings; but also because of the practice of integrating forwards and backwards in the production process, as well as horizontally.

2. INTER-FIRM CO-OPERATION

There are several avenues of co-operation open to enterprises which fall short of the full pooling of sovereignty involved in a merger.

(*a*) *Trade Associations.* Some of the most common arrangements between firms take place through a trade association. This is a very wide term and includes any body of employers who have agreements with each other, such as the Confederation of British Industry, which acts as industry's spokesman on economic and labour matters where a national voice is required.

In individual industries, on the other hand, trade associations usually have a more specific role. Their functions vary from industry to industry and include the carrying out of research and publicity, but may cover activities such as regulating the output or fixing the price of the products in the industry and organizing the machinery for carrying policies through. Some trade associations have made arrangements for allocating shares of the market to constituent firms on a predetermined basis, involving the setting up of a central sales organization, which is often referred to as a *cartel*. Any agreements of this kind can have much the same effect as more complete mergers between firms, in so far as the restriction of competition is concerned, though they may be less stable. And legislation has been passed to try to limit the operation of restrictive agreements (*see below*, pp. 93–5). But an example of a trade association which employed an elaborate system of devices to control the market, including the fixing of prices, the allocation of sales quotas to members punishable by a scale of fines and control of entry, is given in Fig. 4.12, which shows also the known financial links between members of the Electric Lamp Manufacturers'

Association in 1951. It is difficult to assess the effect that trade associations have on industrial concentration in the present state of knowledge, either of their number, or of the precise nature of their activities. Generally, however, industries without a trade association are much in the minority and, where they exist, membership is usually widespread.

(b) *Interlocking Directorates.* Another device for inter-firm liaison, which can exert an important influence on the control of enterprises is where a number of different companies have interlocking directorates. A link between the firms is contrived by one or more persons becoming directors of several of them. This practice is common among banking and finance companies, but varies quite a lot in scope in different sections of manufacturing industry. It is, moreover, another area where incomplete knowledge exists of the extent of such arrangements as well as their influence. In the Midland metal and metal-using industries an independent estimate traced a connexion via interlocking directorates between companies employing a third of all workers in the industries. And, in the steel industry, the directors of the nine largest companies before renationalization held over six hundred directorships in other branches of industry.

(c) *Informal Agreements.* Finally, and at the opposite extreme from the complete merger, there exist in industry many kinds of fairly loose agreements. These may be unwritten "understandings," commonly referred to as "gentlemen's agreements," or more formal undertakings. A good example of this sort of thing is the understanding between Imperial Chemical Industries and Unilever, whereby the former agreed to refrain from competing with the latter in the production of soap. Another type is where a group of local builders decide not to compete for building contracts, but to allocate new orders received by any of them in rotation. A third involves the exchange of "know-how" between companies, extending in some cases to a pooling of patents. Such arrangements are, all too frequently, not well publicized and it is consequently extremely hard to find out how much is going on and to evaluate them.

This section can most suitably be ended by emphasizing that any attempt to assess the degree of concentration in British industry must take into consideration all forms of loose and tight association from the "gentlemen's agreement" to the full merger. No simple measure can be satisfactory on account of differences between industries and uncertainties of the kinds discussed above. But, taken as a whole, there is no doubt that the overall picture is one of very considerable

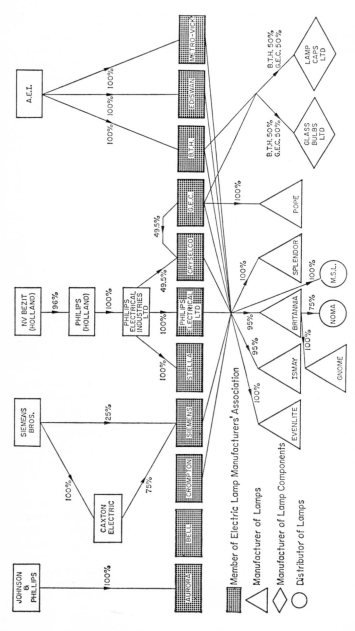

Fig. 4.12. **Links between Members of the Electric Lamp Manufacturers' Association, 1951**

concentration in many sectors, and our earlier examination of the distribution of share ownership should be reviewed in the light of this.

Monopolies, Mergers and Restrictive Practices

The extent of concentration and the powers available to a firm or association of firms which comes to control a large proportion of the output of a particular industry (called *monopolies*) have both been mentioned earlier, but little was done about their possible harmful effects until 1948, when an Act was passed setting up a Monopolies Commission.

The Monopolies Commission was first given broad powers to inquire into industries where monopoly was suspected in order to ascertain whether or not the activities of the firms there operated against the public interest. In the years which followed the Monopolies Commission investigated about thirty industries, from electric lamps to pneumatic tyres and, in almost every case, found some restrictive practices to be operating against the public interest, such as measures to prevent the entry of new firms into the industry or collective agreements on retail prices fixed in advance (later prohibited by the Resale Prices Act, 1964, *see below*).

The government's policy has developed in several ways as a result of a number of Acts of Parliament in the 1950s and 1960s. The Restrictive Trade Practices Act of 1956 was passed to deal specifically with restrictive trade agreements between firms as distinct from single large monopolistic companies. Under its provisions firms must register a wide range of agreements affecting the supply of goods with a Registrar of Restrictive Practices, who may take proceedings against them to a Restrictive Practices Court. The presumption of the law is that all such agreements are contrary to the public interest, unless special circumstances can be shown to exist, such as that they provide a substantial net benefit to the consuming public.

Over 2,000 agreements have in fact been registered, though the vast majority have been subsequently abandoned voluntarily. Some thirty cases have been contested before the Court, of which about a third were allowed to continue. The majority were, however, found to be against the public interest and declared void; including the famous Cotton Yarn Spinners' Agreement where, in spite of the fact that the Court accepted the argument that local unemployment would follow the abandonment of the agreement, it was held that this was not in itself sufficient to offset its detrimental effect of restricting competition.

Another recent development has been the Resale Prices Act of 1964, which prohibits agreements, even by individual manufacturers, to fix minimum resale prices of their goods by retailers in advance, unless granted exemption by the Restrictive Practices Court. This piece of legislation has been particularly effective. About 500 applications for exemption have been refused and only a few have been allowed to stand. As a result of the Act, the previously widespread practice of fixed prices for goods in all shops has virtually disappeared from Britain. By shopping around, one can now usually buy most articles at a discount (*see also*, pp. 155–6).

Further developments in anti-monopoly and restrictive practices legislation include the Monopolies and Mergers Act of 1965, which added services as well as goods to the references which could be made to the Monopolies Commission, which was incidentally enlarged at the same time. The Act also made provision for the Board of Trade (now the Department of Trade and Industry) to withhold permission for mergers between large companies, which might adversely affect the degree of monopoly, and to refer such mergers to the Monopolies Commission for investigation and report. Finally, the Restrictive Trade Practices Act of 1968 added another class of agreements to those which might be registered. These are so-called "information agreements", whereby firms circulate price lists to others in the industry, and which, it has been suggested, might be as effective in some circumstances as actual price-fixing agreements in preventing price-cutting.

The legislation against monopolies, mergers and restrictive practices has been criticized on a number of grounds—the Monopolies Commission, in particular, for the slow pace at which it has operated, and for the fact that its findings do not have to stand up to public inquiry as with hearings before the Restrictive Practices Court. On the other hand, it must be stated that the government has not always accepted the advice of the Monopolies Commission. For instance, the Commission's recommendation that the Imperial Tobacco Co. Ltd. should divest itself of a $42\frac{1}{2}$ per cent shareholding in its rival Gallahers was not followed, though the government did receive a promise from Imperial Tobacco that it would not interfere in the management of Gallahers. (In other cases, too, the government has relied on promises not to abuse monopoly power.) In a different connexion, it was regarded as unsatisfactory by some people that the nationalized industries were not referred to the Monopolies Commission. But this situation has been altered by the decision in 1971 to ask the Commission to investigate and report on gas and electricity connexion charges.

The policy on mergers was held by many to place the government in an impossible position—trying to prevent mergers which might adversely increase monopoly power, at practically the same time as the

Industrial Reorganization Corporation was set up to try to stimulate mergers to increase efficiency (*see above*, p. 90). Partly to avoid this conflict of interest the Industrial Reorganization Corporation was abolished in 1971.

Finally, the work of the Restrictive Practices Court has been criticized on the grounds that lay (i.e. non-economist) judges are asked to make decisions on economic matters, for which they are not qualified. Certainly some decisions have been made which appear to be based on reasoning that at least some economists have found unacceptable. But we cannot consider this issue further in a book of this nature.

The Course of Industrial Production

Continual improvements in technique and the growth of the population are constantly acting to increase industrial output. We have already observed, earlier in the chapter, how the output of different industries changed between 1958 and 1970 and it is now necessary to look at the course of such changes on a year-to-year basis.

The average level of production in industry as a whole is measured with the help of what is called the *Index of Industrial Production*, which is shown in Fig. 4.13. As may be seen, output moved fairly steadily upwards between 1958 and 1970 at a rate of about 4 per cent per annum on average, although there were periods of relatively rapid growth, as in 1958–60 and 1962–4, alternating with others of slower growth, as in 1960–1, 1966–7 and 1969–70. Before the war the fluctuations were very much greater as is also shown in the diagram. In the past a country such as Britain, where the bulk of industry is in private hands, has generally been subject to alternating periods of prosperity and depression. This continuous succession of boom and slump at fairly regular intervals since the days of the Industrial Revolution is known as the *trade cycle*, and its causes are not a matter on which all economists are agreed.

The cycle shown in the diagram covers the years 1927–38, after which, largely as a result of preparations for the Second World War, production began once more to increase. Fig 4.13 does not confine itself to the progress of industrial production generally, but includes also the course of output in the iron and steel industry, in order to demonstrate one very important feature of the trade cycle, namely that fluctuations are not the same in all sectors. In most heavy industries, such as iron and steel, the tendency is for production to shoot up really rapidly in the prosperous years, and to be more depressed than the average in the slump. On the other hand, industries catering directly for consumers, such as foodstuffs, generally have a more even history, neither declining so fast in depression nor expanding quite so rapidly in prosperity.

Since a decline in industrial production means that many firms close down or lay off some of their workers, it also means a decline in employment. Since, also, we know that much of the heavy industry of the country is highly localized in some districts, slumps have traditionally

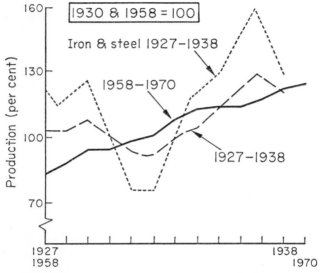

Fig. 4.13. Industrial Production, U.K., 1927–38 and 1958–70
Comparative Changes

given rise to pockets of unemployment in certain areas (*see* Chapter 7). The seriousness of this problem in the 1930s in fact prompted the government to take the special measures, mentioned earlier, to deal with the location of industry.

EXERCISES

(For key to symbols indicating sources, *see* p. 14.)

1. From a library obtain a copy of the latest issue of *The Times 1,000* (a publication containing details of the finances of the largest thousand companies in Britain). Add the profits earned last year in the largest twenty profit earners. Next refer to the *Annual Abstract of Statistics*, and extract the figure for the gross trading

profits of companies for the same year. (Use the Table headed Company Appropriation Account in the section "National Income".) Calculate the proportion of total company profits earned by the top twenty companies. Repeat the calculations for an earlier year. Has the degree of concentration in large companies appeared to change at all between the two dates?

2. Find out how many persons are employed in the firms in which three of your relatives or friends work. Assemble the information derived from the whole of your class, and prepare a table showing the size of firms for everyone concerned, grouping firms by size into the following classifications—

| less than 100 employees | 1,000–20,000 employees |
| 100–999 employees | over 20,000 employees |

Calculate the percentage of the total in each group.

3. Using figures of numbers employed, calculate the proportion of the total workers in the engineering industry and in food, drink and tobacco accounted for by each sub-group under those headings. (For example, the group "Agriculture," consists of sub-groups, agriculture, forestry, and fishing.) (A.S.)

4. Prepare two charts on the lines of Fig. 4.2 showing the relative importance of the major manufacturing industries according to whichever of the following are available—

(a) The value of net output,
(b) The value of sales,
(c) The volume of employment.

Use the latest figures available and compare your results. (A.S.)

5. List six of the most important industries in your locality. Can you offer suggestions as to why they were established there?

6. Using the oldest and latest figures you have available, calculate the proportion of total wage-earners in industrial groups according to whether you consider the product of that industry to be primary, secondary or tertiary in nature, and compare your results. (A.S.)

7. Make a graph showing the course of the index of industrial production and indices of production for the past twelve months in the following groups of industries—

| Engineering and allied industries | Textiles, leather and clothing |
| Chemicals and allied industries | All industry |

Is this a period of prosperity or depression (a) in industry generally, (b) in particular industries? (M.D.S. or E.T.)

8. From the latest edition of Who Owns Whom in your local library, prepare a chart on the lines of Fig. 4.8 for one of the following companies—

Imperial Tobacco Group Ltd.
Cadbury Schweppes Ltd.
The Rank Organization Ltd.
Great Universal Stores Ltd.
British Leyland Motor Corp. Ltd.

CHAPTER 5

Major British Industries

Our brief survey of the British economy in the previous chapter has forced us to overlook much interesting detail and we must, accordingly, spend some time examining the principal characteristics of some of the most important industries.

1. Agriculture

In the seventeenth century there would have been every justification for commencing with agriculture in any survey of British industries, for it was then by far the most important industry in the country, and was responsible for the employment of something like four out of every five working men and women. Even at the beginning of the nineteenth century, over one-third of the population worked on the land, and today the figure is more like one person in twenty-five. Increases in efficiency of methods in farming, however, have prevented a similar fall in the volume of agricultural output and, although we no longer grow enough food to feed our much larger population, it still remains the chief primary industry. In peacetime we have sometimes been apt to overlook this aspect of British agriculture, and to ignore its fairly continuous relative decline. But the experience of two world wars, when we were in danger of being cut off from overseas sources of supply and shipping space was badly needed for carrying troops and weapons, underlined the basic importance of food supplies in this island. Measures to expand the output of agriculture were adopted soon after the outbreak of war in 1939, and by the 1940s we had decreased our dependence on overseas supplies (measured in calories) from about 70 to 60 per cent of our requirements. By 1970 a new pattern had emerged in which home production accounted for approximately half the value of total consumption of food, and we were producing about 10 per cent of our butter, 30 per cent of our sugar, 40 per cent of our wheat, bacon and cheese, and two-thirds of our meat, but virtually all our liquid milk and eggs. It does not, of course, follow that it would be in any sense ideal for Britain to become self-sufficient in foodstuffs, especially since many other countries in the world are able to produce much more cheaply and sell food to us in exchange for our manufactures; but the extent of our dependence should be borne in mind when strategic questions are under consideration.

THE SIZE OF FARMS

In our discussion of manufacturing industry, we noticed a high degree of concentration in large-scale business in several sectors. In agriculture the story is rather different. About two-thirds of the agricultural holdings in England and Wales, for instance, are of less than 50 acres, and only about 3 per cent are of 500 acres or more. That is not to say that British farming is entirely dominated by small units. For one thing large farms have been increasing in relative importance, and those of at least 500 acres occupy a quarter of the total land. Moreover, something like half the total of about a quarter of a million agricultural holdings are worked only part-time by persons with other sources of income. The average size of farms worked full-time is about 160 acres and it is probably more reasonable to look on Britain as a country in which the medium-sized farm is fairly typical. This conveniently distinguishes us from France, where peasant smallholdings predominate and, at the other extreme, from the United States, where the wide expanses of land in the prairies have given rise to the typical large holding.

LAND USE

The United Kingdom is a country where land is scarce. Of the total area of sixty million acres, four million are covered with forest, and another three-quarters of a million are inland water. Seven million acres are used for houses, factories, roads and the like. Even the forty-eight million which remain can by no stretch of the imagination be called good agricultural land. Over a third is either so mountainous or has such poor soil that it is virtually beyond the margin of cultivation. This "rough grazing," as it is officially called, is not, of course, evenly spread over the country. Scotland is unfortunate in having two-thirds of the total for Britain, and much of Welsh agriculture is on land of this type.

Of the remainder of the land, about a quarter is much better permanent pasture, and only just over a third is used for the growing of crops. As can be seen from Fig. 5.1, however, even this is not all under the plough at any one time, but about a third is used as temporary grassland for mowing or grazing in rotation with other crops.

The additional land brought under the plough as part of the war effort after 1939 has been slowly returning to grassland, but the area under tillage is still higher than pre-war. The use made of the twelve

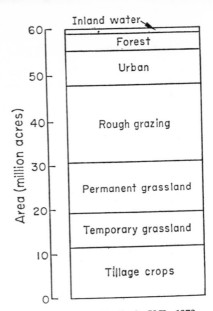

Fig. 5.1. **Land Use in the U.K., 1970**

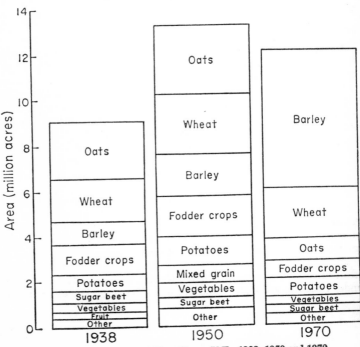

Fig. 5.2. **Land Under Tillage Crops, U.K., 1938, 1950 and 1970**

million acres devoted to the cultivation of tillage crops is shown in Fig. 5.2. As can be seen there, about three-quarters of the total is devoted to the production of cereals for both animal and human consumption. Barley has a higher yield than oats, which it has replaced as the foremost grain crop. Something like 5 per cent of the land is used for potatoes; and sugar beet, vegetables and other crops each absorb less than half a million acres.

LIVESTOCK

The shortage of good land suitable for arable cultivation makes the livestock population of the country a vitally important part of its agriculture. For, by and large, livestock can thrive on poorer soils than

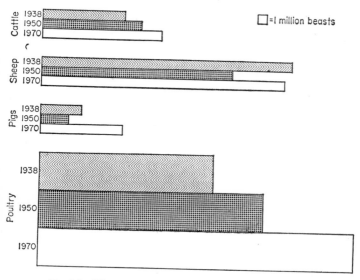

Fig. 5.3. Livestock Population, U.K., 1938, 1950 and 1970

growing crops like cereals or vegetables. There is now more livestock in the United Kingdom than in 1938, as Fig. 5.3 makes clear. The wartime need to save shipping space, however, required the use of more land in cereal production, and severe declines took place in the 1940s, especially in sheep and pig populations. Replacement was a slow process and not until 1959 did the number of sheep pass the 1939 figure.

AGRICULTURAL PRODUCTION

Land use and livestock populations, although important, are not a good guide to the contribution which farming makes to the standard of living. A better method of estimating the importance of the different agricultural products is shown in Fig. 5.4 where the relative values of the outputs of the chief commodities are set out for the farm year 1969–70. The outstanding position of livestock and livestock products,

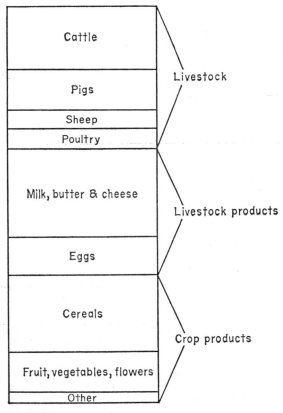

Fig. 5.4. **Agricultural Output, U.K., 1969–70**
Proportion of Individual Products in the Value of
Gross Agricultural Output

which account for nearly three-quarters of the total value of agricultural output, is at once evident. And although throughout the war the policy of bringing more land under cultivation resulted in a considerable increase in cereal and milk production, largely at the expense of meat, the pre-war pattern had been more or less restored by the mid-1950s. That is not to say that the volume of total agricultural output was the same as in 1939. Despite falling numbers of people working on the land, rising yields of crops and livestock have resulted in a level of output which was about double pre-war by 1970.

REGIONAL FARMING

We saw in Chapter 4 that the principal areas in Britain which specialized in agriculture included eastern and southern England and Scotland. We now know enough about the different kinds of farm produce, however, to realize that any broad statement is an over-simplification of the situation. An alternative idea of the pattern of agricultural production in England and Wales is achieved if we imagine a line drawn due south from Newcastle to the coast. Almost all the land on the east of this line is less than 400 ft. above sea level, whereas a great deal west of it is higher. Since mountainous and hilly land is generally unsuitable for growing crops, but at the same time tends to have greater rainfall, we find that specialization in Wales and the West Country is more often in dairy farming, while the greatest concentrations of cereal production take place in the flatter and drier eastern England.

This way of looking at things should not, however, be carried too far. It is intended only as a very rough guide to the principal kinds of agricultural specialization which take place in Britain. In fact, though such specialization does exist, it does so only to a limited extent, for British agriculture is an outstanding example of mixed farming. Even though there may be more wheat grown in East Anglia than in other parts of the country, we should not be surprised to find wheat in a field on a sheep farm in central Wales, or a few cows on a farm in Norfolk. For, though yields may vary considerably, mixed farming is one of the best ways of using a very limited supply of land.

Apart from this partial specialization, a number of products are much more evenly spread over the country. The keeping of pigs and poultry, for example, is quite widely dispersed, for neither is closely tied to special soils or climate, and both can exist on a very small patch of land, feeding on the surpluses of local production. The growing of fruit and vegetables is also subject to less specialization. The chief determinant in their case would appear to be proximity to a sizeable market and, wherever the soil is not too unsuitable, market gardeners set themselves up near to the big towns. It is true that they may need more fertilizers than the vegetable farmers in the rich soil regions, like the Vale of Evesham, but what they lose on this they make up in savings of transport costs.

Scotland does not fit very well into this survey. As already mentioned, the greater part of the land is mountainous and the soil is poor. Over most of the farming area cattle and sheep predominate, the latter mainly in the North-West. Crop production tends to be concentrated in the east, especially in the districts of Berwick, the Lothians, Fife and Forfar.

GOVERNMENT ASSISTANCE AND MARKETING

In the decades before the outbreak of the Second World War, the farming community had, on balance, a fairly difficult time. It is true that every year was not equally bad, but competition from foreign food producers was intense, and even the prosperous years were less marked in agriculture than in most other industries. By the beginning of the 1930s, the situation had become so serious that the government began to adopt a number of piecemeal measures to improve the lot of the farmer, and these were continued until the outbreak of war in 1939, when agriculture came into the front line and, with food production playing a vital role in the war effort, prosperity returned to the industry. After the war, both the major political parties agreed that every effort should be made to prevent agriculture from returning to its pre-war depressed state, and the result was embodied in the Agriculture Act of 1947.

The Act established a policy allowing the free import of foodstuffs into Britain, while subsidizing British producers by means of a "deficiency payment" representing the difference between the price they receive from the sale of their produce in the market and a "guaranteed price" for individual products. Guaranteed prices have been set annually at a February Price Review after meetings between the government and representatives of British farmers. The cost to the taxpayer has been of the order of £300 million in recent years.

The future style of agricultural support, however, is due for a radical change as a result of British entry into the Common Market (E.E.C.) (see below, pp. 281–4). Countries in the E.E.C. have adopted a common agricultural policy which takes the form of placing levies (or tariffs) on imported foodstuffs, which have the effect of raising internal market prices to the levels deemed desirable to support domestic producers. The British government announced its intention to move over to a system of levels for some products in 1971, and full membership implies that this will be extended. It is impossible to forecast exactly what this will mean for the future. It will certainly transfer the burden of subsidizing agriculture from the taxpayer to the consumer, as market prices rise and imports become gradually more expensive in the transitional period. In so far as low-cost foreign (non-E.E.C.) suppliers of agricultural products (such as New Zealand) find their prices less competitive than they used to be, there will also be a tendency for supplies to come from less efficient sources and therefore for the cost of food to rise also in Britain in real terms.

It must be added that the British government operates a number of other measures to assist agriculture—including direct grants for land improvements (drainage, silo construction, etc.) and support for the voluntary amalgamation of small farms. The state also provides, or assists in the provision of, national and regional advisory services for agriculture and sponsors research into agricultural problems.

Finally, mention should be made of the Marketing Boards which assist farmers to dispose of their produce on favourable terms. There are Boards for hops, milk, wool and potatoes, with powers which vary considerably. The Boards are, however, organizations set up by farmers themselves, though their schemes of operation need Parliamentary approval, and the Minister of Agriculture appoints some Board members.

2. The Iron and Steel Industry

The industry which the statisticians call "Metal Manufacture" employs half a million workers, three quarters of whom are in iron and steel. It is hardly more worthy of the title of a major British industry, therefore, than agriculture from the viewpoint of the size of its labour force. Steel, however, is basic to the production of so many articles of everyday life that it can be considered almost a primary industry. For steel is used directly for a wide variety of goods from razor blades to filing cabinets, but it is of great importance as a material for the motor vehicle industry, for machinery and equipment used in factories, and in building (see Fig. 5.5). Because of this, the rate at which output of steel expands is often taken as a guide to the state of industrial development which a country has reached. Thus, production of steel has grown from something under a million tons in the 1870s to 30 million in 1970.

The rather simple title of Iron and Steel conceals the fact that the activities usually considered under this heading are a very mixed lot. It is not easy, moreover, to define the limits of the industry. The basic products of pig iron, wrought iron, and steel ingots and castings form the kernel of the industry, but it is also usually taken to include the later stages in production by rolling steel into bars, plates, sheets, rods, tubes, etc., and also the coating of steel sheets to make tinplate. On the other hand the further manufacture of these products into such items as chains and hardware, nails, screws, pins and needles, wire, cutlery and tools and suchlike, is excluded on grounds of convenience, though they are often closely integrated with the manufacture of the more basic products.

Fig. 5.5.   Steel Consumption, U.K., 1970
Deliveries of Finished Steel

TECHNIQUES OF PRODUCTION

The first process in the industry occurs when iron ore, coke and limestone are fed into a blast furnace and smelted to produce pig iron which is subsequently transformed into steel by the removal of impurities in a second heating operation. A century ago this was a long expensive and laborious process, but the introduction of a new type of furnace—the Bessemer "Converter"—greatly simplified and cheapened the operation. Ten years later a further advance, the Siemens-Martin open-hearth furnace, was made which, while being more expensive than the Bessemer, made possible much greater control of the quality of the steel produced. Quality control is especially important in the case of alloy steels. For, although finished steel has many advantages over crude pig iron in strength and flexibility, even greater superiority can be obtained by introducing a quantity of some other metals during the production process, to make a steel alloy. Thus the addition of tungsten produces an alloy of greatly increased strength, widely used for tools; and, if chromium and nickel are added, a "stainless" steel results, which is not liable to rust or corrosion.

The Bessemer process was widely adopted in Britain and, in the 1880s, was responsible for about three-quarters of total steel production. Just before the end of the century, however, the emphasis had shifted to quality production, and the open-hearth process began to predominate. This trend continued during the twentieth century, and by the 1950s nearly 90 per cent of British steel was produced in open-hearth furnaces. Since the early sixties, however, the number of open-hearth furnaces in use has been declining in the face of further technological advance, in particular the appearance of electric furnaces and the development of highly efficient and flexible processes making use of pure oxygen. Automation has also been quite extensively applied to the industry. The major modern steelworks tend to be highly mechanized and computer-controlled. They are also increasingly integrating several stages in the production process, from the manufacture of iron, through that of steel, to the fashioning of semi-finished and finished steel products, in continuous strip mills, and even continuous casting works, for example.

LOCATION

The location of production in the steel industry has been dictated chiefly by the availability of coal and of the principal raw material—iron ore (though of considerable importance, as ore deposits are worked out, is scrap steel, which can be reconverted into high-grade steel). Of these two factors, the years have seen a change in relative importance and, as more efficient methods of production have resulted in economies in the use of coal, the ore has come to play the dominant part. British deposits of ore vary considerably in metallic content. The richest deposits, in Cumberland and Glamorgan, contain about 50 per cent of iron; but most home ore comes from the Midlands, especially from Lincolnshire and Northamptonshire. This latter ore is of relatively low grade and was little worked until after 1913, when technical advance made it a commercial proposition.

More than half the iron ore used in this country is actually mined abroad. Much foreign ore is a good deal richer in metallic content than British, and is imported from a great many parts of the world. The chief suppliers are Sweden, North Africa, Canada, Venezuela and the U.S.S.R.

The importance of imports should be borne in mind when examining the map of Fig. 5.6, which shows the regional distribution of crude steel output in Britain. It explains, in particular, the continued production of steel in South Wales, the Glasgow region of Scotland, and the north-east coast, where local ores no longer keep the industry going. These districts are well served by ports through which the imported ores can pass, and they are also near to suitable coal supplies. South Wales and the north-east coast are the principal centres of production, responsible for over 40 per cent of total output. The former is renowned for tinplate, and the latter concentrates more on heavier lines of product such as are used in shipbuilding.

ORGANIZATION

For technical reasons the production of steel is on the whole best carried on in very large plants. About three-quarters of the labour force in the industry is employed in establishments with more than 1,000 workers.

For the greater part of the nineteenth century Britain was the foremost producer of steel in the world and enjoyed a large export trade to many countries. During the 1870s, however, one of the principal of these markets, the United States, was lost when American resources were developed and, by the 1890s, the United States surpassed Britain as the leading producer of steel. By 1913, American production had leaped ahead and was about four times the British output. In Germany, too, development was late but by the beginning of the First World War she was producing about twice the British output. Largely as a result of this great increase in competition from foreign producers working with more modern equipment, the decade after the war was one of depression in the British steel industry, which reached really severe dimensions after 1929, when the general world slump in trade set in.

The situation was so serious that the government was forced in the 1930s to adopt measures to assist the industry, such as the levying of an

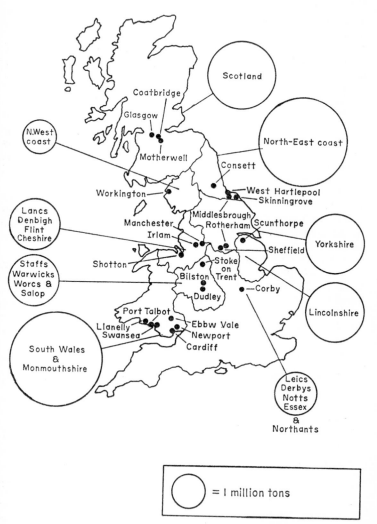

Fig. 5.6. **Crude Steel Production in Great Britain, 1970**

import duty on foreign steel to shield British producers from competition. In addition, the industry itself was not slow in taking action to reduce competition between the individual firms inside the country, with the object of increasing the general level of profits. Much integration through amalgamation and many other interlocking devices took place, covering most of the various stages in production from the actual mining of the ore through all the processes of smelting and rolling, even to such end-products as shipbuilding and engineering. This concentration was greatly assisted by the formation of the British Iron and Steel Federation in 1934, which began immediately to encourage schemes for reorganization and integration and to exercise the sort of control over price and production policies which is now associated with trade associations. The process of concentration continued after the Second World War and culminated in the nationalization of major sections of the industry in 1951. Following the general election of that year, a new Act began the process of selling them back to private ownership, but at the same time an Iron and Steel Board was established to provide some public supervision of the industry, and especially to set maximum prices and keep a watch on development.

In 1964 the Labour party was returned to office, pledged to the renationalization of steel. Three years later the thirteen major steel companies in the private sector, accounting for over 90 per cent of crude steel production, became part of the new nationalized British Steel Corporation—leaving some 200 firms, responsible for about a third of the industry's sales, in the private sector. Britain is now the world's fifth largest steel producer.

3. The Coal Industry

Coal mining employs about 300,000 workers and is our only important primary industry other than agriculture. Still the principal source of power, both for industrial and for domestic purposes, coal is fundamental to the whole economy. It is used to produce heat both directly, by burning as in the home grate, and indirectly to generate electricity and to manufacture gas, and it is also capable of other uses. It may be treated to produce such materials as coal tar, benzene, sulphate of ammonia and other chemicals, which may be used as fertilizers and in the production of dyestuffs, plastics and many other goods.

The coal industry does not, naturally, present the same difficulties of classifying the types of goods produced as, for example, iron and steel. Nevertheless, there are many different types and grades of coal mined in different parts of the country. The principal differences arise from variations in the heat (or calorific) value, in size, in content of ash and of chemicals such as sulphur, and in hardness. Each type frequently has a particular use for which it is best fitted. Thus coal used in steel manufacture should contain as little sulphur as possible, while that required for the production of coke should possess certain coking qualities, but differences should not be over-stressed as, in most cases, a great deal of substitution is technically feasible. As can be seen from Fig. 5.7, only about one-eighth of total coal consumption is used directly for domestic purposes, whereas nearly a half is used to make electricity, and another 15 per cent for gas and coke production.

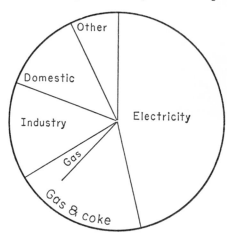

Fig. 5.7. Inland Consumption of Coal, U.K., 1970

TECHNIQUES OF PRODUCTION

Over 95 per cent of the coal produced in Britain is mined at a great depth beneath the earth's surface. Two principal systems have traditionally been employed. The oldest is the "Room and Pillar," which involves driving a number of narrow headings into the coal seam, thus cutting off large blocks or "pillars" of coal, which are then removed to leave an empty space or "room"; this must be supported by props before the next pillar is removed. The system is economical of labour but, as the richer seams are worked out, technical difficulties have decreased its importance in British mines. The method which has taken its place is that known as the "Longwall" system. Here the coal face is attacked on a wide front. The space left behind has then to be filled constantly by packing stones to prevent the roof caving in, and this involves the employment of extra labour and careful planning to prevent production hold-ups.

The chief reason for the greater productivity in coal mining in the last thirty or forty years has been the increasing use of machinery. At the outbreak of the First World War over nine-tenths of the coal was cut by hand; by the 1950s almost all was machine-cut. The heavy work of loading the coal on to the conveyers which take it away from the coal face, on the other hand, was until more recently done by hand. Machines for this task, however, have been increasingly introduced and by 1970 over 90 per cent of the deep-mined coal in Britain was power-loaded. Future increases in productivity will have to come from improvements of a different kind, especially from increases in the speed of ancillary work to keep pace with the highly mechanized coal-face and loading operations.

The remaining 5 per cent of coal is won from the earth by "open-cast" mining. This is only possible where the coal seams are very near to the surface of the ground. The soil and subsoil are first removed, and the coal is then lifted directly by mechanical shovels from a depth of up to about 200 feet below the surface.

COAL OUTPUT

The nineteenth century was the greatest period of expansion that the coal industry has ever seen. Output grew from about 10 million tons to a peak of 287 million tons in 1913, which has never been surpassed. The principal reason for the growth lay, of course, in the tremendous increase in industrial development and in population over this period, but there was also an important and growing demand for coal from abroad. The latter factor assumed a dominant role in the last decades before the First World War, when countries on the continent of Europe were in the full throes of industrialization. British coal exports in 1913 were nearly 100 million tons and accounted for about a third of total production.

The situation after 1918, when the war came to an end, was very different, as Fig. 5.8 shows. Neither production nor exports regained their pre-war position and, indeed, in 1933, the worst year between the two wars, neither was much more than two-thirds of the 1913 figure. Several reasons can be adduced for the depressed state of the coal industry in the 1920s and 1930s, but they all hinge on the decline in the demand for British coal. The export trade was severely hit by expansion of coal production in Europe, especially in Germany and Italy, and by replacement of coal by oil as the most important motive power of the world's shipping fleet. On the home front technical developments economizing in the use of coal had been made in a number of the principal coal-using industries, such as iron and steel. Some of these industries were also depressed for reasons of their own, and the decline in their production was reflected in a reduced coal consumption. Deplorable relations between the miners and the coal owners made matters considerably worse. The recommendations of the Sankey Commission in 1919 for the nationalization of the coal industry were not adopted by the government, and in their attempt to resist wage-cuts the miners came out on strike for long periods, even bringing the whole of industry with them in the General Strike of 1926. The measures adopted by the governments of the day to aid the industry in depression were similar in principle to those given to the steel industry. After a

Fig. 5.8. Coal Production and Exports of the U.K., 1913 and 1927–70

emporary subsidy in 1925–26, the major step was the Coal Mines Act of 1930, aiming at the elimination of competition between individual coal companies in Britain. The provisions of the Act included the establishment of a Central Council of coal owners with powers to regulate output and fix minimum prices, the setting up of a Commission to promote amalgamations between companies, and the repealing of an Act of 1926 which had established the eight-hour day.

RECENT DEVELOPMENTS

Since the end of the Second World War the coal industry has been through two quite contrasting phases. In the period up to 1955 vigorous efforts were made to regain the pre-war level of output and exports. But the industry was facing major problems of reorganization, including a severe manpower shortage. In spite of many improvements in conditions of work the existence of a plentiful supply of cleaner, safer and less strenuous jobs outside the industry was a formidable obstacle to attracting labour back down the mines. As may be seen from the chart, production climbed only slowly back towards pre-war levels, and it was never found possible to approach anything like even the 1939 level of exports.

After 1955, however, the pressure to expand was relaxed. Demand and production declined and exports sank to minute proportions. In 1968, a record low year, they were only 2 million tons. One of the major reasons for the decline was the inroads being made by an alternative source of power—oil. Whereas in 1947 oil provided less than one-tenth of total fuel supplies in this country, by the mid-1960s the proportion had risen to about a third. By 1970, oil had become almost as important as coal, and the development of nuclear power stations and exploitation of natural gas provided additional competing sources of energy. Still accounting for less than 10 per cent of total supplies, nuclear power and natural gas, however, are expected to increase their shares significantly in the 1970s.

LOCATION

The location of the coal industry in Britain, itself one of the major factors in the location of many other industries both past and present, is pretty rigidly determined by the geological conditions which gave rise to the formation of seams of coal in prehistoric times. These as Fig. 5.9 shows, are fairly widely scattered over the country. The largest coalfield by far is that extending across the boundaries of Derbyshire, Nottinghamshire and Yorkshire. Accounting for about half of total coal production, it also includes relatively new coalfields where output per manshift is high. The coalfield of Northumberland and Durham produces about a sixth of total output. Admirably suited to the export trade in coal, this region suffered greatly from the decline in coal exports after 1913. Many of the easiest seams have been worked out and, with fairly low productivity compared with some of the newer fields, it cannot expect to return to its earlier position. The South Wales coalfield accounts for about a tenth of total production but this, too, is a declining area. Like the northern field, its heyday coincided with a flourishing export trade, and it suffered intense depression in the years between the two world wars. Productivity there is particularly low—the result of increasing difficulty in working less accessible seams, but the high quality of much of its coal is a partial offsetting factor.

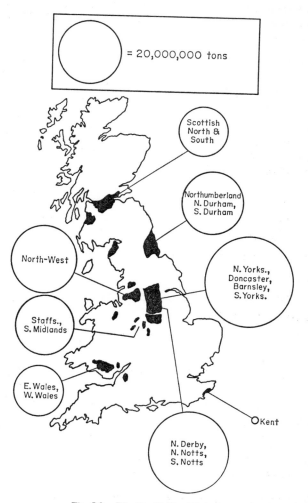

Fig. 5.9. **The Coalfields of Britain**
Regional Coal Output, 1970

There are other coalfields in the West Midlands; in the North-West, where reserves are rapidly being exhausted; in Scotland where production is declining and in Kent, where output is very small.

4. Clothing and Textiles

Clothing and textiles, it may be recalled, have not been among the most rapidly expanding industries in Britain recently. Textiles, in particular, have been losing ground for several decades. Since the mid-nineteen-twenties, employment has fallen by about 50 per cent in spite of the increase in the size of the working population and the development of new man-made fibres. Taking clothing and textiles together, however, they still employ over a million workers. In the textile trades, three-quarters of them are women.

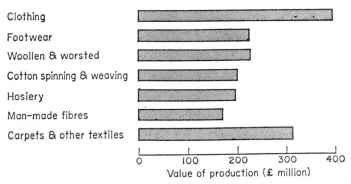

Fig. 5.10. **Clothing and Textiles: Value of Production, U.K., 1968**

The principal sections of the industry are set out in Fig. 5.10. The clothing industry is quite widely spread over the country though there are important centres of the garment trade in London, Manchester and Leeds, and of footwear and hosiery in Northampton, Leicester and Nottingham. Although there are some large firms, for example in men's tailoring, small-scale organization is typical of much of the industry.

The textile sections are principally concerned with the manufacture of yarns and fabrics. Divisions between categories can be based upon materials used and the processes of manufacture themselves. The main materials are cotton, wool, and man-made fibres, and the following discussion is based upon this division. With the modern tendency to produce cloths which are a blend of two or more of these, however, the distinctions should not be exaggerated.

Cotton Textiles

Cotton is the section within the textile group which has suffered the greatest decline of all. Cotton goods are manufactured from the lint of the cotton plant, which is put through a variety of different processes. The first of these is ginning, which involves the separation of the lint from the cotton seed and which takes place near where the cotton is grown. On arrival at the country of manufacture, the lint is cleaned and combed and then goes to the spinning mills where it is converted to yarn. The next operation consists of the weaving of the yarn into cloth on machines called looms, of which there are two principal kinds: the ordinary looms which can most easily be adjusted for changes in the type of cloth desired, and the automatic looms which can produce about three times as much cloth of a standardized pattern but which cannot be quickly adjusted to frequent changes in quality, design, etc. The final stages in the production of cotton cloth then follow; bleaching, dyeing, printing and finishing are the most important of these operations.

LOCATION

The location of the cotton industry in Britain is so heavily concentrated in Lancashire that a map to demonstrate this would be superfluous. In order to understand the reasons for this concentration it is necessary to go back nearly two hundred years in history. Before the great mechanical inventions of the later eighteenth century, cotton came to Lancashire which already had an established woollen and linen industry and was relatively free from contemporary restrictions to which trade was subject. The introduction of power-driven machinery in the cotton mills led to some dispersal of the industry, especially to Scotland where there was plenty of water power in mountain streams. But this movement was reversed with the use of the steam-engine and the growth of the port of Liverpool, convenient for supplies of raw cotton from the southern American states. From about 1800 Lancashire never looked back and by the beginning of the twentieth century over three-quarters of the industry's labour force was already in the county. Within Lancashire, too, geographical specialization had been taking place in the different sections of the industry. Spinning and weaving, the two most important processes, were almost always undertaken by independent firms, the former being located largely in the part of the county south of Rochdale and the latter to the north.

5

GROWTH AND DECLINE

The period of growth in Lancashire's cotton textiles coincided with
an age of overwhelming British supremacy in world production of
cotton goods. In the middle of the nineteenth century this country
owned over half the world's productive capacity and supplied nearly
three-quarters of world trade in cotton goods. Expansion continued
until the outbreak of the First World War, though the dominant
position had begun to be eclipsed somewhat earlier. The war, however
marked a turning point in the history of Lancashire cottons and, as

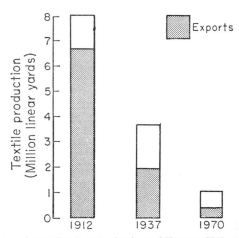

Fig. 5.11.   Cotton Textiles: Production and Exports, U.K., 1912–70
Production of Fabrics and Exports of Piece Goods

Fig. 5.11 shows, commenced the tremendous decline in both production
and exports which continued practically without interruption to the
present day. The principal cause of this change is to be found in the
situation in the export trade. For, even as late as 1913, Britain was
exporting about 80 per cent of her production of cotton goods. By the
end of the 1930s, in spite of a 70 per cent fall in production, only about
a half of this was sent to overseas markets.

Partly this may be explained by the growth of competition from
other exporters, especially from Japan, who, with a very cheap and
plentiful supply of labour, managed to win from Lancashire many of
her traditional markets, particularly in the Far East. More specifically,

he decline in British exports may be traced to a decline in the volume
f world trade in cotton goods which began in the period between the
wo world wars. The appearance of cotton-textile industries in countries
which had previously been the most important markets for Lancashire's
xports was, in part, the result of the war and the consequent cutting
ff of supplies from Britain, but many countries were determined in
ny event to set up new industries, and cotton happened to be one of
he easiest for a non-industrialized country to begin with. Markets were
ost in the United States, Brazil and many other South American
ountries, but above all in India, whose imports of British cotton goods
ell from over 3,000 million yards in 1913 to under 300 million in 1938.

After 1945 the industry enjoyed a period of brief revival, but the
ost-war boom was not long-lived and from 1951 the decline returned
1 both production and exports. In export markets it was the same
tory of competition from foreign low-cost producers in a world where
ne total volume of trade continued to fall. At home, too, foreign
ompetition began to be a serious threat to domestic production. By
960, imports (especially from India, Pakistan and Hong Kong) were
unning at a level more than ten times greater than pre-war. To meet
iis, the industry was successful in inducing the government to put
eilings on imports, which has kept the volume down since 1966.

RGANIZATION

part from some very large-scale organization at the two ends of the
ade, especially in dyeing, calico printing and fine sewing-thread
pinning, cotton-textile production has in the past tended to favour the
nall firm especially in the weaving section. This is less true now that
ie industry has contracted so far at the expense of the smaller units,
nd vertical integration has also taken place. Small-scale production
 not inherent in cotton weaving, as indeed the organization of the
idustry in the United States emphasizes, but was a result of peculiarly
ritish conditions. For the industry tends to emphasize high-quality
oods, for which the more efficient automatic loom is less suitable.
he decline in the British export trade since 1913 has accentuated this
ndency for, as competition became intense in the cheaper grades of
oth, Lancashire became increasingly dependent upon exports of
uality goods, and the substitution of the old looms by the new auto-
iatic ones, which nearly all other countries were using, was held up.

The high degree of specialization and consequent diversity of interests
 cotton textiles help to explain why attempts at integration and
ationalization" in the 1930s were less successful than, for example, in
al or iron and steel. Some combination did, of course, take place and

surplus capacity was reduced in the spinning section, but very little was achieved in weaving where organization was on an even smaller scale. The continued decline of the industry in the 1950s, however, led to the reappearance of more excess capacity and prompted the government to bring in the Cotton Industry Act of 1959. This measure secured the scrapping of nearly half the industry's spindles and looms by providing two-thirds of the finance needed. Government funds to help install up-to-date machinery or equipment were also made available.

Wool Textiles

While the English climate is unsuitable for the growing of cotton, and the development of that industry had to await the opening up of other areas of the world, Britain has had a large sheep population for many centuries, and the woollen industry is naturally very much older than the cotton industry.

The processes to which raw wool is subjected are broadly similar to those for cotton, with a number of additions necessitated by the fact that it is an animal and not a vegetable fibre. Woollen fibres are not all of the same length or quality, and this gives rise to a division of the industry into two main sections: woollen goods proper and worsteds. Briefly, the difference between them is that the worsteds are made from top-quality long fibres, which are combed parallel to produce a fine woven cloth, while the coarser short fibres are left for the rougher woollens. The industry as a whole is organized in smaller units than cotton, except for the combing, dyeing and finishing trades. There is, however, a contrast between the woollen and worsted sections. The typical firm in the woollen branch has undertaken both spinning and weaving, whereas in worsteds these functions have tended to be specialized among firms, though integration has been taking place in recent years.

LOCATION

Until the eighteenth century the woollen industry was quite widely dispersed over the country although concentration was to be found especially in East Anglia and the West of England where sheep farming and, hence, the raw material predominated. With the development of textile machinery, which for a number of reasons came rather later to wool than to cotton, concentration began in the West Riding of Yorkshire about the 1830s. Dependence on foreign supplies of wool (mainly from Australia, New Zealand and South Africa) has at the same time increased, and today less than 20 per cent of home consumption of vool comes from British sheep. Within the West Riding itself further pecialization has taken place. Worsteds have tended to be located n the western district around Bradford and Halifax, with woollens nore popular in the east and south around Leeds. Woollens are not quite so exclusively confined to the West Riding, and some other egions, of which the Scottish Border, the Hebrides, the West of England and Wales are the most important, produce certain special lines n wool cloth, especially tweeds.

CONOMIC DEVELOPMENT

he growth of the woollen industry in the nineteenth century began to low down rather earlier than that of the cotton industry and reached a

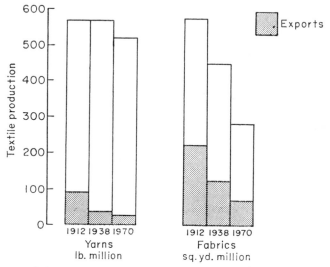

Fig. 5.12. **Production and Exports of Wool Textiles, U.K., 1912–70**

eak in the 1870s. This was largely due to the fact that the chief arkets abroad were in countries settled by Europeans who set up eir own wool-textile industries long before such relatively backward untries as India established their cotton mills. The distinctly lesser ependence of the woollen industry upon exports is the principal reason hy the depression in the years following the end of the First World ar was not so severely felt as in cotton. Some decline indeed took ace, as Fig. 5.12 shows, but this was not nearly so catastrophic.

In recent years, output and exports of fabrics have tended downwards, while both production and trade in yarns have held up much better.

Man-made Fibres

The production of man-made fibres has at least as much right to be considered part of the chemical industry as of textiles, but its products compete directly with the natural fibres of cotton and wool, so it may receive attention here.

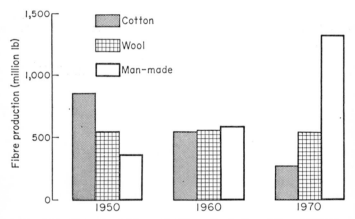

Fig. 5.13.   **Natural and Man-made Fibres: Production of Yarn, 1950–70**

Measured by the yardstick of the employment of labour it hardly stands out in its correct perspective, since only about 50,000 persons worked in the industry in 1970. This is an understatement of its importance for at least two reasons: first, its production involves not so much labour as a great deal of capital equipment; and second, in marked contrast to most of the other branches of the textile industry its output has been expanding rapidly since the last war. Fig. 5.13 shows how its importance has increased since 1950 and the extent to which man-made fibres have displaced conventional ones.

PRODUCTS AND PROCESSES

There are two principal types of synthetic fibres, which differ both in method of manufacture and raw material.

1. *Rayon* is the oldest and still the largest of the main products. Its development can be traced back about 100 years, although it was not a commercial success until the 1890s. The first factory in Britain was built near Coventry in 1905. Rayon has a vegetable base (cellulose) and is made from wood pulp or cotton linters. There are two methods of manufacture, known as viscose and acetate production, both of which involve pressure-feeding through a small jet to produce the filament. Over three-quarters of output is of the viscose variety.

2. The newer *non-cellulose* fibres are sometimes referred to as "true" synthetics in contrast to rayon, because they are derived entirely from chemicals. They have very largely been developed either during or since the Second World War, and by 1970 accounted for roughly half of man-made fibre production. The processes involved in their production are generally more complex than in rayon. There are several different types of fibres in this category, and the number and variety change almost yearly with research. The original, and for long the leader, nylon, and its rival Terylene, can be derived from by-products of coal and petroleum. There are also more recent so-called acrylic fibres such as Orlon, Acrilan and Courtelle, which share a common base and have similar properties.

LOCATION AND ORGANIZATION

The organization of synthetic-fibre production contrasts with that of cotton and wool. Heavy capital and research expenses are involved and the major producers tend to be vertically integrated, for example, backwards into oil-cracking to produce the raw material, and forward into weaving and finishing, and even in some cases into garment manufacture. The degree of concentration in large enterprises is, in consequence, exceptionally high.

Imperial Chemical Industries manufacture nylon at Pontypool, Doncaster and Gloucester, and Terylene at Wilton in Yorkshire. Courtaulds dominates the production of rayon, which takes place largely in the Midlands and Lancashire, though they also make other synthetics, e.g. Courtelle.

USERS OF MAN-MADE FIBRES

Most man-made fibres are produced in two forms for different purposes: as a continuous filament and, as natural fibres, in short lengths known as staple. The principal consumer of synthetic fibres is, of course, the clothing industry, where they are employed either on their own or in blend with natural fibres or with each other.

Rayon staple is a particularly good example of a fibre used in blend in fabrics for the lower-priced garment trade for both men and women. It has also been successfully adopted for conventional and tufted carpets. Continuous-filament rayon was originally important for ladies' stockings, where it has lost some ground to nylon, but an important new use was found in the manufacture of vehicle tyres.

The non-cellulose fibres have attractive qualities such as strength and crease-resistance, which have earned them a special place in the manufacture of apparel. They compete with both wool and cotton; and the acrylic fibres, in particular, are warm to the touch.

In addition to domestic uses, over 10 per cent of British production of man-made fibres is exported as raw material.

5. The Chemical Industry

Our discussion of man-made fibres has been undertaken, for convenience, under the heading of the textile industry. But the processes by which synthetics are manufactured are much more comparable with those of many chemicals than with wool or cotton, and it is worth while taking a look at some other aspects of the chemical industry, which produces nearly a tenth of total manufacturing output. It is important to emphasize, too, that, as we saw in Chapter 4 (Fig. 4.3, p. 70.), the chemical industry has been one of the most rapidly expanding sectors, with output advancing roughly twice as fast as in industry as a whole. Exports have risen also, and chemicals accounted for 10 per cent of the total value of all exports in 1970.

STRUCTURE AND DEVELOPMENT

The main groups in the industry are shown in Fig. 5.14, but the interrelationships between them are complex, and too much should not be made of the divisions. For example, both organic and inorganic chemicals may be counted as earlier stages in the production of many plastics, fertilizers, detergents, paint, etc.

The plastics section of the industry has been one of the fastest growing in recent years. Plastics are not capable of simple definition, but may be taken to include materials the shape of which can be controlled at some stage in the production process, usually by moulding or extrusion. Development, especially of thermoplastics like polyvinyl chloride (P.V.C.), polyethylene, polystyrene, etc., with their widespread uses as materials for packaging foodstuffs, cable coverings, domestic utensils, toys and other mouldings, etc., has been linked with the supply of organic chemicals, the great bulk of which are now petroleum based.

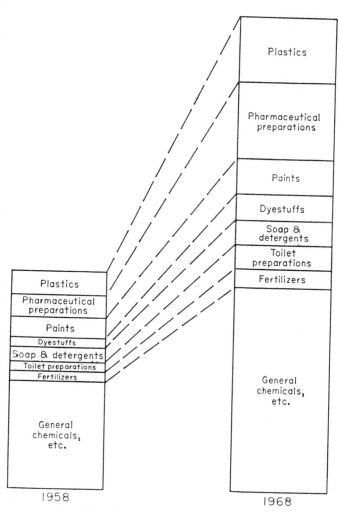

Fig. 5.14. **The Chemical Industry, U.K., 1958–68**
Main Sectors by Value of Net Output

Petro-chemicals are produced during oil-refining as a result of distillation and the catalytic, or steam, cracking of the petroleum molecules. They yield a wide range of plastic materials, but also liquid detergents, solvents for the paint industry, industrial alcohol, fertilizers, synthetic rubber, fungicides and many others. Pharmaceutical preparations, including drugs, account for about a sixth of the value of the industry's output. Other important products are paint, dyestuffs, toilet preparations, soap and detergents, explosives, pesticides, polishes and a wide range of other chemicals and chemical products.

ORGANIZATION

The great diversity of products of the chemical industry in Britain precludes any very useful discussion of the way in which it is organized. And indeed the difficulty of drawing hard and fast lines between industries is well illustrated in the case of chemicals. The production of petro-chemicals, for instance, really cuts right across the oil industry. On the one hand, the Shell Co. operates subsidiaries which make it self-sufficient in the manufacture of certain specialized chemicals from the earliest refining stages, while, on the other hand, I.C.I. has its own catalytic cracking plants. Extensive equipment is needed and a high degree of automation exists in the small number of firms concerned. Much the same is true of many other products, and the chemical industry is dominated by I.C.I., though there are other quite large firms like Monsanto, and Albright & Wilson. A number of them, especially in the pharmaceutical section, are subsidiaries of foreign companies. There are also a considerable number of smaller firms in certain lines, such as paints and plastic moulding. The location of many individual products is quite highly concentrated. Petro-chemical production, for instance, tends to be close to the oil refineries. Other products are more widely dispersed, as, for instance, paint. Taking the industry as a whole, the bulk of employment is in the north-west, north-east and south-east of England.

6. The Engineering Industry

Engineering is at once the largest and in many ways the most complicated of British industries. Depending on how it is defined, it employs a quarter to a third of the labour force in manufacturing, and includes such a wide variety of different products, from radios to ocean-going liners, that no general discussion of techniques is possible. While common features are limited, the outstanding one which binds various firms together, and permits the examination of an engineering group at all, is the fact that they are all concerned with the fabrication of some sort of machinery, largely from iron and steel. Although this helps to explain the inclusion of several of its branches, it does not enable us to draw a hard and fast line defining the limits of the industry. Different and arbitrary limits are taken for different purposes. The manufacture of electrical machinery, machine tools and scientific instruments, for instance, is always included; so too, often, is shipbuilding and marine engineering. Vehicle production, on the other

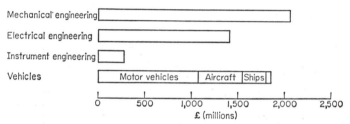

Fig. 5.15. **Engineering and Vehicles, U.K., 1968**
Value of Net output

hand, is frequently considered a separate industry on account of its size, though it is fundamentally in the same category as shipbuilding. Some idea of the scope of engineering may be gained from Fig. 5.15, which shows the value of the output of major sections.

LOCATION

Taking the engineering industry as a whole, the first impression one gets is of a fairly wide dispersion of production over the country. None of the major regions in Britain has less than 10 per cent of its labour force in engineering of one sort or another. At the same time a considerable amount of specialization does take place in the individual sectors of the industry, as Fig. 5.16 shows.

Thus, the bulk of motor-vehicle production is concentrated in the West Midlands, especially around Birmingham and Coventry, and in the South-East, though some dispersion has occurred in recent years, with plants in Merseyside, Scotland and Wales. Aircraft production predominates in the South-East, the Midlands, the South-West around Bristol, and in Lancashire. Agricultural machinery tends to come from East Anglia, where agriculture is important, but also from the South-East and the Midlands. Shipbuilding is highly localized, especially on the Clyde, the north-east coast, the South-East,

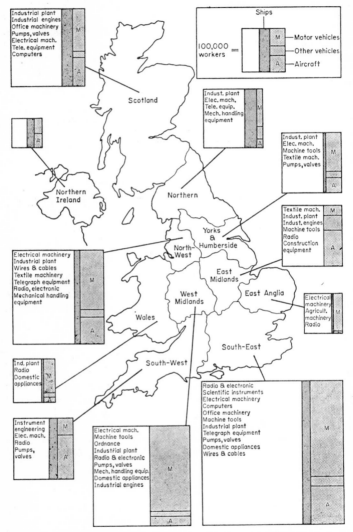

Fig. 5.16. **Engineering Industry, U.K., 1970, Location of Employment**
(Some important sections of engineering are indicated.)

at Barrow and Birkenhead in the North-West, and at Belfast in Northern Ireland.

The South-East region, the largest by far it will be remembered, leads the field in many lines but especially in radio and electronic equipment, scientific instruments, computers, office machinery, industrial plant, and telegraph and telephone apparatus and equipment. The West Midland region is the second biggest, and predominates in the production of motor vehicles, machine tools, electrical machinery and industrial engines. The North-West region follows closely in total production, and has for long been the chief producer of textile machinery, stimulated by local cotton and woollen industries. It is the leading producer also in locomotive and track equipment, and has expanded more recently in several other lines, being now an important producer of electrical machinery and industrial plant.

ECONOMIC DEVELOPMENT

The diversity of production in engineering makes it difficult to tell a simple story of the progress of the industry. Some of the products, such as the steam engine, have their origin in the "industrial revolution" of the later eighteenth century, when motor power was first applied to industry. The majority, however, are newer and their development can rarely be traced back much before the middle of the nineteenth century, and often only to considerably later than that. It is useful to distinguish between the relatively older and newer branches, for the inter-war years saw the beginning of a shift in emphasis between them which has since been continued.

The great expansions in the newer manufactures were in motor vehicles and electrical goods, where important inventions like the internal combustion engine and wireless had become commercial propositions and had opened up great new possibilities. The same groups (motor vehicles, electrical machinery, radio, etc.,) provided the bulk of the expansion after the end of the Second World War. Production of some of these (cars, T.V. and radio sets, for instance) had begun to lag behind the leaders by the 1960s, however, and the pace has more recently been set by certain rather specialized sections of the industry, e.g., especially, electronic equipment and computers, some machine tools, mechanical handling equipment, chemical plant and instrument engineering.

The older parts of the industry, such as shipbuilding and steam engines, were the ones to suffer most from the depressed conditions of the 1920s and 1930s. Most of these, too, have continued their decline since the end of the Second World War. In shipbuilding, for instance, British production in 1913 had amounted to about 40 per cent of the world total. By 1939 it had fallen to 25 per cent, and by the beginning of the 1970s to 5 per cent.

The relative newness of many engineering products, however, is in marked contrast to some of the other leading industries so far examined —agriculture, coal, and wool and cotton textiles. The pattern there, of British pre-eminence in the eighteenth and nineteenth centuries and gradual eclipse in the twentieth, cannot therefore apply to all engineering. It is true that, in 1913, Britain and Germany were the principal world suppliers of engineering products, and that even before the Second World War the United States had shot far into the lead. But losses have been considerably less than in some other fields and production has kept up reasonably well. In fact, as far as the export trade is concerned, the greater decline in exports of other industries has been reflected in an increased importance of engineering products. In 1970, these accounted for over 40 per cent of the total value of British exports. Transport equipment, especially, deserves mention in this connexion. For some years now it has made up about one-third of the engineering contribution to exports. Motor vehicles are, of course, among the most important. In 1970, more than 40 per cent of British output of one and three-quarter million cars and half a million commercial vehicles went overseas.

ORGANIZATION

While generalization is dangerous in an industry as widely diversified as engineering, it is true to say that large-scale business predominates here. In the field as a whole, about half of the entire labour force is in establishments with over a thousand workers. Although some branches, for instance the manufacture of mechanical handling equipment and textile machinery contain a fair number of small firms, concentration in others is very great. This is especially the case where the existence of large markets for standardized products in sections of the industry have made mass-production techniques economical. Automation has been introduced to the manufacture of engines and other engineering products, for instance, by installing transfer machines to organize sequences of assembly operations. In the vehicle industry three-quarters of the labour force is in establishments with more than a thousand workers. In the motor section four large groups—British Leyland (Austin, Morris, Wolseley, etc.), Ford, Chrysler (U.K.) (Hillman, Humber, etc.), and General Motors (a U.S.A. concern making Vauxhall and Bedford)—manufacture about 95 per cent of British output. The five largest firms sell more than 70 per cent of the industry's production of valves, machinery for the chemical industry, and electrical equipment for motor vehicles; more than 80 per cent of output of ball bearings, television sets and batteries; and more than 90 per cent of the production of telephone wires and cables, locomotives, aircraft, vacuum cleaners and gramophone records.

7. Transport

Although the provision of transport constitutes a tertiary service rather than a primary or a secondary industry, it qualifies for inclusion in this chapter on two grounds. In the first place, it is an important employer of labour and accounts for approximately one out of every fourteen members of the employed population. In the second place, transport occupies something of a key role in the economy. Even a relatively minor hold-up in the system can have far-reaching and dislocating effects on industry generally. The vital importance of the railways, for example, has prompted governments to assume direct responsibility for their operation for the duration of two world wars, and was one of the major arguments put forward for their nationalization, together with other forms of transport, in 1947 (*see above*, Chapter 3, pp. 58–9).

INLAND TRANSPORT

Transport is used to convey people and goods, and in Britain the vast majority of journeys are made either by road or by rail. Fig. 5.17 is no more than statistical confirmation of the well-known fact that the bulk of both passenger and goods traffic in the sixties goes by road, a lot more, of course, than used to. Not too much importance should be attached to the exact relative shares, which depend significantly upon the actual measure used. Since journeys by road tend to be shorter than by rail, for instance, the use of goods mileage, rather than just tonnage, as an indicator, would increase the apparent share of rail in freight traffic.

Apart from road and rail a small amount of traffic is carried by air and on the water. Canals had their hey-day in the last quarter of the eighteenth century and the first quarter of the nineteenth, before the coming of the railways, which largely superseded them. Being both less accessible and much slower they gradually went out of use, and in 1970 carried less than one per cent of the total tonnage of all inland transport. Coastwise shipping, on the other hand, retains a small but significant share in goods traffic. For the island nature of the country and the fact that so many centres of industrial activity are situated near to ports means that the shipping of bulky merchandise between such places as Cardiff and London, though slow, is relatively cheap and can still be quite convenient. Transport by air possesses the obvious advantage of speed which can sometimes offset the generally higher costs incurred. But in spite of an approximate threefold increase in traffic since 1960, the volume is still too small to show in Fig. 5.17 in

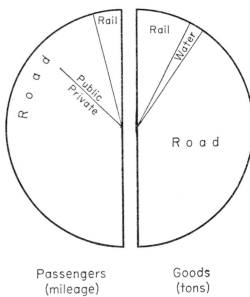

Passengers
(mileage)

Goods
(tons)

Fig. 5.17.   Inland Transport, U.K., 1970
Share of Road, Rail and Waterways (including Coastal Shipping)

comparison with other forms of transport. No doubt the relatively short distances in Britain are partly responsible for the fact that road and rail remain the major means of transport, and we should, therefore, look a little more closely at each of these.

RAILWAYS

The application of the steam-engine to vehicles, which heralded the development of railway transport in Britain, is usually traced to the famous Stockton–Darlington Railway which was opened in 1825, although it was not until about 1840 that rapid expansion really began. The period of extension of the railways, however, is now economi history. Since the beginning of the twentieth century additions have been very few and far between, the tendency being rather to close down less frequently used lines than to open up new ones. The changeover from rapid growth in the mid-nineteenth century to decline in the mid-twentieth is largely due to the revolution in road transport which followed the invention of the internal combustion engine, the most recent features of which have been the post-war private car boom, and the expansion of road freight and passenger services competing successfully on price.

The continuously unsatisfactory financial position of the railways led to major closures of branch lines, and British Rail began to concentrate its attention on inter-city main line services. Various schemes for reorganization were also tried, including the Transport Act of 1968

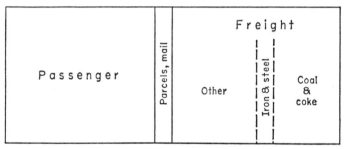

Fig. 5.18.   **British Rail, Traffic Receipts from Passenger and Freight Services, 1970**

(see above, p. 59), which introduced, among other measures, a system of government grants for unremunerative branch lines, which it is considered desirable to retain on social grounds.

As Fig. 5.18 shows, the railways derive about half their revenue from the carriage of freight. The bulk of such receipts comes from the transport of heavy iron and steel, and coal and coke. The last of these is, however, a diminishing source of income, as the coal industry itself is, as we noticed earlier in this chapter, declining. Passenger receipts are, therefore, becoming relatively more important. The Railways Board has been engaged in trying to raise the quality (including speed) of its services by electrification and other means. At the end of the 1960s, its policies showed some signs of success as the volume of passenger traffic started to turn up; though it has doubtless been aided by the lengthening delays and increasing frustration that congestion has brought to the roads of Britain.

ROAD TRANSPORT

The great developments in road making which are usually associated with the names of Telford and McAdam actually preceded the growth of railway transport, but they were not fully used until after the "railway age." It was not until the internal combustion engine was invented by Lenoir in 1860 and developed to produce the first British petrol-driven car in 1895 that road transport became a really serious proposition.

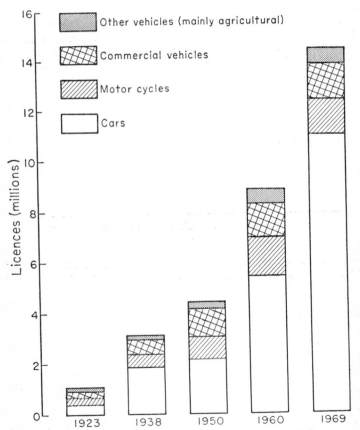

Fig. 5.19.   **Motor Vehicle Licences: Great Britain, 1923–1969**
Numbers of Current Licences

Even so, much had still to be done, and it was the stimulation of the First World War and the large-scale use of lorries to transport men and materials that startlingly revealed the possibilities of the new form of transportation. Fig. 5.19 shows the fourteen-fold increase in the number of motor vehicles on the roads of Britain which took place between 1923 and 1969.

Road transport was soon to prove itself admirably suited to the carriage of persons and goods, especially over relatively short distances. Much more flexible than the railways, lorries can go direct from door to door, effecting a great saving in time and permitting more careful treatment of any goods liable to damage. Commercial vehicles headed the advance. Many ex-servicemen went into the business, buying an old army lorry with their gratuity and a loan to cover the balance, even before new vehicle production had time to get going after the war.

The growth of road transport, and particularly of goods transport, was so rapid in the 1920s, and the consequent loss of traffic by the railways so serious, that pressure was brought upon the Government to take some action to hold up the advance. The most important measure consisted of the Road and Rail Traffic Act of 1933. Apart from certain provisions regarding the fitness of vehicles on the roads and conditions of work for driver employees, the main purpose of the Act was to limit the entry of new hauliers into the business of transporting goods by road. This was achieved by a system of licensing under which applicants for licences to carry goods for others had to show a need for their services—a need which competitors could contest (licences for users to carry their own goods being given automatically on satisfaction of the fitness conditions). The Act undoubtedly had the effect of slowing down the development of commercial goods transport by road in the remaining years before the Second World War, but the transfer to public ownership of long-distance road haulage in 1947 greatly reduced the significance of the licensing system. Denationalization of the major sections in 1953 restored it, although amendments made then and in the Transport Act of 1968 increased the latitude of the authorities in considering applications. Long-distance freight services remaining in public hands were run by British Road Services until 1968, when they were taken over by the National Freight Corporation run, in conjunction with British Rail, to promote a nationally integrated road and rail system for the carriage of goods.

For road passenger transport, a licensing system somewhat similar to that for goods was introduced by the Road Traffic Act of 1930. Public transport of passengers by road in England and Wales is in the hands of both state authorities and private enterprise. The Transport

Act of 1968 established the National Bus Company, which operates some 20,000 vehicles, and set up local Passenger Transport Authorities, which control the buses previously run by municipal authorities, and are given the task of co-ordinating all passenger transport services in their areas, both road and rail.

INTERNATIONAL TRANSPORT

Britain being an island, transport to and from our shores must be either by air or by sea. Shipping is of great importance from the viewpoint of foreign trade, where Britannia used to rule. While Britain is still a major maritime nation, her position of overwhelming dominance has now been lost. In 1913, this country was responsible for over forty per cent of the world's tonnage of merchant ships. By 1939, this had fallen to less than a quarter, and by 1970 to about a tenth. Our changed position may be traced in part to the Second World War, which stimulated shipping in other countries, especially the United States, at a time when our resources were fully occupied. But since the end of the war Britain has continued to lose ground as Norway and Japan, in particular, have added to their merchant fleets. The practice has also grown up of registering ships under the so-called "flags of convenience", particularly that of Liberia, to obtain certain tax advantages. While we, therefore, have heavy payments to make to foreigners these days on account of shipping charges and can no longer count on a substantial net credit balance, receipts for the services of British shipping still make a sizeable contribution to this country's foreign earnings.

Air transport plays a larger part in the carriage of passengers than of goods though more than ten per cent of the *value* of the United Kingdom's foreign trade now goes by aircraft. This form of transport is, however, most important for relatively light valuable articles, where higher costs do not act as a strong deterrent. Passenger services bring in most revenue, and these have been growing on a world scale. Approximately twice as many persons now enter and leave the country by air as by sea. The organization of the nationalized air corporations, B.E.A. and B.O.A.C., was referred to in Chapter 3 above.

EXERCISES

(For key to symbols indicating sources, *see* p. 14.)

1. Obtain figures of the total coal output in Britain last year and three years ago, and also of the labour force engaged in coal mining in the same years. Calculate the number of tons produced per man for both years. Can you think of any reasons for such differences as you may find? (*A.S.*)

2. Prepare a graph showing the trend in the production of cars and commercial vehicles over the last five years. (*A.S.* or *E.T.*)

3. Prepare a chart on the lines of Fig. 5.12, showing the production of cotton cloth and man-made fibres for the years 1913, 1924, 1937, 1950, 1960 and the latest year for which you have figures. (*K.S.* and *A.S.*)

4. Calculate the proportions of total output of the following goods which were exported last year and five years ago—

Coal

Cars and commercial vehicles

Agricultural machinery

Alcoholic spirits

Finished steel

Woollen and worsted yarns

Electric wires and cables

Soap and detergents

Rubber tyres and tubes

Machine tools

(*A.S.*)

5. Prepare a chart showing the proportion of the total number of steel furnaces in the ten main regions of Britain in the last year for which statistics are available, and ten years before then. (*A.S.*)

6. Obtain figures of the size of the harvest and the acreage devoted to the production of the following crops, for the most recent year and the earliest year available. Compare the outputs per acre for the two years. Why do you think they may have changed?

Wheat

Barley

Oats

Potatoes

Sugar beet

(*A.S.* or *W.A.*)

7. Calculate the percentage increase or decrease in the production or sales of the following products, over the last two years, and over the last seven years.

Soap

Detergents

Paint

Fertilizers

Sulphuric acid

Thermoplastic resins (all)

Polyvinyl chloride (p.v.c.)

Synthetic rubber

Synthetic dyestuffs

Which are the fastest growers? Are they the same in the longer period as in the shorter? (*A.S.*)

8. Prepare a chart showing the number of new vehicle registrations for private cars in Britain for each of the last ten years. (*A.S.*)

9. (*a*) Calculate the percentage change in the tonnage of goods carried by U.K. airways and by British Rail between last year and the previous year.

(*b*) Calculate the percentage change in the total number of passengers carried by U.K. airways domestic services and British Rail between last year and the previous year. (*A.S.* and *W.A.*)

10. Arrange a visit to one or two local factories. Try to find out in each case—

(*a*) How long it has been situated in its present site.

(*b*) Whether it is an independent company or a subsidiary of another.

(*c*) What proportion of its output is exported.

(*d*) How many employees it has on its books.

(*e*) How fast its output has been growing.

Where possible, compare any answers you get with the average for the industry and for all industries together. (*A.S.*)

11. Prepare a table showing the total gross tonnage of merchant ships—
    (a) Owned by the following countries,
    (b) Launched by the following countries,
for the year 1960 and for the most recent year available—

United Kingdom	Germany (West)
United States	Liberia
Japan	Sweden
Norway	U.S.S.R.

and calculate the percentage of total world tonnage in each case. (*W.A.*)

CHAPTER 6

Distribution

ɪᴛ is clear that the actual production of goods, with which we have so far been largely concerned, is insufficient unless these goods are somehow made readily available to consumers, and this entails their passing through what are known as the channels of distribution. As we have seen, for the country as a whole the distributive trades account for the employment of approximately one in every ten persons in the labour force. For individual commodities, on the other hand, the chain may be long or short. The market gardener, who sells his produce direct to the public in his own shop or stall, does his own distribution, while the butter from a farm in Australia passes through grading and packing stations, is carried by land and sea and by land again, and is handled by exporters, importers, wholesalers and retailers before it is finally put on sale to the consumer.

It is difficult to say which stages in the process of distribution are the most important, since each is necessary to ensure that the goods finally reach the consumer. The organization of transport has, however, been dealt with in the previous chapter, and we shall concern ourselves here mainly with the important links in the chain—the wholesale and retail trades.

The Wholesale Trade

Wholesale merchants may best be regarded as middlemen who act as links between retailers and producers. They tend to specialize in particular lines of business and, as they are spread over all parts of the country, they are able to act as focal points for orders from local retail traders which they can submit in bulk to manufacturers. Their existence thus obviates the need for a multitude of small orders. Each individual retailer of confectionery, for example, has no need to send to several manufacturers for relatively small supplies of each of their different brands of chocolates and sweets, but is able to order all at the same time from one or two wholesalers, who in their turn may collect orders from many retailers and indent for much larger quantities from individual manufacturers.

In addition to acting as a channel for orders and thus also supplying manufacturers with useful information on current trends in consumers' demand, wholesalers frequently carry fairly large stocks of a certain limited range of products for which the retailer generally has neither the space nor the financial resources. Since most retailers are almost certain to be situated nearer to a wholesaler than to manufacturers, this enables them to obtain supplies at very much shorter notice. Some

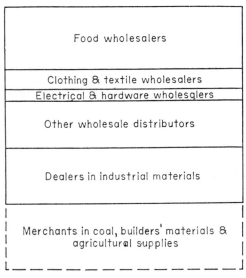

Fig. 6.1.   **Wholesale Trades, Great Britain, 1965**
Number of Business Units (*Note:* Merchants include Retailers)

wholesalers also perform other useful services such as arranging for the packaging and transportation of goods and extending credit facilities to retailers.

While the importance of the wholesaler in the distributive process has been declining in the twentieth century, there is still a substantial amount of activity going on. It is not easy to be very precise about the amount involved, since some retailers also engage in wholesaling operations. Some of the larger coal merchants, for instance, often supply other retailers as well as the general public. The Department of Employment, however, recorded a labour force of over half a million in wholesale distribution in 1970. And the last official Census, covering the trade in 1965, classified some 20,000 firms in the business of wholesaling, and nearly as many more dealing in coal, builders' and agricultural supplies, and industrial materials and machinery. The chief lines of consumer goods are fruit and vegetables and groceries, but clothing and textiles, hardware and electrical goods also use wholesale channels quite extensively (*see* Fig. 6.1). The main industrial materials involved include timber, metals, hides and skins, and scrap materials of all kinds.

The growing tendency to by-pass wholesalers in recent years has been associated with the growth of large-scale organizations in retailing, which have been able to secure for themselves better terms with manufacturers than the small independent shops. Some manufacturers, also, have shown a preference for dealing direct with retailers in order to keep a tighter control over the sale of their products to the ultimate consumer, or have even entered the field of direct selling to consumers, cutting out both wholesaler and retailer in an attempt to charge very competitive prices.

Resistance to such pressures by wholesalers has taken a number of forms. Some have sponsored the establishment of buying associations among chains of small retailers to cut costs and secure favourable trading terms. Others have reacted by opening up self-service wholesale cash-and-carry warehouses, especially for foodstuffs, which keep costs low for the small shopkeeper who is prepared to use his own transport.

COMMODITY MARKETS

For most commodities, merchants who act as intermediaries maintain individual contacts with manufacturers, but in a few cases there exist special commodity markets where most of the business is carried on. These are of greatest importance with certain primary products, like food grains and non-ferrous metals, which lend themselves to easy trading by quality. Thus, there is the Liverpool Cotton Exchange, the London Metal Exchange (tin, lead, zinc and copper), the London Commodity Exchange (coffee, cocoa, sugar, hides, copra and rubber) and the Baltic Exchange (grains, shipping and air transport) to mention some of the most important. Most of these commodities are not produced in Britain at all, and it is through the appropriate exchanges where importers and dealers gather that business can most easily be conducted. Indeed, so convenient a market do they provide that transactions between foreign buyers and foreign sellers frequently take place there. For purely domestic dealings there are also many local agricultural markets and the meat, fish, fruit and vegetable wholesale markets in London and the provinces. Mention was made in an earlier chapter, too, of the special agricultural Marketing Boards which act as channels for the sales of certain kinds of produce (*see above*, p. 105).

Some of the commodity exchanges discussed in the last paragraph provide facilities, known as *futures* markets, for the purchase (or sale) of commodities in advance of actual requirements. This can be particularly useful, for instance, in the case of goods where future supplies are uncertain and the possibility exists that prices may change appreciably. It means that a purchaser on the Liverpool Cotton Exchange, for example, may assure himself of supplies of cotton at a price fixed in September, even though delivery is not to take place until December. Avoiding the risk of future price changes in this manner is called *hedging*. And, of course, the futures price will contain a certain element of premium against risk.

The Retail Trade

The part of the economy with which we, as individuals, are probably most familiar is the last link in the chain of distribution, where we do our own shopping—the various shops and stores which make up the retail trade. These are really of two kinds: first, the shops which sell actual goods—the retail trade proper—and second, those places which *do* things for us rather than sell them and where, for example, we get our hair cut or our clothes cleaned, which are known as the *service* trades.

The last detailed count of the number of retail shops was made in 1966. It showed that there were rather more than half a million in Britain, representing something like one shop to every eighty adult persons in the country. The Census of Distribution is also useful in that it allows us to see the numbers of shops selling different kinds of goods. The main categories are set out in Fig. 6.2. This shows, surprisingly enough perhaps, that food shops are of really outstanding importance and account for nearly half of all retail outlets. These include all branches of the food business, though grocers are by far the most numerous. The diagram also shows the relative numbers of the other main food retailers, with the exception of the confectioners which cannot be easily picked out from the ubiquitous newsagent-cum-tobacconist-cum-confectioner, which we know so well.

Turning to the non-food items, we may observe the prime position of clothing, which accounts for every sixth shop in Britain. The remaining shops provide for somewhat less essential needs and are considerably fewer than food stores and clothiers. There are in fact approximately 20,000 shops each dealing with one of the following

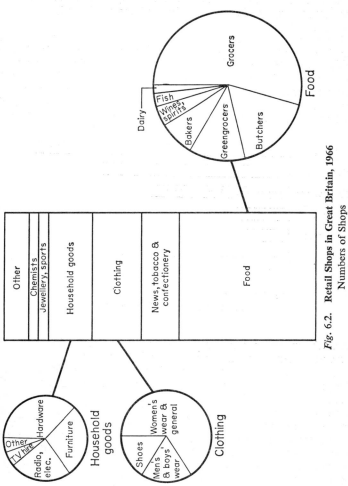

Fig. 6.2. **Retail Shops in Great Britain, 1966**
Numbers of Shops

groups of merchandise: hardware, furniture, fancy goods, jewellery and toys, radio and electrical articles, and chemists' goods.

THE SERVICE TRADES

It is rather artificial in some ways to try and distinguish between the supply of goods and the provision of services at the retail level, since quality of service can be an important part of all retailing. The distinction can be made, however, and it has the advantage of allowing us to assess the relative importance of these two main sectors. Looking at figures of total employment, for instance, we may say that very roughly half the employees in distribution work in retail shops, a fifth in

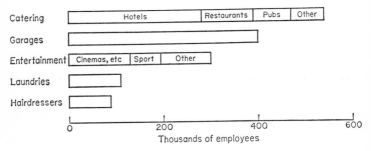

Fig. 6.3. **The Service Trades of Great Britain, 1970**
Employment in the Main Sections

wholesaling, and a third in the service trades. Fig. 6.3 shows the number of persons employed in the chief service lines.

After what we saw of the outstanding importance of food shops in the previous section, it should come as no great surprise to see the dominant position of catering among the service trades. It might not have been so easily guessed, however, that about half of all receipts in the catering business comes from the sale of alcoholic drink. Some 50,000 garages in present-day Britain employ about 400,000 persons. There are approximately the same number of hairdressers, though the number of their employees is, of course, much lower. Similarly the figure for workers in laundries does not fully reflect the substantial increase in do-it-yourself laundrettes that has appeared in recent years. Other service trades too small to show in the diagram include shoe repairers. These have tended to decline, and are now in the position of employing fewer workers than television rental outlets (classed incidentally in the Census as shops rather than service trades), which have been one of the most rapidly growing sectors (though still small) in distribution.

This catalogue of the types of goods and services sold by shops is important in establishing the structure of the retail trade, but it might suggest that there is only one retail store for the supply of all goods. In fact, the organization of retailing is more complex, and there are a

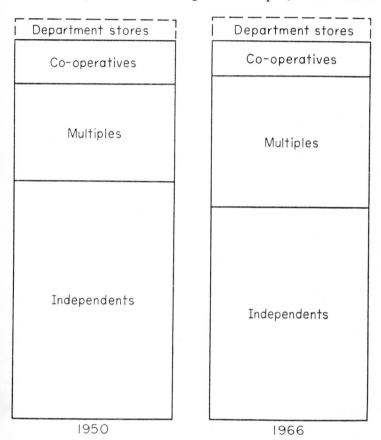

Fig. 6.4.   **Business Organization in the Retail Trade, Great Britain,
1950 and 1966**
Proportion of Total Sales

number of quite distinct types of business. The main groups are
indicated in Fig. 6.4, and it is to them that attention must now be
directed.

Types of Retail Organization

1. THE INDEPENDENT RETAILER

Everyone is familiar with the small shop, often owned by the man who
runs it. The term "independent retailer," however, is generally used
to include shopkeepers who operate up to nine branches and, so
defined, the independents account for over three-quarters of the total
number of retail outlets. Since these shops tend to be on the small side,
however, their importance from the viewpoint of the amount of
business done is diminished, though they still supply more than half
of the total value of all goods sold at the retail level.

In spite of the fact that they do not offer many of the facilities of
some of the other types of retail store, they are still popular with
shoppers for a variety of reasons, among the more important of which
is the fact that many are situated conveniently in residential districts
and enable small everyday needs to be met without making a special
journey "into town". They also sometimes offer personal services,
such as short-term credit, and the restricted scope of their clientele
permits them to get to know their customers and, though keeping only
small stocks, to cater quite well for individual needs.

Independent retailers are very much more important in some lines of
retail trade than in others, and nearly all of the most numerous, such as
newsagent-tobacconists, greengrocers, ironmongers, repair businesses,
etc., are of a type where the amount of capital required is relatively
small. The life which such a business offers is not unattractive when
compared with a routine factory or office job, though at least some of
those who choose it earn distinctly less than they could in other
occupations, for competition from others with similar ideas sometimes
keeps profits quite low.

Fig. 6.4 brings out the fact that the independents have been suffering
a relative decline in recent years. Their share in total sales fell by
about 10 per cent between the Censuses of 1950 and 1966. The independents' loss has been the gain of larger-scale retail organizations with
certain cost advantages which accompany their size. More extensive
price competition, too, has exposed their position. What is perhaps
equally remarkable is that the decline of the independents has not gone
further than it has. In part, this must be due to a growth of demand for
services like hairdressing and do-it-yourself stores which favour the

mall man, as well as to the formation of *voluntary chains* of independent
etailers which have given such groups some of the advantages of
arger firms—especially that of bulk-buying. A notable spurt in the
growth of these groups (many of which are wholesaler-sponsored) has
aken place in the last decade. This has been particularly so in the
grocery trade. By 1966, over 40 per cent of independent grocers'
purchases of stock were made by such voluntary chains; but there are
imilar arrangements in most other sections of retail business.

. THE MULTIPLE CHAIN STORE

Chains of (ten or more) stores under a single ownership have been the
most rapidly expanding retail outlets for a generation. Between the
Censuses of 1950 and 1966, the sales of the multiples rose from just
ver a fifth to well over a third of the total at retail level, and they
ave continued to press still further ahead since then. Based on the
rinciple of economical large-scale operation, each has tended to offer
he public a fairly narrow range of fast-moving lines of merchandise at
ow prices. Today there are remarkably few areas into which the
multiples have not penetrated.

In the grocery trade, where they made their first appearance, firms
ke Tesco's and Sainsbury's account for about 40 per cent of all sales.
Multiple dairies, like the Express and Unigate in London, sell about
he same proportion of the milk. Multiple shoe shops like Dolcis and
Freeman, Hardy and Willis are even more important, and dispose of
more than half of shoe sales; while as much as three-quarters of the
television rental business is done by Radio Rentals and the other
multiples. Men's outfitters have their Montague Burtons, women's
heir C. & A. Modes, butchers their Dewhursts, fishmongers their
MacFisheries, booksellers their W. H. Smiths, and even tobacconists,
hose sales are so popular with independent shopkeepers, are not
mmune from inroads from the multiples, which account for more than
0 per cent of total sales.

Organization within most multiple chains is on a branch basis with
he main decisions taken by a staff of specialists in a central Head Office,
ut the small size of many individual shops gives them also some of the
dvantages of the independent retailer. Each has a branch manager
ith much the same opportunity of getting to know the peculiarities of
s own local market as the one-man concern.

While the multiples have been described as if they all confine their
ade to a single line of merchandise, it should be added that the
ndency in recent years is for some of them to introduce a wider range
 goods to their shelves—food stores offering household goods,

clothiers adding foodstuffs, etc. To some extent this has brought them
into competition with what used to be called variety chain stores, such
as Woolworth's and British Home Stores, but which can hardly still be
considered as a sufficiently distinctive type of business to deserve
separate treatment.

3. THE RETAIL CO-OPERATIVE

The remaining major type of retail organization to be considered is
the co-operative. The origins of the co-operative movement are usually
associated with the name of Robert Owen and the first successful
experiment in Rochdale in 1844, but co-operation in retailing has
expanded greatly since then. Today there are about 600 retail societies
although their number is gradually being reduced by amalgamations.

The distinctive feature of co-operative societies lies in their owner
ship; for, while all other shops are privately owned by individuals or
joint-stock companies, the co-operatives are owned by the people who
shop there, who become members by paying a minimum deposit on a
share in the business. The co-operatives also sell to the general public
but it is the members who supply the capital and, as there are so many of
them (about thirteen million), the amount which each individual con
tributes is small and need not in fact be more than a few pence. In
contrast again with the organization of joint-stock companies, there is
an upper limit on the amount of share capital which may be held by
any individual, and voting rights at meetings are not proportional to
shareholdings. Most districts have their own local "co-op," and the
members elect a committee of management from among themselves
who decide upon the general policy of the store and appoint a manager
and full-time staff to do the work.

The principle on which the co-operative societies grew up was one
whereby goods were sold at normal retail prices and, at the end of each
half-year the profits were distributed to members in proportion to their
purchases during the period, in the form of a "dividend" of so many
pence per pound of purchases. Recently, some societies have switched
to a policy of giving trading stamps at the point of sale instead. In so
far as stamps are offered to all customers, this naturally reduces the
incentive to join the co-op, and societies have been urged to give an
additional bonus to stamps redeemed by members. The size of the
dividend, or the exchange value of the stamps depends on the amount
spent at the store but also on the size of the profits. The last of these
can differ, of course, from society to society according to the efficiency
of their operations. But it should also be mentioned that "co-ops" have
still retained some of the ideals of their founders, and some funds are

devoted to the provision of scholarships for members and employees, and other social aims.

The share of the co-operatives in total retail business has been falling now for a considerable number of years. In 1950, the movement had about 12 per cent of retail sales. At the 1966 Census, this had fallen to 9 per cent, and all the indications are that it was lower still by 1970. This is in spite of the fact that the falling growth rate had led to the appointment of an independent Commission into the Co-operative Movement in 1958, which drew attention to the fact that declining market shares had tended to be most evident in the majority of small

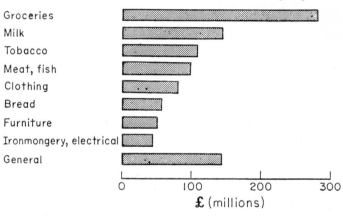

Fig. 6.5.   **Retail Co-operatives in Great Britain, 1966**
Value of Sales by Commodity

independently run retail societies, which were not in a position to exploit the advantages of large-scale production as had the multiples. Some of the largest co-operatives have had most impressive records. The London Co-operative Society, for instance, opened the first self-service store in Britain in 1942. Large stores have the advantage of being able to strike good bargains with manufacturers, though some of these have in the past refused to trade with co-operatives, or stipulated that no dividend could be allowed on their goods. To compensate for this, in 1873 the Co-operative Wholesale Society was set up to manufacture goods itself.

The strength, and perhaps also the weakness, of the co-operatives lies in their sales of particular commodities. They are heavily dependent on food and tobacco, as Fig. 6.5 reveals, and these products account for nearly three-quarters of total sales. They are responsible for a third of all fresh milk sold and a sixth of all groceries. They also sell a significant amount of furniture, clothing, ironmongery and household articles. Many of these latter items are sold in large stores in populous districts, for they operate shops of very different size, from the local provision stores to really big department stores in cities like Manchester and London.

4. THE DEPARTMENT STORE

The distinctive feature of the department store lies in the wide range of goods offered under one roof. This feature, coupled often with an efficient delivery service, is indeed their greatest attraction, though many stores also provide special "departments" designed to encourage custom, such as cafés and restaurants where friends can meet for a meal, information bureaux and exhibitions. Most department stores, such as Selfridges and Lewis's, are situated in central positions in large towns and cities, in the West End of London, and in nearly all of the major suburban and provincial shopping centres. Consequently, it is not uncommon to find quite a number of them side by side, each offering roughly the same varieties of goods, from departments dealing in food and provisions and clothing to cosmetics, radio and furnishings. The general standard of quality may be the chief difference between these adjoining shops, but this is not indeed always the case and quality often varies, as in London, from district to district, the shops inside each locality being more nearly similar to each other than to those of another area.

Department stores are not very numerous. There are only a few hundred of them in the whole of the country—an insignificant fraction of the total number of shops. Their importance to the community should rather be judged by the value of their sales, which represents roughly one-twentieth of that of all sales at the retail level. On average each sold in 1966 goods getting on for a million pounds. Their history stretches back to the 'sixties and 'seventies of the past century, when they started to evolve as a separate type from medium-sized grocery or drapery shops. Gradually they extended their range of influence, diverting custom from the small independent shops and sometimes consolidating their position by amalgamation.

Department stores cut across the boundary lines already drawn between different types of retail outlet. Two in every five of them are independent, and the remainder are run by the co-operative societies and the multiples in roughly equal numbers. Since the Second World War, they have roughly maintained their share of an expanding retail market—selling about one pound in every twenty pounds' worth of goods sold, throughout the 1950s and 1960s.

OTHER TYPES OF RETAIL TRADING

The broad categories used in the previous descriptions conceal certain other types of retail organization which deserve mention.

Supermarkets. Supermarkets are large self-service stores, usually defined as having a floor-space selling area of over 2,000 square feet. The growth in their number has been so rapid in the last few years that it is virtually impossible to discuss their importance in a general kind of way. At the start of the 1960s there were less than 1,000, but by the end of the decade they had increased to more than 3,000 at a rate of roughly five per week. Run largely by multiples and co-operatives, supermarkets are handling about a quarter of all grocery trade. They offer the shopper keen prices, which their size allows, together with the advantage of a wide selection of merchandise. Their success suggests that people rather favour unhurried self-service in such stores, and they have encouraged the habit of shopping less frequently for larger quantities. Many people expect the trend towards supermarket shopping for groceries to continue to follow the pattern of the United States and to absorb the great bulk of the trade. If so, this will also mean a tendency towards even larger supermarket premises, with five or ten thousand square feet of selling space.

In the sphere of household goods, as distinct from groceries, the supermarkets have not made any comparable advance. The American pattern of *discount stores* selling basically non-food merchandise at cut prices was held up in Britain on account of difficulties over securing supplies of goods from manufacturers practising resale price maintenance (*see* pp. 155–6). But although the law was changed in 1964 and resale price maintenance largely abolished, price cutting in Britain has tended to be more general, and discount stores rather uncommon.

Mail-Order Trade. Another very different method of conducting retail business, but which has also been expanding considerably, consists of selling goods through the post. Although the proportion of total sales accounted for by mail-order is still small, the 1966 Census reported over £400 million passing through this channel—a ninefold increase on 1950. The bulk of the business is in the hands of general mail-order houses, especially the large ones like Great Universal Stores and Littlewoods, which operate mainly by appointing agents who are given elaborate catalogues. There are, however, also several hundred specialist houses handling a limited number of commodities, and department stores often engage in mail-order business, bringing merchandise to the attention of the public by means of advertisements in the daily and weekly press. Certain manufacturers, too, sell direct to the consumer in this way, as well as by employing door-to-door salesmen.

The expansion of mail-order selling cannot be simply accounted for by reference to increasing traffic congestion in shopping centres, though that may well have played a part. In some cases the appeal is one of price, but there is no evidence that this is the prime attraction, and against it must be set the obvious risk of dissatisfaction when the goods arrive. The risk is lessened with standardized and well-known branded items and with those, such as dress materials, where patterns are often available beforehand, but reliance on the reputation of the selling firm is of great importance. Willingness to send goods on approval must similarly be a factor, especially as sales of clothing account for over half of total business. Presumably some people prefer trying clothes on at leisure in their own home.

Mention should perhaps also be made of sales from mobile shops, of which nearly 12,000 were counted at the Census, and of street traders operating in recognized markets, as well as increasing numbers of automatic coin-operated vending machines (selling a widening range of merchandise) in offices and factories as well as in shops. All these forms of retail trading are mostly used for the sale of foodstuffs but their overall importance is not great.

The Seasonal Nature of Retail Trade

The volume of business carried on by the retailer is not by any means evenly spread throughout the year. A number of influences are at work which make for busy and slack seasons, and some of these vary from trade to trade. Common to all of them, however, is Christmas, with the December boom in buying presents, and the slackest period of the year in January and February, when economy is the watchword of families who have spent a lot of their savings. The decline is more marked in some trades than in others, foodstuffs being outstandingly stable, with toilet requisites, such as perfumes and bath salts, at the other extreme. A second important factor, which affects clothing, is the weather, and sales rise in spring when new outfits are bought, and are low in August before winter buying begins; in any event most surplus cash from the weekly wage goes on holiday spending. Sales may also be affected by other factors, such as uncertainty regarding changes in the rates of taxation on particular commodities before the Chancellor of the

Exchequer announces them in the Budget. Month-to-month fluctuations in retail trade are illustrated by Fig. 6.6, but it should be realized that day-to-day trade is hardly more stable. A recent private inquiry into the trade of four supermarkets in the Midlands showed that well over half their sales were made on Fridays and Saturdays.

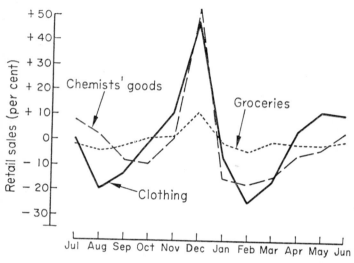

Fig. 6.6 **Retail Sales, Great Britain, 1970**
Percentage Difference from the Average for the Year

Advertising

The great development in advertising that has taken place in the twentieth century has been the result of the effort by businesses to expand the volume of their sales. Advertising can bring about this expansion in two ways—by spreading information about the existence of a commodity, or by somehow persuading people that an article is worth buying. The way in which this persuasion is achieved is not important from the point of view of the advertiser's profits. Whether you are induced to buy a particular brand of toothpaste because you are told it contains a substance which has been proved to prevent tooth decay, or whether it is because you have seen a picture of a pretty girl using it, the effect on the sales of that toothpaste is the same. The tendency to emphasize persuasion is at the back of much of the criticism that is continually levelled at advertising, although it is also argued that the provision of information, especially about new products, is valuable and may help to build up sales to the point where costs begin to fall.

The scale of advertising expenditure in this country, after a period of fairly steady growth, seems to have settled at a level representing about 2 per cent of total consumer expenditure, or roughly the same as the amount spent on furniture. Most of the advertising is done by manufacturers and is directed at final consumers, but some is done by retailers. The Press is the most important single medium for advertising. In fact, revenue from advertisements is a larger source of income for

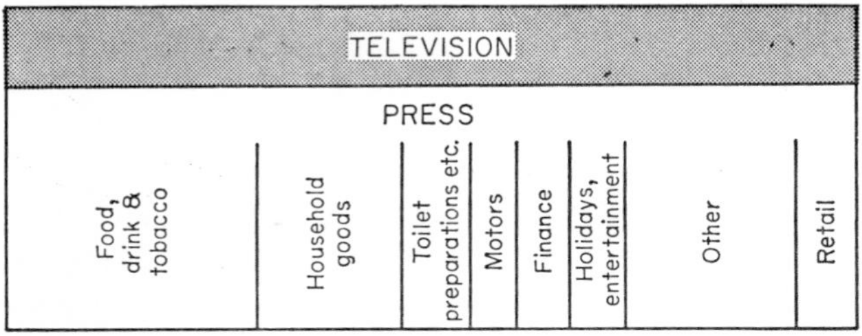

Fig. 6.7.   **Advertising Expenditure by Product and Media**
Estimated Expenditure 1970, Proportions of total

many newspapers than proceeds from sales. Television advertising was introduced in 1955, and expanded swiftly for the first few years, but still does not rival the Press in relative importance. The addition of commercial radio, announced by the government in 1970, might raise advertising expenditure through broadcasting. A number of other media deserve mention—mail-order catalogues, free samples, special offers, outdoor posters and films. In addition, retailers employ a variety of devices to attract custom, including window displays, "sales," and "loss-leaders"—one or two exceptionally low-priced standard articles to which great publicity is given in order to interest customers, who will buy other goods as well.

All products are not, of course, equally advertised, as Fig. 6.7 shows. Leading lines include food, drink and tobacco (especially chocolates and sweets, breakfast cereals, cigarettes, beer, soft drinks and meat extracts, such as Oxo); household goods (from floor polishes to home heating, but outstandingly detergents and other cleaners); toilet preparations and patent medicines (including toothpastes, deodorants, pain killers and indigestion remedies); motors and motoring (where the accent is sometimes, perhaps surprisingly, as much on appearance—sleek cars in glamorous surroundings—as on information concerning performance); and, of course, a wide range of other products, from pet foods to slimming aids.

Many services are also subjects of considerable advertising expenditure, especially travel and entertainment of various kinds and the more austere facilities offered by institutions like building societies, insurance companies and banks. Finally, one should perhaps mention the rather different kinds of advertising by manufacturers in technical journals directed at other traders, as well as the "prestige" advertisements in the Press by large companies, not so much to sell their products as to publicize their "image" for recruitment and other purposes.

Credit Sales

The expansion which has taken place in retail trading has been materially assisted by a parallel growth in this country of selling on credit through the hire-purchase or instalment system. By this method the purchaser is able to take possession of the goods on payment of a relatively small deposit. He then pays off the balance by regular weekly or monthly instalments, although in return for what is really a loan, the eventual cost to him will be rather larger than if he had paid cash outright.

In 1970, the total outstanding balance of instalment credit was approaching £1,500 million; and at the Census of Distribution in 1966, it was revealed that nearly a tenth of retail trading was credit financed. Instalment trading is, however, mainly important in quite a small range of goods. Generally such articles are fairly expensive, for it would not be worth while buying a pencil on hire purchase, and they are usually fairly durable, for it is not so easy to get people to make continued payments for things they have enjoyed in the past but no longer possess, such as foodstuffs or permanent waves. Thus it is not surprising to find that the most important items include cars, furniture, durable household goods and radio and television sets, in which credit selling accounts for over a fifth of all sales. Retail traders finance about one-third of the total hire-purchase business themselves. The remainder, and particularly the business in motors, is done by specialized finance houses who provide the necessary funds.

Resale Price Maintenance

The careful reader will have noticed that much advertising is concerned with branded products—that is, with goods which have a prominent trade-mark by which they are known. We often ask for a "Hoover" or a tin of "Nescafé" rather than for a vacuum cleaner or for instant coffee. This branding of products can be of advantage to the manufacturer, since it means his product is well known by name and is in general demand, but it can also be attractive to a retailer, especially if he knows that all or most of his compettitors are going to charge the same price for a branded article, and not try to undercut him. It is only to be expected, therefore, that many manufacturers, acting partly in their own interests and partly in response to requests from retailers, long ago took steps to ensure that their products were sold everywhere at the same price. General conformity to these fixed prices used frequently to be maintained by collective agreements between the appropriate trade associations of manufacturers and distributors, involving such effective methods as "blacklisting" retailers who cut prices below those agreed and withholding further supplies from them.

The practice of Resale Price Maintenance (known often as R.P.M.) is estimated to have applied to goods representing about a third of total consumer expenditure shortly after the end of the Second World War. Since the effect of R.P.M. is clearly to restrict the scope for price competition which might benefit consumers, the government passed the Resale Prices Act in 1964, which abolished the practice, except in any cases where exemption might be granted by the Restrictive Practices Court (*see above*, p. 93). The result of the Act has been that legally imposed minimum prices have virtually disappeared from shops in Britain (the outstanding exception being the price of books, granted exemption by the Court). Many manufacturers of branded goods now publish instead "recommended retail prices" which, though not enforceable, are commonly adopted by many retailers.

THE CONSUMER MOVEMENT

The growth of advertising together with other sales promoting techniques and the bewildering selection of goods, offered to an increasingly rich public, were responsible for the appearance of what can only be described as a movement for the protection of consumers which took hold in Britain in the late 1950s. One of the earliest expressions of this feeling was the establishment of the Consumers' Association—an independent organization, devoted to comparative testing of products on the market, designed to guide prospective purchasers as to which brands and makes of commodities were likely to provide good value for money. Its monthly journal *Which?* has included reports on goods from aspirins to washing machines and, by 1970, it was being distributed to over half a million subscribers. Central and local government authorities are also involved in consumer protection through their operation of the provisions of Acts of Parliament relating to such matters as hire-purchase and weights and measures control, and misleading trade descriptions. The government also set up an official Consumer Council in 1963, specifically to help safeguard consumers' interests, but it was fated to have a short life and was in fact wound up by the new government in 1971.

EXERCISES

(For key to symbols indicating sources, *see* p. 14.)

1. Select a street in your local shopping centre, and walk along it with pencil and paper making a note of the number of shops of each of the following types—

Grocers and provision dealers	Off-licences
Greengrocers and fruiterers	Confectioners, tobacconists, newsagents
Butchers	Boot and shoe shops
Bread and flour confectioners	Furniture shops
Fishmongers	Chemists and photographic dealers
	General stores

Collect the information obtained by the whole class and work out the proportion of the total (for each different kind of shop). Compare your results with the national figures. (*A.S.*)

2. Again go along the same street, and this time notice how many shops there are of the following kinds—

Department stores	Co-operatives
Multiple chain stores	Other shops

Once more collect the information for the whole class, and work out the proportions of the different types of shops. What difference would you expect to find in your proportions if you had been able to find out the value of the sales of the shops instead of merely counting them?

3. Using figures of the number of persons engaged instead of the number of shops, prepare a chart on the lines of the centrepiece in Fig. 6.2 showing the importance of the different types of shops in Britain. What differences, if any, do you find? (*A.S.*)

4. Calculate how many persons per shop there are in Britain of the main types listed in Exercises 1 and 2 above. If you were able to divide the figures of shops into groups of town and country, what changes would you expect to find? (*A.S.*)

5. Find out the total instalment credit outstanding last December and the total value of consumers' expenditure on goods and services last year. Express the former as a percentage of the latter. Repeat the calculation for any earlier years for which you can obtain figures, and comment on any trend. (*M.D.S.* or *F.S.*)

6. Allocate a different daily newspaper or weekly magazine to each student in the class, and make a note of the number of advertisements for the following main types of goods. Award one, two or three marks to each advertisement

according to its size, and add together the marks for each group of merchandise. Compare the separate results for daily and for weekly papers—

Food and drink	Toilet goods
Household supplies	Financial advertisements
Medicines	Entertainment
Clothing	Smoking
Motoring	Other

7. Go carefully through the advertisements in the current number of *The Building Trades Journal* or *Wireless World*, and make a note of the proportion of advertisements which appeal to the intellect by offering information about the product, and of those which, rather, try to catch the eye without giving any real information at all. Then do the same for the advertisements in *Radio Times* or *T.V. Times* and compare your results.

8. Estimate the proportion of total advertising time on commercial television between the hours of 7 p.m. and 10 p.m. on any two or three nights of the week devoted to the main classes of goods in Exercise 6 above. Set out your results in the form of a table beside those of Exercise 6.

9. Make a list of the principal articles for which comparative test reports were published in *Which?* during the last six months. Compare the prices of recommended products with the average of all those tested.

10. Find out the total cost, including interest and other charges, of buying the following commodities on hire-purchase from a local shop over a period of one year—

a bicycle	a suit of clothes
a gas cooker	one other article

Find out also the cash price, and express this as a fraction of the total hire-purchase cost.

11. Ascertain the current (or "spot") price and the "futures" price for three months' forward delivery of standard units of the following commodities, and sort them into two groups according to whether the "futures" price is greater or less than the "spot"—

Tin	Rubber	
Lead	Cotton	
Zinc	Wheat	
Copper	Cocoa	(*F.T.* or *T.*)

CHAPTER 7

Labour

THE production of the goods and services which make up the economic activity of a country is achieved by a combined effort of many types of resources, known as the factors of production. Among the principal of these are raw materials, land and buildings, machinery and equipment, and labour itself. Now, when goods are produced jointly by several factors of production working together, it is not too meaningful to describe one of them as being more important than the others. It may be true that there is a sense in which we may say that labour is of primary importance in the production process. For other factors are useless if there is no labour to work with them, even if only to push a button, while even without machines men and women may be able to produce some things, if less efficiently. But the reason for giving labour a chapter to itself is other than this. For inanimate factors are brought into use as a result of decisions by persons who own or control them, and it is only indirectly that a human being is involved. Labour, on the other hand, enters directly into production itself and each individual is therefore in a position to act to look after his own interests in the course of the production process.

The limited capacity of individuals, acting separately, to influence their conditions of employment led men to realize that power increased enormously if they joined forces with others doing the same type of work in a common effort. The movement towards the combination of workers which gathered strength with the Industrial Revolution has produced the powerful trade-union organizations of the present, and we may well begin our discussion of labour by considering them.

The Functions of Trade Unions

The activities of trade unions are concerned with all aspects of the employment of their members, but priority is usually given to questions of wages. Before the Second World War they included the prevention of wage-cuts, but these have become so much rarer since the 1930s that the attention of each union has been directed to securing wage increases for its own members in an economy in which incomes have generally been rising. Trade unions are also concerned with the prevention of unemployment among their members, even though this sometimes conflicts with their other aims. This is another area where conditions are very different from those existing before the war. The presence of higher levels of employment nowadays has diminished the importance of unemployment as a general trade-union problem, but it has certainly not disappeared completely, and unions in declining industries are well aware of their particular vulnerability.

In addition to questions of wages and unemployment, trade unions try to look after other interests of their members. They may, therefore, look into such matters as factory lighting and working conditions, seniority and redundancy policy, and what are termed "fringe benefits," like holidays, sickness pay, medical services, time off for attending classes, and so forth. Hours of work might come in the last category and they have certainly not been neglected in recent years. However, the unions' main objective has seemed to be really one of securing higher wages in the majority of cases by obtaining reductions in the "normal" or "standard" hours with a corresponding increase in hours paid at higher overtime rates, rather than an actual reduction in hours spent at work. Normal hours have indeed come down from about 47 or 48 to about 40 to 42 per week, but the average hours worked by adult men at the end of the 1960s was about 46½, compared to a figure of about 47½ at the beginning of the 1950s. Some unions also have an interest in obtaining for labour a share in the management of the businesses in which they work, through the establishment of works councils. Finally, it should not be forgotten that British trade unions have political aims of wider general significance. They play an important part in the formation of Labour Party policy, and many trade union officials are themselves Members of Parliament.

The Growth of Trade Unions

The early history of trade unionism, from the first local trade clubs in the eighteenth century, is one of tremendous struggle by working men to gain recognition, in the eyes of the law, of their organizations. For the law was not always on their side. Anti-combination Acts were passed in 1799 and 1800 inflicting the most severe penalties on any workmen who tried to form a union, and many suffered before public opinion was slowly won round and changes in the law were made.

No sooner had legal victory been gained by a number of Acts of Parliament between 1824 and 1876 than trade-union membership grew with rapid strides, from something under a million members in 1876 to a pre-war peak of over eight million in 1920. The years between the two world wars, however, were times of depressed industrial activity, whereas trade unionism flourishes in periods of general prosperity. Membership, consequently, began to fall off again in the 1920s and 1930s and, at its lowest ebb, in 1933, was little more than half the 1920 figure. With the revival in activity in the later 1930s, however, trade unionism soon expanded again as Fig. 7.1 shows. The

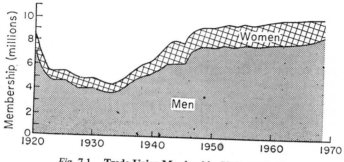

Fig. 7.1. **Trade-Union Membership, U.K., 1920–69**

1920 peak was passed at the end of the second World War, and membership has held up well since and now exceeds ten million.

The Growth of Political Action

The political activities of trade unions did not begin to assume great importance until about the beginning of the present century, when a special committee was formed to promote the direct representation of labour in Parliament. In 1906 this committee became known as the Labour Party, and soon began to make its influence felt, though it was not for nearly twenty years that a Labour government first held office. The links between the trade unions and the Labour Party still exist. The majority of unions, with some important exceptions, are affiliated to the Labour Party, and a substantial number of Labour candidates are sponsored by the trade-union movement. It should be remembered, however, that the two organizations are quite separate bodies, though there is a great overlap in the membership of both. A joint committee exists, but differences in policy are by no means infrequent.

Trade-Union Membership

In 1970, trade-union membership was about ten million. As there were, at the same time, about twenty-five million in the labour force this represents only about half of what is technically possible, and the opportunity for continued growth is therefore, in principle, considerable. The relative importance of men and women in the unions is quite another matter and, as Fig. 7.1 shows, the male unionists outnumber the female by roughly three to one. This, of course, is in part no more than a reflection of the fact that there are more men than women in the labour force as a whole; but it is not the only reason for, whereas about half the men belong to a union, only every third woman worker is a trade unionist. Even this difference is to some extent explained by the fact that about 15 per cent of women work only part-time, and when allowance is made for them, nearer to a third of full-time women employees are union members. However, there still remains a substantial difference in membership rates between the sexes, which must be because it is generally more difficult to recruit women into trade unions. This is probably due to their attitude to work. Many women regard their jobs as temporary features of their lives, to be forgotten as soon as they get married, while men, on the other hand, usually having to work continuously until they retire, take their employment more seriously and are consequently more concerned with trying to improve their conditions.

Strength and Weakness of Trade Unions

Trade union membership varies substantially between industries, as Fig. 7.2 shows. Before discussing this matter it is important to warn the reader that the figures on which the diagram are based can only be taken as giving the roughest idea of the relative strength of trade unionism. The number of unions with mixed industry membership has been growing considerably, and this means that the allocation of union membership to any industry group becomes increasingly arbitrary.

Nevertheless, Fig. 7.2 does help identify some of the strongholds of trade unions—especially in coal mining, where a long tradition of solidarity exists, on the railways, and in engineering and printing. On the face of it, there is little that these areas of trade-union strength have in common as far as the product of their respective industries is concerned, and there are often special historical circumstances to account for the growth of unionism. But it is worth noticing that trade unions tend to flourish when fair numbers of workers spend most of their time together and are, therefore, able to discuss and compare conditions of work with each other all the time. It also helps if they regularly congregate in the mornings and evenings to clock on and off in a yard or other place which can be used for union meetings without special arrangements.

On the other hand, unionism is notably less strong in the distributive trades, agriculture, and among clerical workers in offices. The causes here are doubtless complex, and to an extent social. But there is probably some partial explanation in the fact that workers in these

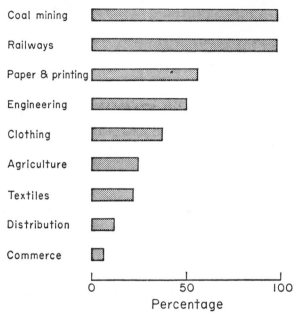

Fig. 7.2. **Trade-Union Membership, U.K., 1969**
Trade-Union Members as Percentage of the Numbers Employed

industries tend to spend most of their days working alone or in small groups dispersed in many shops, farms or offices over the country. They often have no convenient meeting place in which they can congregate, and many of them work under widely different conditions of employment—whether of wages, hours of work or anything else. Even if they had a common meeting place it would be much less easy to find a common ground for policy than, for example, among factory workers or miners. It should be realized, too, that part of the reason for relatively low trade-union membership in some industries may be found in the fact that they employ large numbers of women.

Types of Trade Unions

The study of trade unions according to industry is not entirely satisfactory for the simple reason that unions are not all organized on an industrial basis. The earliest forms of workers' organizations were, in fact on a craft basis, corresponding roughly to clubs, the members of which were all doing the same kind of work, such as blacksmiths, cabinet makers or tailors. *Craft unions*, such as the Amalgamated Society of Woodworkers and the Musicians' Union, have persisted into the present day. But the growth of large-scale production and the decline of the individual craftsman in so many trades have reduced the importance of such narrow craft unions. Generally, the process has been one of amalgamation. The Amalgamated Union of Engineering and Foundry Workers is a good example of this process. Traced back to 1920, when its predecessor the Amalgamated Engineering Union was formed, as a result of the merging of ten smaller unions each concerned with a particular job within the engineering trade, it is now what might best be described as a multi-craft union and, with well over a million members, is the second largest union in Britain.

Some unions are organized on an industrial basis, including quite large ones, such as the National Union of Mineworkers and the Union of Post Office Workers. *Industrial unions* are not always, however, clearly different in practice from craft unions. Although a union's membership may be confined to a single industry, it does not necessarily represent all the workers there. The existence of both the National Union of Railwaymen and the Associated Society of Locomotive Engineers and Firemen (to which engine drivers belong) is a good illustration of the way in which particular craft skills influence union organization and cut across attempts to fit unions precisely into those of different types.

In addition to unions organized on a craft and an industrial basis, it is necessary to distinguish a third category of union—the *general workers' union*. In most industries there are some employees who are not skilled in any particular trade, and it is easy to understand that general labourers, for instance, may have more in common with other unskilled workers than with other employees in their own industry. Principally to cater for them, a few general workers' unions have been formed; as they are not confined to unskilled workers it is not surprising to find that they tend to be very big. In fact the largest union of all, the Transport and General Workers' Union, is of this kind and has over a million and a half members. It was formed as a result of amalgamations of several smaller unions. In 1922 eighteen different unions, of which the dockers were one of the most important, merged into a single union, which continued to expand by further amalgamation for the next quarter of a century. Several others joined before 1930, and by the outbreak of war in 1939 there were over forty former unions merged into the T.G.W.U. Further development during and after the war brought the number up to its present strength—a merger of over fifty separate unions comprising a million and a half workers— and there is no reason to believe that the period of growth has ended. The second largest general union is the National Union of General and Municipal Workers, with over three-quarters of a million members, and all general workers' unions account for nearly a quarter of total trade-union membership.

Union Demarcations

One result of the way in which trade-union structure has developed in Britain is the existence of a degree of rivalry between certain unions. Those organized on a craft basis, for instance, often pay a great deal of attention to protecting their particular trade from encroachment by outsiders. This takes two basic forms, one aimed at restricting the supply of workers with a particular skill by insisting on minimum age at entry and length of apprenticeship service; the other at reserving certain types of work for members of a particular union. The electrician who comes to mend a fuse but will not tighten a loose bolt under the washbasin because it is the plumber's job, has been a music-hall joke for very many years.

Disputes between unions as to which shall represent a group of workers have also brought the trade-union movement some rather bad publicity. A major reason for restrictive practices (and for inter-union disputes too) has been to try and maintain the bargaining power of the craft unions. Fear of redundancy may sometimes also be relevant. But it has become quite common in recent years for craft unions to agree to eliminate some restrictive practices in a productivity agreement forming part of a wage settlement.

In 1970 the government established the Commission on Industrial Relations (C.I.R.) among whose functions is that of trying to help settle differences over the way in which workers are organized into unions. This was followed, in 1971, by the Industrial Relations Act, which caused profound controversy. The Act set up a National Industrial Relations Court (N.I.R.C.), made up of people with special knowledge or experience of industrial relations, under the chairmanship of a Judge. The N.I.R.C. is intended to be available for the settlement of disputes of national importance, while additional powers were given to existing Industrial Tribunals to settle more local issues of these kinds. The intention behind the Act, however, is that the Court should operate much more flexibly, and to an extent more informally, than most courts of law.

The Act introduced a new registration scheme for unions (as well as for employers' organizations) and identified a number of so-called unfair industrial practices. Many of its provisions are concerned with the conduct of disputes between unions and management, especially those leading to strikes (*see below*, pp. 71–3). But included among the unfair practices are some relating to the internal organization of unions, such as restrictions on the right of qualified individuals to join or not to join a union (though workers preferring not to join may be required to pay an appropriate contribution to it or to a charity).

To qualify for registration, a union must adopt policies which satisfy the Registrar of Trade Unions on these matters. Registration is not compulsory, but unions which fail to be registered lose exemption from income tax, and forfeit protection against legal actions for damages, most of which is of very long standing. Registered unions have corporate status and are liable only to a limited scale of compensation payments on actions which they lose, while unregistered unions may be sued for unlimited sums with union officials losing their freedom from personal liability. At the time of writing, it is not known whether the majority of unions, many of which are bitterly opposed to some of the principles in the Act, will register or not. (Technically, they were all put on a provisional register, and would have to deregister, if they so wanted.)

The Size of Trade Unions

The total number of trade unions in the country in 1969 was just over 300, a figure which the amalgamations mentioned in the previous section had brought down from over a thousand in 1938. With a total membership of ten million, this might imply that the average union had over 30,000 members. Such an assumption is very misleading, for the size of individual unions varies so widely that the average is quite meaningless. This is demonstrated in Fig. 7.3. There it is clearly shown that the great majority of unions are of very much smaller size than this. Over 100 of the smallest have less than 500 members each, representing altogether less than 1 per cent of the total membership. Well over half of all the unions have fewer than 2,500 members and still account for only a fraction of the total number of trade unionists. At the other end of the scale, however, we find a small number of really big unions, nine all told, each with a minimum of 250,000 members, representing

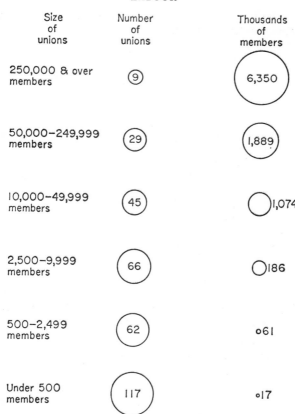

Size of unions	Number of unions	Thousands of members
250,000 & over members	9	6,350
50,000–249,999 members	29	1,889
10,000–49,999 members	45	1,074
2,500–9,999 members	66	186
500–2,499 members	62	61
Under 500 members	117	17

Fig. 7.3.   **The Size of Trade Unions, U.K., 1969**

ess than 3 per cent of all the unions, but accounting for well over half f the total membership. Here, of course, we find the really important nions—the two mammoth general workers' unions, mentioned earlier, nd the largest of the industrial and multi-craft unions.

he Trades Union Congress

he central body of the trade-union movement is known as the Trades nion Congress (T.U.C.). Established in 1868, in Manchester, rimarily for political purposes, its activities were restricted in the nineteenth century, and it was not until the 1920s that it began to assume the importance that it undoubtedly has today.

Like most trade unions, the T.U.C. has a full-time salaried General Secretary, but the other members of the General Council consist of part-time officials from individual unions, who are elected at the annual conference, when delegates from all over the country attend and discuss the current business. Nearly all the large unions are affiliated to the T.U.C. and have a say in the formation of general policy. Voting is on what is known as a "block" basis, according to which each delegate is given a number of votes roughly corresponding to the total membership of the union which he represents. Control of policy is thus effectively in the hands of the largest unions.

Although the T.U.C. has come increasingly to be regarded as the representative voice of the trade unions—the government frequently consults it on questions of national policy, not only on such matters as factory legislation, health, pensions and national insurance, but also on general economic issues. The public announcements of the General Council of the T.U.C. are considered as authoritative, but its formal powers are surprisingly limited. There is, for example, no obligation on individual unions to observe any decisions that may be taken at the annual conference. This considerable weakness is the result of the traditional reluctance of many unions to sacrifice their own independence and it is not impossible that, with their gradual disappearance, the powers of the T.U.C. may sometime be increased.

The Trades Councils

In addition to the T.U.C. as a meeting place for individual unions nearly every locality that is to any considerable extent industrial has its own trades council. Organized on a geographical basis, rather more than 500 of them in England and Wales are composed of branches of the different unions in the area. Each branch decides independently whether to join and there is no reason to suppose that all the branches of any one union will take the same decision, but it is estimated that rather more than half the total trade-union membership does in fact do so.

Although it was a trades council (in Glasgow) which called the first national meeting, as a result of which the T.U.C. was founded, relations between the councils and the T.U.C. are not always as good as might be expected. For over fifty years the trades councils have not been allowed a vote at the T.U.C. conferences, on the ground that to do so would give all members of both a double vote.

In spite of this, trades councils play an important part in the trade union movement. They generally hold monthly meetings and organize many activities in the locality. For example, their role in the organization of the General Strike of 1926 was outstanding. This is all the more surprising when it is realized that their income is very small—on average the affiliation fee per member is a few pence per year—so that with very few exceptions they are not able to employ any full-time officials and they have, consequently, to rely mainly upon voluntary support.

Trade-Union Finances

A useful way of examining the functions of trade unions is by looking at their main items of income and expenditure.

INCOME

Total income of all trade unions in 1969 amounted to nearly £40 million. Nearly 90 per cent of this was derived from contributions from members for the current year, and the remainder was mainly interest on accumulated funds. The average contribution per member works out at about £4·43 per year, or 8p per week. This average figure, again, is apt to be deceptive for there was quite a wide divergence between the contributions actually paid by different unions. The annual payment in the chemical industry was £1·25, in clothing, textiles and agriculture about £3, while at the other extreme it was over £7 in paper and printing and over £8 in educational services. Even these figures are averages, and many unions have a number of different scales of contribution according to the specific job of each member.

The principal cause of these differences in size of weekly subscription lies in the benefits which each union offers.

EXPENDITURE (*see* Fig. 7.4)

Apart from the item of working expenses (which covers such matters as the salaries of full-time officials, expenses of delegations to conferences, and other sundries), the remaining income was largely returned to the members themselves in the form of one benefit or another. Many of these are what are termed "friendly" benefits, and at one time were the main means by which workers could make financial provision for possible misfortunes like unemployment, sickness and death. The development of national social services, especially since 1945, has greatly reduced the significance of such benefits in most cases, but many are still paid. Superannuation is one of the most important, though benefits vary considerably between unions. Some printing unions provide relatively high pensions for members, and this is one of the reasons why their rate of contribution is above average. Some others, such as the general workers' union, provide only very small amounts for superannuation while still others, including the National Union of Agricultural Workers, pay nothing at all. Other benefits paid by nearly all unions are for sickness and accident and for death. Dispute benefit is paid by most unions and covers the expenses of members arising out of disputes with employers, such as compensa-

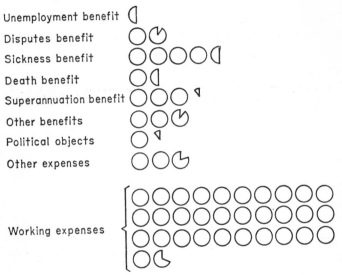

Fig. 7.4. The Finances of Trade Unions, Great Britain, 1969
Average Expenditure per Member
(Each circle represents 10p.)

tion for short-time working or unemployment resulting from a strike, and the amount depends, accordingly, on the number of disputes in any year. Unemployment benefit is also still paid by a large number of unions, but it is a relic from the days before national unemployment insurance was introduced, and has lost its former importance.

The only other expense item of interest is that for political purposes, and the average contribution to the political fund was about 25p per head in 1969. A small part of this may be ued by the individual union, but the bulk goes to a central fund administered by the T.U.C. and helps, among other things, to pay for general election expenses of trade-union sponsored Labour Party candidates. The total amount contributed to the political fund went up sharply in 1946–7 by about 80 per cent when Parliament repealed a twenty-year-old Act which required the permission of a member of a union to be obtained before the political levy could be charged. After the new Trade Disputes Act all members paid the political levy automatically in their general subscription, but they were free to ask for its return if they wished. It is an interesting reflection on the attitude of the British worker that a large proportion took the line of least resistance both before and after the Act and did not go to the trouble of making a special request either to pay or to have a refund of the political levy.

In 1969, expenditure per member in fact exceeded union income. The accumulated funds of trade unions, however, amount to over £100 million. They are therefore able to draw upon this in some years and add to it in others—largely depending on the amount of dispute benefit paid in any particular year.

Labour Disputes

Disputes arise over many matters: general conditions of work, victimization of individuals by management, demarcation lines between jobs, sympathetic action in support of other workers, hours of work; but by far the most important are those arising out of differences connected with wages. The traditional weapon of the trade union in these disputes has been to strike, the counterpart of the employers' lock-out. For a number of reasons, chiefly related to the establishment of new machinery for regulating wages and settling disputes, which are discussed below, strikes, although still quite numerous, have been considerably less common since the 1930s, than they were in earlier years. This is evident from Fig. 7.5 which shows the number of working days lost as a result of stoppages of work due to disputes since 1911. The average number of days lost per annum has fallen from the high figure of thirty-three million in the 1920s to about three to five million since the end of the Second World War. Further inspection of Fig. 55 shows that the prevalence of strikes appeared to mount towards the end of the 1960s. In 1970, there were nearly 4,000 stoppages involving nearly $1\frac{3}{4}$ million workers directly and indirectly in the loss of about 11 million days' work.

A significant feature of many post-war strikes has been the fact that a substantial number were "unofficial," in the sense that they were called by shop stewards (union representatives at the place of work) without the approval of union headquarters. The Royal Commission on Trade Unions (the "Donovan Commission," which reported in

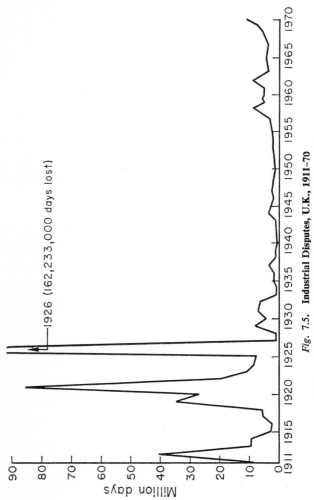

Fig. 7.5. **Industrial Disputes, U.K., 1911–70**
Number of Working Days Lost as a Result of Industrial Disputes

1968) found this prevalence of unofficial strikes arising from disagreement between local shop stewards and officials at headquarters, to be one of the crucial problems of current British industrial relations. Many of the Commission's recommendations were designed to lead to the development of orderly procedures for dealing with all industrial disputes and to promote the growth of collective bargaining at the factory level. One recommendation, which was swiftly adopted, called for firms employing more than 5,000 workers to make arrangements for dealing with disputes at plant level, and to communicate them to the government, which might refer unsatisfactory cases to the Commission on Industrial Relations (see above, p. 165) for investigation.

The Conservative government, which took office in 1970, however, went a good deal further and passed its Industrial Relations Act the following year, setting up the National Industrial Relations Court, and registration system outlined earlier (see above, p. 165). The Secretary of State for Employment also published a Code of Industrial Practice, setting out a number of guidelines for good industrial behaviour which, while not having the force of law, can yet be cited in cases before the N.I.R.C. Certain provisions of the Act were concerned with the position of the individual worker. Some of these have already been discussed, but they include also the right to extended notice for long-service employees, and protection from unfair dismissal. One of the prime purposes of the new system of registration, unfair practices and court procedures of the Act, however, was to reduce the incidence of unofficial strikes, by ensuring that financial protection from damages during a dispute is only enjoyed by the union deemed appropriate to represent a particular group of workers. It will be some time before any reasoned assessment of the effectiveness of the Act can be made.

Machinery for Negotiation in Disputes

It is possible that the machinery for the settlement of disputes will change in the next few years, with the passing of the Industrial Relations Act, but it appears to be the government's intention that established and satisfactory arrangements for collective bargaining between unions and management should continue to operate. Many of these have developed as a result of voluntary agreement between the two sides of industry. They vary from one industry to another, but usually involve the establishment of some permanent committee of the two sides to which any disagreement is referred and argued to a conclusion acceptable to both. In other industries, existing arrangements were the outcome of proposals made by the Whitley Committee, which reported during the first World War, that industries which had not provided themselves

with some permanent machinery for settling disputes should set up
Joint Industrial Councils. Over a hundred of these were formed in the
years immediately following. Weakness of organization on both sides
and the trade depression of the 1930s, caused over half of them to
collapse, but a great revival took place after the Second World War
and by the 1960s some two hundred were in operation (in government
service, the gas, water and electricity utilities, road transport, etc.).

Government Intervention in Disputes

Collective agreements are presumed to be legally binding (unless the
parties expressly stipulate otherwise) since the passing of the Industrial
Relations Act of 1971, and it will be a matter for the courts to deal
with disputes arising over past agreements. Where, however, the parties
fail to agree, the government has a number of courses of action open to
it. When the failure to agree is due to questions of the appropriate
organization to represent a group of workers, the Commission for
Industrial Relations may be called in, and/or the National Industrial
Relations Court or local Industrial Tribunals left to settle the matter.
The Department also employs a number of Conciliation Officers to
try and help the parties to a dispute to reach a settlement. Other cases
may be referred, if both parties agree, to the Industrial Arbitration
Board (originally called the Industrial Court) established in 1919 for
this purpose.

In the most serious cases of disagreement the Secretary of State for
Employment may appoint a special Court of Inquiry, without the
consent of both sides. Moreover, the Industrial Relations Act gives
the government additional powers in cases of national emergency. In
the first place, the Minister can apply to the National Industrial
Relations Court for an order restraining strike action for up to sixty
days, where national health or security is endangered, or where the
community would be deprived of the essentials of life, or where
deferment would help to reach a settlement. In the second place, the
Secretary of State for Employment can apply to the Court for the
ordering of a secret ballot among workers, if there is reason to believe
that a majority do not really support a strike but cannot give adequate
voice to that view.

Finally, it should be added that the Minister has the power to set up
Wages Councils for industries with inadequate negotiating machinery
and to fix minimum wages where necessary. Some sixty Wages Councils
were operating at the end of the 1960s, but they are considered by the
government to have outlived their usefulness and will probably be
gradually wound up. Apart from the Wages Councils, the Minister

power to fix minimum wages has been rarely used in recent years, and the only sector where it is important is agriculture. The Office of Manpower Economics was, however, set up to advise the government on the pay of certain, initially rather restricted, groups of workers in the public sector.

Unemployment

Since the question of unemployment is obviously of the utmost importance to the individual worker, and its prevention is one of the aims of trade unions, it is necessary to consider the extent of unemployment in Britain. Before doing so, however, it will be useful to distinguish between the principal types of unemployment, even though in any particular case we may be unable to decide how much is of each kind.

1. SEASONAL UNEMPLOYMENT

In some industries—agriculture and building, for instance—production varies greatly according to the time of the year. Farmers take on extra labour for the harvest, and we may expect to find a rise in agricultural unemployment as men are laid off when the corn is in. On the docks, too, employment tends to come in peaks as the ships come in for unloading. To some extent this seasonal nature of production in some trades is met, not so much by actual unemployment as by men working overtime in the peaks and short-time in the slack periods, or by "dovetailing," e.g. the switching by seaside hotels to catering for conferences in the tourist off-season.

2. VOLUNTARY UNEMPLOYMENT

There is no doubt that some unemployment exists because the people concerned just do not want to find jobs. This may be due to the fact that some are so lazy that they prefer to eke out a bare living on social security benefit or to the fact that they are rich enough to live comfortably without taking on a job at all. This kind of unemployment is not very important in this country, though we may all know someone who falls into this category.

3. STRUCTURAL UNEMPLOYMENT

As we saw in Chapter 4, the structure of industry is constantly on the change, in that some industries are expanding while others are on the decline. These changes are responsible for what is called structural or *frictional* unemployment. For as an industry contracts it is only to be expected that some of the workers may be unemployed until they find new jobs in other industries. Thus, since we know that the shipbuilding industry has been contracting, we may be fairly sure that some of the unemployment among workers there has been of this kind. It should also be added that when the unemployment is due to the adoption of a new technical process which makes men redundant it is commonly referred to as *technological*.

These descriptions of structural unemployment may perhaps suggest that it is temporary in nature and, while this is often the case, in times of general depression when most industries are contracting it may, on the contrary, be prolonged and much more serious. It is beyond the scope of this book to deal with the causes of such prolonged unemployment, sometimes referred to as *cyclical*, because of its association with the trade cycle (*see above*, p. 95).

4. LOCALIZED UNEMPLOYMENT

It frequently happens that the unemployment resulting both from seasonal and from structural causes occurs in industries which are highly concentrated in one or more districts. This is liable to cause pockets of chronic unemployment in particular areas and, in fact, prompted the government to take the special measures to deal with them outlined in Chapter 4.

Unemployment in Britain

The extent of unemployment in Britain in the period since the end of the Second World War has, on the whole, been relatively slight.

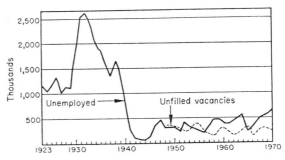

Fig. 7.6.   **Registered Unemployed Persons 1923–70 and Numbers of Unfilled Vacancies, 1948–70, Great Britain**

As Fig. 7.6 shows, until the late 1960s the total number has been around three or four hundred thousand, representing about 1½ to 2 per cent of the labour force out of work, although it exceeded half million occasionally for relatively short periods. From 1967 to 1970, however, unemployment climbed to a significantly higher level, reaching 3 per cent of the work force in early 1971 and, at the time of writing, fears have been expressed that it may even exceed one million. Before the war, as the chart shows, the situation was very different—with unemployment continually in excess of a million (out of a smaller labour force) throughout the period 1923–39. In 1932, at the bottom of the trade depression, the number rose to two and a half million, representing about one in five of the working population.

It is also sometimes useful to compare the numbers of unemployed persons not with the total labour force but with the numbers of vacancies reported unfilled. It is true that the available jobs at any time may not fit the qualifications of those seeking work, or they may be in totally different parts of the country, but any given level of unemployment tends to be more serious if there are relatively few unfilled vacancies than if there are a lot. Fig. 7.6 also shows the number of jobs available, as well as the number of unemployed, for the years since the war for which statistics are available.

INDUSTRIAL UNEMPLOYMENT

This very general picture of the total numbers unemployed conceals the very important fact that unemployment is not equally spread over the whole of industry. Fig. 7.7 gives details of the differences in the major industries for 1932 and 1970. The latter year was one with relatively high unemployment by post-war standards, but differences are much less striking than in 1932. Comparing the percentage unemployment in different industries with the national average for 1932 of 22 per cent we find unemployment well above average in industries like shipbuilding, coal mining, and iron and steel, and relatively less in light industries such as baking, the distributive trades and the professions. This is no more than a reflection of the fact that, as we noted in Chapter 4, heavy industries tend to hold up less well during a slump than those catering directly for the consumer. It suggests, too, the reason why in 1970, itself a year of relatively high unemployment, the construction industry was particularly badly hit.

REGIONAL UNEMPLOYMENT

Comparison of the extent of unemployment in different parts of the country again produces divergencies, as the details in the map (Fig. 7.8) show. The depression of the inter-war years, with unemployment tending to be highest in the declining heavy industries concentrated in Wales, Scotland and the north of England, can be seen to have left a

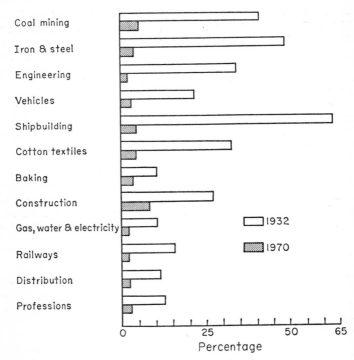

Fig. 7.7.   **Unemployment in Selected Industries in Great Britain, 1932 and 1970**
Percentage Unemployment

legacy even into the 1970s. Unemployment rates in April 1971 were still relatively high in these areas, and relatively low in the South East and the Midlands, though the various measures taken by the government since the 1930s (*see above*, pp. 79–80) have somewhat diminished the relative imbalance in regional unemployment.

Employment Exchanges

The existence of significant differences in unemployment rates both by region and by industry emphasizes the importance of assisting workers to move into new jobs. One institution, first introduced over half a century ago, which encourages such labour mobility by reducing the

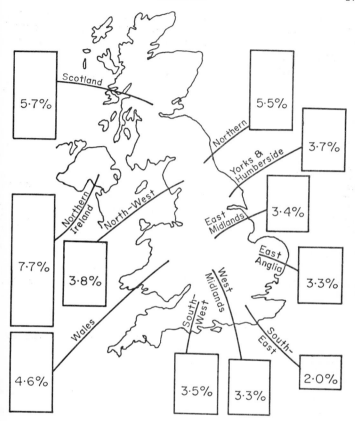

Fig. 7.8. **Regional Unemployment, U.K., 1971**
Percentages of the total number of employees registered as
unemployed on 5 April, 1971

ngth of time spent by the unemployed in looking for a job, is the
nployment Exchange. About a thousand of them are operated by
e Department of Employment in the industrial districts of Britain.
ey receive notices of vacancies from employers and pass this informa-
n on to unemployed persons who register with them. The Depart-
nt also operates certain other rather specialized services having
nilar objectives, of which the Professional and Executive Register,

which is concerned with posts of a managerial nature, is one of th
most important. In addition to these governmental services, privatel
run employment bureaux perform a similar function, which is o
particular importance in secretarial and other office work.

EXERCISES

(For key to symbols indicating sources, *see* p. 14)

1. Prepare a table showing the membership of trade unions for every yea
since 1960, making a note of the separate numbers of men and women. Ha
there been a fall in the numbers of either? If so, can you suggest a possibl
explanation? (*A.S.*)

2. Find out the number of trade-union members in each industry and the tota
membership. Work out the average size of industrial unions, including those fo
"general workers". List them in rank order by size. (*W.A.*)

3. Collect figures showing the number of industrial stoppages of work in th
six main industrial groups in Britain for the past two calendar years. Work ou
the proportion of total stoppages accounted for by each group, and compar
your results. Are there any big changes, and do you know why? (*A.S.*)

4. Prepare a graph showing the number of working days lost as a result o
industrial stoppages for the past ten years. (*A.S.*)

5. For the latest year for which statistics are available, find out the total numbe
of workers and the total number of unemployed persons in each of the followir
industries—

Agriculture and horticulture	Iron and steel
Bread and flour confectionery	Mechanical engineering
Catering contractors	Locomotives and railway track equipmen
Chemicals and allied industries	Pottery
Distributive trades	Shipbuilding
Footwear	Woollen and worsted

Work out the percentage unemployment in each case and compare your resul
(*A.S.*)

6. Prepare graphs showing the percentage of the working population that w
unemployed in Scotland, and the United Kingdom, in the following years—

1924, 1929, 1932, 1937, 1948, 1955, 1960, 1966 and a later year, if availabl
(*K.S.*)

7. Prepare a graph showing the excess or deficit of employment vacanci
unfilled over the total number of registered unemployed in Britain for the pa
twelve months. (*E.T.* or *M.D.S.*)

8. Trace an outline map of Great Britain from any atlas and divide it rough
into regions. Shade areas where unemployment rates are equal to the avera
for the whole country, and hatch those where they are below. Compare the resu
with the map on p. 179. (*E.T.* or *M.D.S.*)

9. Construct a graph showing the percentage unemployment for each mon
in the past calendar year for the whole of Great Britain and for the region in whi
you live. Do you know why the percentage should be higher (or lower) in yo
area? (*E.T.* or *M.D.S.*)

10. Construct a chart showing the average weekly hours worked by men and women over 21 for as many years as you can obtain statistics since 1960. (*A.S.*)

11. Prepare a table for the last two years showing (*a*) the numbers of workers unemployed, (*b*) the numbers working overtime, and (*c*) the numbers on short-time. Calculate the percentage changes from one year to the other. Which appear to change more similarly, (*a*) and (*b*) or (*a*) and (*c*)? Have you any idea why?

CHAPTER 8

Income and Wealth

FROM what has been said in previous chapters we should, by now, have some idea of the total volume of production of all goods and services in the country as a whole. It is usual to refer to this total over a period of time, such as a year, as the value of the National Output or Product. Moreover, since the factors of production engaged in producing all the goods and services receive incomes for doing so, the total can equally well be referred to as the National Income.

THE NATIONAL INCOME

Estimating the size of the national income involves a number of problems, some of which are of a statistical nature. One, in particular, is worth mentioning briefly in order to understand better the meaning of the British national income to be discussed in this chapter. For compiling the national income at all must involve adding together in some way all the outputs of the various goods and services produced—tons of steel, gallons of milk, television sets, restaurant meals and so on. The only convenient unit of measurement for adding such obviously different things is their money values (the prices at which they sell) and the national income is, therefore, really the money value of all the goods and services produced over the period under consideration, normally a year.

Other statistical problems cannot be discussed in detail. But they may be taken to imply that the official figures of the national income published by the Central Statistical Office, whether derived from the addition of total outputs or of the total incomes of all the factors of production, are no more than estimates and should be treated as such, though they may be good enough for many purposes.

It is of prime importance to have some idea of the major components of the national income, since the way in which it is distributed critically affects relative living standards, both as between different individuals and between individuals at different points of time. We shall consider the distribution of personal and factor incomes shortly. First, we may discuss the way in which income may be allocated as between the present and the future. In this connexion, it is useful to distinguish between two kinds of goods and services which can be produced, *consumer* goods and *investment* (or *capital* or *producers'*) goods.

The difference between them is fairly straightforward, though there are in practice borderline cases to be settled. Consumer goods are things like food and household goods which are wanted for their own sake and which are capable of immediately and *directly* affecting present living standards via current consumption. Investment goods, on the other hand, affect consumption only *indirectly*. They include things, such as factories and machines, which are not in themselves desirable,

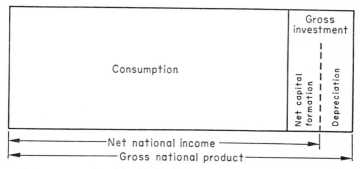

Fig. 8.1. **National Income, U.K., 1970**

but which are wanted because they indirectly assist in the satisfaction of consumer wants in the future. The distinction between consumer goods and investment goods, then, is between things which satisfy consumer wants directly and those which do so indirectly. It should be noted that the difference is not simply one of durability. Some consumer goods, such as food, are in fact capable of satisfying a want only once, while others, like cars and cameras, can go on providing a benefit over a length of time. Likewise investment goods include disposable raw materials as well as longer-lasting machinery.

Roughly four-fifths of the national product of the United Kingdom takes the form of consumer goods, as Fig. 8.1 shows, and the remainder is used for investment. If we wish to continue to enjoy at least our present living standards in the future it is important that such investment takes place. Machines, factories and other capital equipment are all part of the assets of the country which make it possible to produce many of the things in the mechanized and relatively efficient ways which we do now. In principle, we might be able to push up current living standards for a short while by ceasing to produce investment goods and by using all our resources to make consumer goods for present enjoyment. But soon existing capital equipment would be run down and we should suffer, if we did not make good the deterioration and depreciation which is continually taking place. As Fig. 8.1 shows, roughly ten per cent of our national income, nearly half the investment, is used to make good such depreciation. It is usual to refer to the *Net* national income after deducting this in order to distinguish it from the *Gross* national income (or Gross National Product, G.N.P., as it is more often called) before depreciation is allowed for. The net national income, then, can be regarded as representing the total output of goods and services produced in the year which could, in principle, be consumed without sacrificing the future to the present. But, as can be seen, we usually devote more resources to the production of investment goods than we strictly need, merely in order to replace existing capital equipment. This is because we are not generally satisfied with existing living standards but seek to raise them by saving and investing for the future. Any extra investment is called net capital formation and is available for growth—for the construction of new, better and more efficient equipment, which becomes possible as technology advances.

Personal Incomes

As has been stated, each factor of production earns an income for its part in the production of the goods and services which go to make up the national product, and we must now consider the way in which total income is divided among persons. Before doing so, it must be emphasized that the sum total of personal incomes is not the same thing as the national income. There are two main reasons for this. In the first place, it may be recalled that, while part of the income of joint-stock companies is paid out in the form of dividends to shareholders, some is usually retained in the business itself and is not passed on to individuals (*see above*, Chapter 3). While we shall, accordingly, exclude undistributed business profits from our consideration of personal incomes, we shall, in the second place, have to deal with certain incomes accruing to persons which arise for reasons other than in return for the production of goods and services. These are referred to as *transfer* incomes and include payments made by the State such as pensions, unemployment benefit and so on.

The total value of personal incomes in 1970 amounted to over £40,000 million, and the way in which this was divided among the different groups of income recipients is shown in Fig. 8.2.

1. Income from Employment

The most important group by far are those whose incomes arise as payment for employment. Their share amounts to something like two-thirds of the total, and they consist of two sub-groups, wage-earners and salary-earners.

(A) WAGES

The distinction often made between wages and salaries is a rather arbitrary one. Wage-earners are defined as "operatives" and include manual workers and shop assistants, as distinct from administrative and clerical employees. They are the larger of the two groups, and have received about 40 per cent of total income for a very considerable number of years. Although mention is often made of the "average wage," there exist, within this category, considerable differences as between individuals. These will be easier to understand if the principal methods of wage payment are first made clear. Two main systems may be distinguished—

(i) *Time Wages.* The most common form of paying wages is according to the length of hours actually worked in any one week. Generally a certain minimum number of hours are stipulated in the conditions of employment of each individual wage-earner, for which a fixed weekly wage is paid, with provision for payment of a higher rate for overtime, week-end and holiday work.

Fig. 8.2. **Distribution of Personal Incomes, before Tax, U.K., 1970**

(ii) *Payment by Results.* While a worker on a time-rate basis receives the same wage regardless of the amount of work which he actually does, a worker who is paid according to the amount he produces is offered a special incentive to work hard. Not that this method of wage payment is necessarily desirable. Sometimes it is difficult to measure the amount of work done, and in any case it does not always follow that output would be increased by an incentive scheme. It is all very well to pay strawberry pickers a certain sum for every pound of strawberries that they gather, but it would be impossible to pay a cinema box-office attendant according to the number of tickets she sells. This would make her earnings high when a good film was being shown and attendance was up, and exceptionally low when a very poor one was being screened.   Not only would it be extremely unfair; it would not even serve a useful purpose. For, while the application of payment by results may give the strawberry picker an incentive to work harder, it is very unlikely to have the same effect on the box-office attendant.

Systems of payment by results are numerous, and several are quite complicated. They generally fall into one of two principal types. The first gives a worker, or group of workers, a previously stipulated sum for every unit of output produced, and is called a *piece rate*. The second sets the worker a standard "task" or job with a set time to do it in, and he can earn a *bonus* which is related to the time "saved." This should not be confused with the bonus given to employees of some companies which operate profit-sharing schemes with all their workers; the size of such a bonus is determined by the total profitability of the company over the year.

Systems of payment by results have a long history, and a new wave of popularity extended their use in Britain after the Second World War to about a third of all wage-earners. In more recent years, however, piece work has become less common again partly, no doubt, because the increasing use of mechanization in industry has made it less useful.

DIFFERENCES IN WAGES

Bearing in mind the fact that workers are paid in a variety of different ways and that this, in itself, is responsible for variations between the wages of individuals, we may now turn to examine some other sources of wage differences. Four of the most important are as follows—

1. *Differences in Respect of Skill.*   In many cases these are almost too obvious to mention. The head chef at the Savoy Hotel naturally earns much more than the cook in a small café, and an electrician more than a road sweeper. Frequently, however, differences in the degree of skill attaching to a particular job may be very much a matter of opinion. Thus, in the engineering industry, how is one to decide whether a welder, for instance, should get a higher or a lower wage than a fitter? Sometimes the decision may be left to the employer who will then probably pay the higher rate to the worker whom he has the greatest difficulty in securing. In nearly all industries where trade unions are strong, however, the employer has much less say in the

fixing of these skill differentials. For most trade unions have gradually evolved a hierarchy of skills which they are usually reluctant to see altered, and collective agreements with employers normally stipulate that the same differentials will be retained for the same skills in an industry whenever there is a general alteration in wage rates. However, the fairly common practice of maintaining the same differentials in absolute terms, by awarding equal *money* increases rather than equal *percentage* increases to workers with different skills, has meant that such differentials have become relatively smaller in many occupations than they were before the war.

2. *Differences by Industry*. A second source of differences in wages is related to the particular industry in which one happens to work. Fig. 8.3 shows details of the weekly earnings of wage-earners in a number of the more important industries. *Earnings* are the total amount of money income which an individual receives each week. They take account of any overtime or short time which may be worked and are, therefore, more suitable for this purpose than the simple wage rates on which they are based. Differences are considerable. The average weekly earnings of male manual workers in British industry in October 1970 were over £28 per week. Compared to this some of the most highly paid industries were vehicles, iron and steel and chemicals while, at the other extreme, earnings were £5 or £6 per week lower in clothing and textiles. Too much attention should not be paid to the exact ordering of industries at this or at any other particular time, since there are often changes in relative positions as individual businesses expand or contract, and are able or unable to pay higher wages. In addition, it should be emphasized that inter-industry differentials are, in part a reflection of the skill differentials already discussed, since the proportion of workers with different degrees of skill certainly varies from one industry to another. Moreover, variations in hours worked, in opportunities for overtime, in methods of wage payment and other matters, make it difficult to draw simple conclusions about the reasons for any particular industry having above- or below-average earnings.

3. *Differences in Respect of Sex*. As Fig. 8.3 also reveals, you are much more likely to earn more if you are a man than if you are a woman. Average earnings of women in all industries in October 1970 were actually 50 per cent below those of men, and though they differed from industry to industry, the figure is fairly representative. The reasons for this are many and complex, and to a certain extent reflect the fact that the figure for women relates to those aged 18 and over, while that for men to those of 21 and over. The latter, therefore,

includes a smaller proportion of lower paid young persons. However, there is little doubt that a substantial differential does exist. The Equal Pay Act of 1970 establishes the rule that a woman shall have the right to equal treatment with a man doing broadly similar work in the same or an associated establishment, as from 1 January 1976. But even this law will not necessarily ensure that women's earnings rise, on average, to the level of men's for in many cases the actual jobs that women do are different from those done by men.

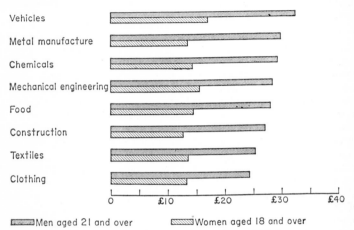

Fig. 8.3.   **Average Weekly Earnings Manual Workers Selected Industries, U.K., October 1970**

An important influence maintaining feminine inferiority is the traditionally held belief that women actually need less pay than men. There is no doubt, however, that the comparative weakness of trade unionism among women restrains the opposition to this view which is now more strongly felt. It is also true that many girls leaving school look upon their employment as a temporary phase of their life, which will cease when they are married. They are, therefore, less inclined to go to the trouble of learning a profession or a trade and thus take advantage of the higher wages which usually accompany an increase in skill.

4. *Regional Differences.* A final explanation of wage differential relates to the region in which one works. As Fig. 8.4 shows, earning tend to be highest in the West Midlands and the South-East, an

lowest in Northern Ireland, East Anglia and Yorkshire and Humberside. In part, this is again a reflection of some of the things already discussed, like inter-industry and skill differentials, for regions vary in the proportions of their labour forces in various industries and with different

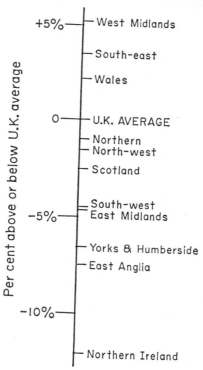

Fig. 8.4. **Regional Wage Differentials**
Average weekly earnings of adult male manual workers.
Manufacturing industry U.K., October 1970

skills. But an additional factor keeping earnings higher in some areas than in others is undoubtedly the differences experienced by employers in getting labour to work for them. Regions with below average levels of unemployment such as the West Midlands and the South-East, for instance, tend to be those with general labour shortages, where higher pay has to be offered, and it is hardly an accident that Northern

Ireland is bottom of the "league" in both average earnings and un-employment rates.

(B) SALARIES

Persons in non-manual employment are classified separately and known as *salary-earners*. The distinction between them and manual wage-earners is, as stated earlier, often arbitrary and not infrequently merely snobbish, based on the whiteness of the collar worn for work. Although many salaried employees actually receive less than the better-paid wage-earners, the highest-paid employees of all are generally in the salary group. It is a very diverse category including, on the one hand, senior executives of large companies and, on the other, office boys, but security of employment is often greater than for wage-earners.

The share of salary earners in the total at the present time is roughly 25 per cent. This figure represents a substantial increase on earlier years and, in fact, the share of salaries has been rising pretty steadily since the 1870s, if not before. The explanation is very largely one of a shift from manual to non-manual jobs, as the numbers employed in clerical, administrative and technical occupations have grown. Average salary earnings have also grown over the last decade and a half almost as fast as those of manual workers.

2. Forces Pay

The total value of the pay and allowances of the armed forces amounts to rather less than 2 per cent of the total of personal incomes, but merits separate treatment, not only because the nature of the work is different but because the actual money pay of the forces is only a part of the "income" which they receive. Unlike most other types of workers, they are given their board and lodging and most of the necessities of life in addition to the pay which they draw each week, so that it is difficult to draw comparisons between them and other groups.

3. Incomes of the Self-employed

There are three main groups of persons whose incomes are treated as those of the self-employed. They are farmers, professional persons and unincorporated sole traders and partnerships.

The share of farmers has been declining over a very long period, as agriculture has diminished in importance in the British economy, and is now no more than half of what it was a century ago.

Professional earnings are the smallest category. They are usually grouped separately since the incomes of these accountants, solicitors, architects, doctors, and the like, are not normally received in the form of regular wages or salaries, but as fees for their services, which vary with the success of their practices. The share of professional earnings in the total is about the same as that of the armed forces. It has also been kept from rising to some extent by the tendency of some professional people to begin trading as joint-stock companies, because of certain tax advantages that have sometimes been given to that form of business organization.

Similar in general character to professional persons are those individuals, like small retailers, who have businesses of their own, which have not been turned into joint-stock companies. Their share of the total is now about 5 per cent. This, too, has been declining, probably for similar reasons, but also, no doubt, because of the relative increase in the importance of large-scale enterprise in British industry.

Rent, Dividends and Interest

The majority of personal incomes which appear under this heading are usually known as *unearned*, since they are derived from the ownership of shares or property of some kind rather than from the actual performance of work. Thus the dividends paid to shareholders in joint-stock companies are included here, and also the interest which moneylenders receive on their loans. Altogether, these account for very roughly a tenth of personal incomes of all kinds. Their share has fluctuated over the years with, for instance, variations in the proportions of company profits distributed to shareholders (*see above*, pp. 47–8). Rent control and decontrol measures of successive governments have also affected the size of the rent element in the total.

Transfer Incomes

The incomes of the previous groups account together for about 90 per cent of all personal incomes. The remainder comprise those already referred to as transfer incomes, which are paid by the State to individuals in the form of pensions, unemployment and health benefits, etc. Their name arises because taxes are frequently used to finance them, and this involves a transfer from those paying taxes to those receiving benefits. In fact there is an element of transfer income in certain other incomes previously dealt with. Some of the interest payments made by the government, for instance, are financed in the same way. We shall discuss these matters again later in the chapter when we look more closely at government finances.

THE SIZE OF INCOMES

So far we have managed to discuss the various types of incomes which people receive without going into the details of how much they earn as individuals. The latter is, of course, of fundamental importance; for it usually matters less to a person whether he receives, for example, a salary or a wage, than whether he earns £500 a year or £5,000.

Some idea of the number of persons who have incomes of different size is given in Fig. 8.5, although it should be pointed out that it is based on returns made to the Inland Revenue for tax purposes, by whose practice the income of a married man includes that of his wife. The number of incomes referred to, therefore, in a considerable number of cases approximates more closely to the number of families than to that of individuals receiving income.

Of the 22 million incomes recorded in this way in 1968–9, the great bulk—13½ million in fact—were in the bracket between £500 and £1,500 per annum. At the bottom of the scale there were nearly 3 millions, including a lot of women, retired and young persons, receiving less than £500 per annum. And at the other end of the scale in the same year, there were about 2 million incomes of £2,000 a year and over; and these included some 7,000 incomes of £20,000 or more.

There are many reasons why such inequality in incomes exists, but we can do no more here than to note the inequality and mention that it can be explained only if we can answer two questions: why some people have better-paid jobs, and why some have more property than others. Something has already been said about the former, and the ownership of property will be discussed later in this chapter.

Distribution of Income after Taxation

Our previous consideration of the distribution of income has assumed that everyone is allowed to keep all that he earns for his own personal expenditure. This is, of course, quite untrue, for the Government steps in and collects a proportion of nearly every individual's income in the form of income tax, which takes the form of a levy of so many pence in every pound of income. Generally the tax is *progressive*, by which is meant that the rate at which it is levied rises the higher a person's income, and special allowances are also made to take care of individual circumstances. Very small incomes are completely exempt from this tax, while very large incomes have been subject to rates of over 90 per cent for those in the highest brackets (*but see below*, p. 197).

In view of the progressive nature of these taxes the distribution of personal incomes after income tax has been deducted is considerably less unequal than the distribution of gross income. The difference can also be appreciated from a study of Fig. 8.5. The change is most noticeable at the top end of the scale. There are, it will be seen, proportionately fewer high incomes after tax has been deducted. Thus

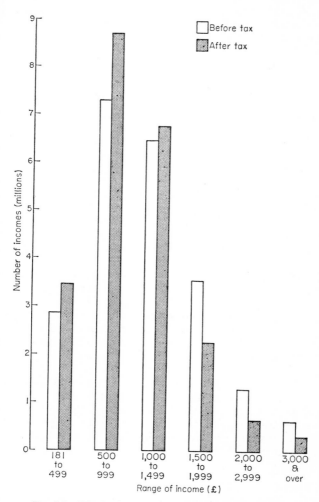

Fig. 8.5. **Distribution of Personal Incomes, U.K., 1968–9**

there are about half as many incomes of £2,000 and over after tax has been deducted as there were before. At the bottom end of the scale taxation makes less difference since low incomes are, as explained, subject to very little tax, but a few of those in the next highest bracket are brought into the lowest class.

It would not be appropriate to leave the question of the distribution of income without making some reference to the changes which have taken place since pre-war days. It is not easy to compare incomes today with those of the 1930s, because wages and prices have both risen so much that it is hard to find a stable basis of comparison. But there seems little doubt that, if we were able to draw up a chart for 1939 which was comparable with our Fig. 8.5 we should find the pre-tax distribution less equal at the former date.

This reduction in the degree of inequality is partly the result of the very much smaller amount of unemployment in post-war Britain, and of the general tendency towards declining skill differentials mentioned earlier. But the extent of any apparent reduction based, like Fig. 8.5, upon income tax returns would, in all probability be an exaggerated one because such figures may be quite seriously affected by tax avoidance devices, and in addition exclude many fringe benefits which have become increasingly popular in recent years.

Moreover, the post-tax distribution of income for the same period does not also exhibit the same trend. Although the statistics are capable of more than one interpretation, it is probably a fair generalization to say that the effect of higher income taxation in the war, and earlier post-war years, also worked to make the income distribution more equal, but that more recently the direction of influence has been reversed, and by the early 1970s the tax system had become less progressive again.

It must be stressed that the outline of the size distribution of personal incomes given above should not be taken to imply too much about the relative standards of living of different income groups. This is a much more complicated matter and involves also considering such matters as the ownership of property, which will be dealt with later in the chapter, and other forms of taxation and state-provided benefits, to which we now turn.

STATE INTERVENTION

The intervention of the government in the economy has been discussed in several places in this book in connexion with the nationalized industries, the regulation of private enterprise and divers matters, and we have just seen how the levying of income tax can affect the distribu tion of incomes. But government activity influences the standard of living of individuals in more ways than this, and in particular because there are a number of goods and services which the State itself undertakes to provide directly for its citizens.

The scope of government action has increased considerably in the present century and now involves about two-fifths of the national income. Today it includes services that are supplied for collective use, like the armed forces, the police force, fire brigades and road maintenance and a number of others which are available to individual citizens as of right, such as education, medical treatment and pensions.

Now the government is not, unfortunately, a fairy godmother blessed with a magic wand which can conjure things like armies, schools and hospitals out of thin air. These things all have to be paid for, and it is our immediate concern to examine the principal goods and services which the State provides and the ways in which it manages to pay for them. It is convenient to consider the matter in two sections, distinguishing between the activities of the central government and those of local authorities.

1. Central Government

The main items of income and expenditure of the central government are shown in Fig. 8.6. It should, however, be stressed at the outset that the figures upon which the chart has been based refer only to one particular year—in this case 1970—while in reality they may be changed quite considerably from time to time. In practice, if there are going to be any important changes, these are generally announced by the Chancellor of the Exchequer in March or April. It is traditionally at this time that the government makes decisions on its economic policy for the ensuing year, and draws up its estimates of income and expenditure over the period, which are known as the *Budget* proposals and are presented to Parliament by the Chancellor himself. While the government is not precluded from introducing further changes at any time that it pleases, it is mainly at Budget time that alterations in taxation are made.

INCOME

While the government has a relatively small amount of trading and investment income, by far the most important source of its revenue is taxation. This takes two principal forms—direct taxation and indirect taxation.

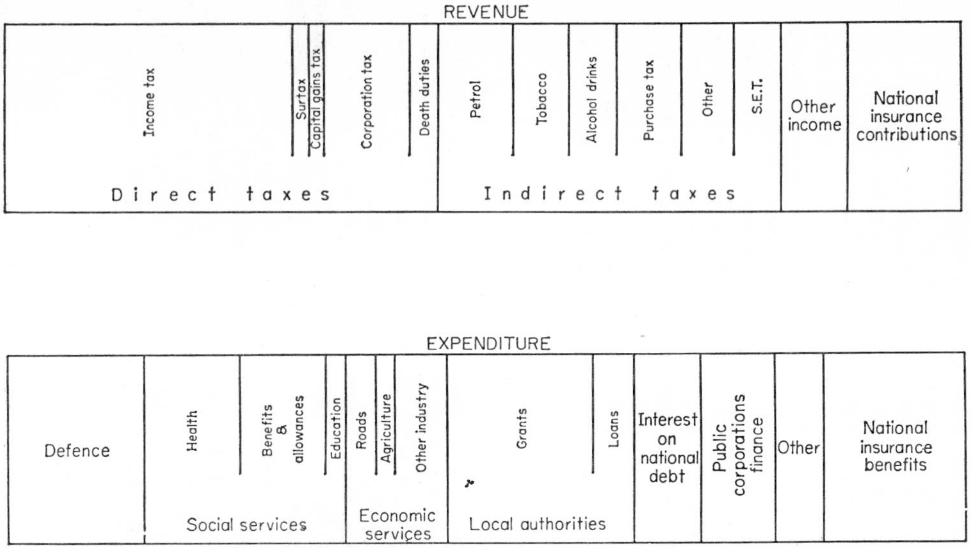

REVENUE

Direct taxes: Income tax | Surtax | Capital gains tax | Corporation tax | Death duties

Indirect taxes: Petrol | Tobacco | Alcohol drinks | Purchase tax | Other | S.E.T.

Other income | National insurance contributions

EXPENDITURE

Defence | Social services: Health | Benefits & allowances | Education | Economic services: Roads | Agriculture | Other industry | Local authorities: Grants | Loans | Interest on national debt | Public corporations finance | Other | National insurance benefits

Fig. 8.6. Central Government Revenue and Expenditure, U.K., 1970

Direct taxation provides just over half the total tax income of the government. Included under this heading are all the taxes on the income or property of individuals, and of bodies, such as joint-stock companies, where a proportion must be paid to the State. Easily the most important of these taxes is the *income tax*, which has already been mentioned. This, it will be remembered, is levied on a person's income, not the whole of which is, however, liable to tax. A number of allowances are made, which are deducted from gross income to give a figure of *taxable* income, on which the tax due is calculated. The chief of these allowances are in respect of a man's wife, children and other dependants, but there are other deductions, such as life assurance premiums and mortgage interest on loans made to individuals for house purchase, which single persons may also enjoy, so that those with very low incomes are not liable to tax at all. Earned incomes, as distinct from investment income (*see above*, p. 191), are also given favourable treatment. After the deductions have been allowed for, tax is then payable to the Board of Inland Revenue. Since 1944, when the system known as P.A.Y.E. (Pay as you earn) was introduced, the tax payable has been deducted at source by each employer, who pays it directly to the Collector of Taxes.

In 1971, the Chancellor of the Exchequer announced that he was embarking on a major reform of personal taxes. One of the reasons for doing so was to simplify the complex system of rates and allowances, so as to make quite clear to the individual what his own tax liability actually is. The changes are to take effect from 1973–4. Prior to that date, personal income has been liable to two separate taxes, known as *income tax* and *surtax*. The former applies a standard rate of tax, effectively about 30 per cent, on all taxable incomes. Surtax, at a graduated rate, is additionally levied on higher incomes, depending on individual circumstances, raising the total liability for those in the top bracket to nearly 90 per cent.

The new system that is to supersede the existing one in 1973 will substitute a single uniform progressive tax for the income tax and surtax. Details of the precise rates are still to be settled, but the Chancellor has already announced that there will be a "basic" rate of 30 per cent in 1973–4, and it is widely expected that the top rate for earned incomes will be around 75 per cent. Investment incomes will be subject to an additional surcharge.

In addition to the taxes on income as conventionally defined, taxes have also been levied since 1962 on *increases* in the value of the capital assets owned by an individual. Such increases are, after all, in a sense, equivalent to income, since a person can, if he wishes, spend any gain due to a rise in the value of his assets between the beginning and the end of a year, without leaving himself any worse off from the point of view of his accumulated wealth. *Capital gains tax* is levied at a flat rate (30 per cent for persons in 1971) on net realized gains from the actual disposal of assets, after the deduction of any realized losses from sale of other assets. There is an exemption limit of £50, and certain property, such as cars, chattels worth less than £1,000 and a private house, are exempt from capital gains tax.

Fig. 8.6 shows that taxes on personal incomes and capital gains account for about three-quarters of revenue from direct taxation. The other major source comes as a result of treating joint-stock companies as separate legal entities from their shareholders. Companies are assessed for *corporation tax* on their profits (and capital gains), though they also act as agents for the Inland Revenue and deduct income tax from the sums that they pay out in the form of dividends, etc. The base on which tax is calculated for companies is their *taxable* profits, a notion similar in some ways to that of taxable income for private persons. Companies do not, of course, qualify for personal allowances, but they are permitted to deduct all expenses properly incurred in the earning of profits, and additionally to offset sums to help provide for the depreciation that continually occurs in the value of their capital. Standard depreciation allowances are given and, in the past, the government has permitted the deduction of *investment allowances* (and investment grants) for industries and regions where expansion is desired. In 1971, however, the government decided to end the system of investment allowances in favour of alternative means of encouraging investment.

The level of corporation tax is fixed annually in the Budget, the current rate being 40 per cent. The system, however, tends to discriminate in favour of profit retention by companies—a policy that has been espoused in the past as a means of encouraging investment. At the same time, it is recognized that such discrimination tends to help companies that have earned high levels of profits in previous years, as against growing firms which need to attract capital by borrowing from the private sector. For this reason, the Chancellor of the Exchequer, in his 1971 Budget, declared his intention to remove the discrimination against distributing profits. Corporation tax also treats profits paid out as dividends on ordinary shares less favourably than those paid in the form of interest on debentures. It therefore discourages the use of equities for raising capital, which is thought by many observers to be another disadvantage of the existing system.

Direct taxes are levied not only on income but also on property or capital. The oldest capital taxes are the *estate duties*, which have to be paid at a person's death on the property he leaves behind him. The tax is a progressive one and the rates on large estates are very high, rising from 25 to 85 per cent on those of three-quarters of a million pounds or over, though there is an exemption limit of £12,500 below which no tax is payable. Estate duties have not, however, been a very important source of government revenue, notably because of the existence of various perfectly legal devices by which the liability to tax could be substantially reduced. There are other forms of death duty which have not, however, been used in Britain since 1949. They include the legacy and succession duties, which are not charged on the total estate left, but on the values of bequests received by individuals at rates varying with the closeness of the relationship between the deceased and beneficiary. They have some advantages over estate duty, and are recurrently discussed, as is the suggestion for an annual wealth tax on the property of the living as distinct from the dead.

Indirect Taxation. The other main source of the government's income comes from taxes on expenditure, often called indirect taxes, because they are not levied directly on persons or companies, but on items of expenditure, such as that on particular commodities or on the employment of labour. Thus, the amount of tax paid by a person, for instance, is not related to his income, but to the quantities of goods and services subject to indirect taxes that he chooses to buy. It may be possible, therefore, in theory to avoid paying such taxes by refraining from buying taxed goods, but as the range and number of goods covered by expenditure taxes widens, this is not a seriously practicable proposition. A more important observation is that some indirect taxes tend to be *regressive*, the opposite of progressive, in so far as they may take a higher proportion of a poor man's income than of a rich man's.

The chief revenue earners for many years have been the duties levied on petrol, tobacco and alcoholic drinks. Their relative importance can be seen in Fig. 8.6. Together they brought in over 20 per cent of total receipts from indirect taxation in 1970. Other expenditure taxes on particular goods and services are those on betting, entertainment and television advertising. In addition, payments have to be made to the government for the right to do certain things. We need licences to operate a television set, to keep a dog and to run a car, and there are many legal documents, such as those transferring ownership of property, which require the affixing of a special stamp.

The most general indirect tax is the *purchase tax*, which is charged on different kinds of luxuries and semi-luxuries, such as cars, umbrellas and sports equipment, at four rates varying from $13\frac{3}{4}$ per cent to 55 per cent in 1971. These rates are said to be *ad valorem* because they are calculated on the value of the commodity, in contrast to *specific* taxes which are fixed according to the quantity of the good in question, e.g. the duty per gallon on petrol, or per pound of tobacco. In 1971, the Chancellor of the Exchequer announced that, as part of the reform of the British tax system he was undertaking, purchase tax would be abolished. It is to be replaced in 1973 by a *value added tax* (V.A.T.). V.A.T. is of far more general coverage. It is levied on all firms on the amount that they themselves add to the value of the goods they produce, i.e. on the difference between their sales revenue and their costs arising from the purchase from other firms of (intermediate) goods and services brought in. These latter, of course, will have already been subject to V.A.T. by the firms operating at earlier stages in production. V.A.T. is essentially a tax on consumer spending, which is levied in instalments at each stage in the production process. For example, the manufacturer of a starter motor for a car pays tax on his value added. When he sells it to a car manufacturer, the price he charges reflects the tax already paid. The firm producing the car is then permitted to deduct the cost of this (and other items brought in) from its revenue from sale of cars, when calculating its liability to V.A.T.

V.A.T. is used by countries in the Common Market, and Britain's entry into the E.E.C. entails its adoption here. The cost to the government of administering the tax may be quite high, but V.A.T. has the advantage of falling more evenly on all goods and services (though some, such as food, will be exempted or given special treatment) than the purchase tax, which concentrates the burden on a relatively small number of items.

In addition to replacing purchase tax, the government declared, at the same time, that V.A.T. would also supersede the *selective employment tax* (S.E.T.). S.E.T. was introduced in 1966 as a tax on all employers of labour, and to that extent may be regarded as one of a family of so-called *payroll taxes*. However, the particular form of the tax adopted in the U.K. has been selective. One of its intentions was to favour manufacturing businesses, as distinct from those engaged in distribution, where it was considered by some economists (notably Professor Kaldor) that rates of productivity growth tended to be lower. Eligible firms in the manufacturing sector of the economy have, therefore, been able to obtain refunds of S.E.T. In addition, the S.E.T. system has been used to help manufacturers in the development areas, by granting them a regional employment premium based on the numbers on their payrolls, as well as the refund of S.E.T. The discriminatory nature of S.E.T., not to mention the anomalies which it is said to have caused, led the Conservative government to the decision mentioned earlier to do away with it. In preparation for its complete abolition in 1973, rates of S.E.T. were halved in 1971, to £1·20 per male employee and appropriately lower rates for women and boys.

Unlike direct taxes, the majority of expenditure taxes are collected by the Board of Customs and Excise. *Customs* duties are imposed on articles imported from overseas. The remainder are known as *excise* duties. The former are quite likely to increase in importance as tariffs are used instead of subsidies to support British agriculture (*see above*, pp. 104–5).

The rates of expenditure taxes actually applied to individual goods and services have been varied from time to time in the Budget. But the Chancellor of the Exchequer also has the power to vary rates by up to 10 per cent in either direction without the prior approval of Parliament. This provision is known as *the Regulator*, and its speedy use is intended to help the government control the level of activity in the economy.

Other Income. The government earns a certain amount of income from property, and finances some expenditure by borrowing. The total outstanding balance owed is known as the National Debt and is now enormous—in the order of £30,000 million. It has accumulated very largely as a result of expenditures needed for the waging of past wars, and is not normally used as a major source of government revenue in peacetime.

National Insurance Funds. Before ending this description of the main sources of revenue of the central government, we must note one special category. For a separate account is kept of what are called National Insurance Funds. These consist of receipts of national insurance contributions—weekly payments by employers and employees which are used to provide certain social security benefits, especially for the old, the sick and the unemployed. As can be seen from Fig. 8.6, contributions have tended to be less than benefits, so that the Fund has needed to be supplemented from general taxation. When first introduced, national insurance contributions and benefits were levied and paid at a flat rate for all participants. The principle of payments being graduated and related to earnings was introduced in the 1960s, and in 1971 the government announced that contributions would be made at rates of $5\frac{1}{4}$ per cent by employees and $7\frac{1}{4}$ per cent by employers, with an upper limit of one and a half times national average earnings, with effect from 1975.

EXPENDITURE

The expenditure side of the government's budget, as it appears in Fig. 8.6, is rather easier to summarize and it is convenient to enumerate the principal categories.

Defence expenditure absorbs about 15 per cent of total income for the central government but it is the one major item that has been declining in real terms for several years.

The Social Services is a term used to cover the major items of welfare expenditure other than national insurance benefits, referred to above, which are kept in a separate fund. The National Health Service was introduced in 1946 to provide medical treatment free to any citizen who needed it. Some charges have since been imposed for prescriptions and other items, but the principle of a free health service has remained relatively unimpaired. The cost to the government of providing it absorbs about 10 per cent of its income. The item Benefits and Allowances include personal grants of family allowances, help given in the form of Supplementary Benefits to the very poor and pensions to war widows and others outside the contributory National Insurance Scheme. Education and children's services of all kinds are, of course, important, but large educational expenditures are made by local authorities rather than the central government.

The Economic Services include the provision and maintenance of roads, the operation of governmental services concerned with employment, the promotion of industrial research and such items as expenses incurred pursuing policies designed to influence the location of industry and the subsidizing of agriculture.

National Insurance Benefits are the counterparts of the National Insurance Contributions. For most years since the end of the Second World War unemployment has been relatively low in Britain, and easily the most important category has been the provision of retirement pensions. Other benefits payable under the scheme are for widows and orphans, for sickness and injury, and there are grants for both maternity and death.

Interest on the National Debt is the cost to the Exchequer of servicing the Debt, as it is called, that is to say of paying interest to existing holders. It currently absorbs about 7 per cent of total income.

The remainder of the income of the central government is used for a large number of miscellaneous purposes including administration, tax collection, and the provision of aid to overseas countries. Finance is also provided for some of the capital needs of nationalized industries, and substantial grants and loans are made to local authorities, whose finances will be examined shortly.

Central government expenditure has been discussed so far on the basis of the classification used for Fig. 8.6, which is based upon a set of programmes for specific purposes, such as defence, social services' provision, support for industry, agriculture, etc. It should be noted. however, that there are other ways of classifying government expenditure which can have important economic significance. In the first place, we could distinguish between *current* expenditures such as retirement pensions and drugs for use in hospitals, and *capital* expenditures, such as the provision of new schools or prisons. The former are concerned with immediate effects on the distribution of income or resources. Capital items, on the other hand, as we know, have lasting effects.

The second alternative classification has rather different implications. It is based on a distinction between what are called *exhaustive* expenditures on goods and services, and *transfer* payments, mentioned earlier (*see* p. 191). The difference may be illustrated by comparing the various social security payments, family allowances, educational grants, etc., which are transfers, with expenditures used for the provision of roads, hospitals and police services, which are exhaustive. Only the latter are important when considering the public sector's claim on resources— the proportion of the nation's output pre-empted, as it were, by the State. But total expenditure, including both exhaustive and transfers, must be taken into account when questions of the government's need to raise finance by taxation and other means for its whole programme are involved. As a point of interest we may note that the importance of transfer payments relative to exhaustive expenditures on goods and services has tended to grow substantially in recent years.

FISCAL POLICY

The greater part of the discussion of governmental income and expenditure so far in this chapter has been associated with its objective of influencing the distribution of income on grounds of social justice, and with the provision of special kinds of goods and services. Before proceeding to examine the finances of local authorities, it is necessary to expand a little on the government's other budgetary role, whereby it attempts to regulate the general level of activity in the economy. This aspect is usually referred to as *fiscal policy*. The goal of fiscal policy is perhaps best described as one of stabilization, of evening out the booms and slumps of the trade cycle which we noticed in Chapter 4 (*see* p. 95). Intervention is called for because excessive fluctuations tend to be associated, on the one hand, with unemployment, and, on the other, with a rapidly rising price level, both of which have some undesirable features.

Fiscal policy is designed to secure alterations in the level of total spending in the community. In the very broadest sense, it is possible to distinguish two means whereby this may be accomplished. The first is one which we have already touched upon when we were dealing with the encouragement of investment and the use of the Regulator (*see above*, p. 201). More generally, the Chancellor of the Exchequer can use the whole range of taxes and subsidies in his Budget to stimulate or discourage spending, by businesses and/or the general public, both on investment and on consumption. Raising taxes (or lowering subsidies) tends normally to discourage spending and is the natural policy in times of excessive boom, while lowering taxes (or increasing subsidies) tends to stimulate expenditure and is, therefore, more appropriate when the level of economic activity is on the low side.

The second means of influencing total spending in the economy relates not to the private sector at all, but to the government itself. For there is no very good reason why the State has to balance its own budget—raising in taxation exactly the same amount as it spends. In times of booming activity, when it wants to reduce the pressure of demand on the price level, it can quite easily run a *Budget surplus*. Conversely, in periods of relative depression, when extra stimulus is called for, the State is in a particularly favourable position to borrow and can just as simply run a *Budget deficit*.

Fiscal policy in practice is not, however, without its problems, and it would be wrong to give any other impression. Not the least of these is the fact that the objectives of fiscal policy are not always mutually consistent. Ideally, stabilization involves aiming for a high rate of economic growth together with full employment and price stability. These goals are by no means simultaneously attainable, so that some compromise is frequently inevitable. Moreover, there are also intricate problems of timing, of deciding precisely when and exactly how much of a surplus or deficit to budget for. It is for reasons such as these that alternative means of controlling the level of activity in the economy and the price level are resorted to. The most important are monetary policy, which is discussed in connexion with the banking system in the next chapter, and attempts at an incomes policy, outlined in Chapter 3 (*see* pp. 61–2).

2. Local Authorities

The administration of local government in Britain is in the hands of several types of organization, ranging from the Greater London Council, through county boroughs to parishes. The total expenditure of all local authorities is only about a third of that of the central

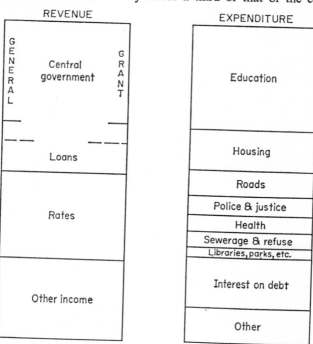

REVENUE   EXPENDITURE

REVENUE	EXPENDITURE
GENERAL / Central government / GRANT	Education
Loans	Housing
	Roads
Rates	Police & justice
	Health
	Sewerage & refuse
	Libraries, parks, etc.
Other income	Interest on debt
	Other

Fig. 8.7. Local Authorities Revenue and Expenditure, U.K., 1970

government. Briefly, there are the following main sources of income, which are illustrated in Fig. 8.7.

(i) *Central Government Grants and Loans.* About half the total revenue of local authorities comes from the central government. 80 per cent of this is in the form of a grant, and the remainder are loans. The General Grant from Whitehall is based on an estimate of the general needs of each area, and accounts for 90 per cent of the total. The specific grants are in some way tied to particular types of expenditure, such as that on roads, the police and the administration of justice.

(ii) *Rates*. In much the same way as the central government collects taxes, so local authorities levy what are called rates on the owners of land and buildings in the district; the only major exceptions being those used for agricultural purposes. Property is assessed from time to time by the Board of Inland Revenue, and a value placed on each. It is on this basis that the rate is calculated—and usually expressed as *poundage*: pence per pound of rateable property. The importance of rates as a source of revenue is a matter of considerable variation from district to district. The larger the amount of valuable property there is in a region, the more important is the income from rates. But this is offset partly by the size of grants from the central government, which are larger for authorities where there is relatively little valuable property, but which have heavy needs for services, such as education, because of having a relatively large number of children in the community.

(iii) *Other income*. Most local authorities, especially the larger ones, earn a supplementary income from the ownership of property, including rents from council houses, and from the operation of such municipal services as public baths and water supplies. They are also able to obtain some finance from borrowing.

On the other side of the account, the expenditure of local governments covers a great many different items, as can be seen from Fig. 8.7. One of these is of really outstanding significance. This is education. The cost of running schools and providing scholarships to universities and other institutions accounts for about a third of total expenditure. A second important category of expenditure is that on housing, but there are also a lot of small items which we would nevertheless be quick to notice if they suddenly ceased, such as the disposal of refuse, the lighting of streets, the maintenance of local roads, the provision of local police, fire, civil defence and other services, and of public libraries, baths and municipal parks which we enjoy.

GROWTH AND LIVING STANDARDS

A major aim of economic policy in recent years has been to try and foster a high rate of growth of output and income in order to raise living standards. We can examine the extent to which this aim has been achieved by observing trends in the national income over a period of years. This can only be a very approximate operation in view of the nature of the national income statistics themselves. The longer the period under consideration, too, the more difficult it is to attach any real meaning to comparisons, as the entire way of life of a country may undergo radical changes. It should be emphasized, also, that living standards depend on the size of the population among whom income has to be shared. A rising income may be needed simply to maintain the status quo with regard to *income per head* if the population is also rising. Finally, it should be recalled that the national income is a measure of the goods and services produced over a year in money terms. Unless the value of money itself is stable, we may find that what looks like a rise in income is nothing more than a rise in the general level of prices at which things are valued. The point may be illustrated by considering the situation of a single individual.

Suppose that we wanted to find out whether the standard of living of a certain Mr. Jones is higher today than it was in, say, 1960. Let us imagine that Mr. Jones is a garage mechanic and that he does not possess any personal property worth speaking about. Then the first thing we must do is to find out how much money he earns each week now and how much he earned in 1960. Suppose we find that at the earlier date he used to take home about £15 a week and that now his earnings have doubled to £30. Clearly it would not be true to say at once that Mr. Jones's standard of living has also doubled, for the simple reason that we have not taken into account the possibility that prices may also have changed in the meantime. If, in fact, the prices of everything that Mr. Jones buys have also doubled in price then we would have little hesitation in drawing the conclusion that Mr. Jones enjoys much the same standard of living as he did before. In other words, the standard of living depends not only upon the money which we earn, but also upon the *cost of living*.

Every individual is in the position of being able to work out for himself how his own standard of living may be changing. Naturally we cannot do this for all the people in Britain, but we can get a rough approximation with the help of some statistics which are published regularly by the Department of Employment. This government department makes calculations of the average level of wages and earnings over the whole of industry, and also of the average level of retail prices of some of the most important things that people buy. Thus if we put the series together we can see very roughly whether wages are keeping step with prices. If the two have moved exactly the same amount up or down, then we say that *real* wages have not changed in spite of a change in *money* wages. Alternatively if wages move at a different rate from prices, then changes in money wages will not be reflected by similar changes in real wages.

TRENDS IN INCOMES AND OUTPUT

Fig. 8.8 traces the course of wages and prices for the period 1955–70. It shows that, although average money wage rates had doubled fifteen

years after 1955, real wages had been rising more slowly, since price
had risen by roughly 60 per cent. Such *inflationary* upward pric
movements have been a fairly regular phenomenon of the last quarte
of a century or so. They contrast sharply with the unemployment o
the inter-war years as a major problem facing the government, whic
has tried to eliminate them by fiscal and other means, and by th
attempts at an incomes policy, outlined in Chapter 3, to dissuade trad

Fig. 8.8.   **Retail Prices, Weekly Wage Rates and Earnings of Manual Workers,
U.K., 1955–70**
Percentage Changes since 1955

unions and employers from raising wages and prices out of line wit
the growth of national output.

A rather better indication of changing living standards can b
obtained by comparing prices with average *earnings*, which represer
more closely take-home pay. Earnings have generally been risin
significantly faster than wage rates as Fig. 8.8 shows. We can relat
this fact to matters discussed in the last chapter—in particular to th
tendency for hours worked at overtime rates to increase. Some pa
is also due to the pressure by employers, especially at times and i
areas where labour is scarce, to pay more than nationally agreed wage
This differential rise in earnings over wage rates is referred to as *wag
drift*.

What we have done as far as average wages are concerned can als
be done for individuals and for the nation as a whole. From the latte

ewpoint we can compare estimates of the national income in money
rms with changes in the general level of prices. Fig. 8.9 does this in a
ightly different way from Fig. 8.8, by recalculating the national income
r each year since 1950 in terms of the prices ruling at a single year
963 prices are the ones used here). This removes the influence of

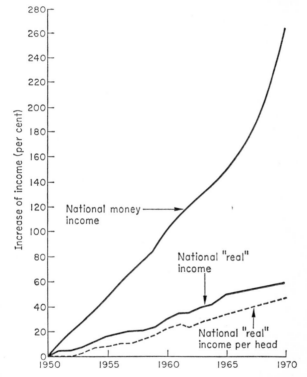

Fig. 8.9. **National Income in "Real" and Money Terms, U.K., 1950–70**

sing prices on the national income figures, and the resulting series
timates movements in the *real volume* of goods and services produced
ver the years. Thus, although the national income in money terms
ore than trebled in the two decades after 1950, since prices were also
sing, the total real income was only approximately 65 per cent higher.
his implies that total output was, in fact, growing on average at

roughly 2½ per cent per annum, and is a figure which may be compare
with some of the higher targets set from time to time. Even this,
course, does not represent the extent to which living standards ha
increased for a number of reasons. One is simply the fact that t
population has also been growing. In 1970 the larger national incor
had to be shared among about 10 per cent more people. Fig. 8.9 sho
the approximate difference this implies for income per head, thou
too much significance should not be attached to any of these preci
figures, which, as mentioned earlier, are subject to considerable margi
of error.

FAMILY EXPENDITURE PATTERNS

The picture of the standard of living drawn so far is, it must be stresse
only an average and, like all averages, may not in reality quite represe

Fig. 8.10.   Family Expenditure Patterns, U.K., 1969

the exact situation for any one individual. There are several reasons for this. One is connected with the way in which we as individuals apportion our expenditure over the different goods and services which are available. The average of retail prices (called the *index* of retail prices) used for most purposes as the most appropriate measure of changes in the general price level is not a straightforward average of the prices of every single article which is available for sale to the general public. It is based on an inquiry into expenditure designed to reflect the pattern of that of the majority of households in the country, and it gives relatively more weight to articles which form a high proportion of total expenditure. The "average" family represented is one which spends its income in the way shown in Fig. 8.10 (i.e. about a quarter on food, one-tenth on clothing, etc.). For any family which allocates its expenditure differently from that of the average used for the calculation of the index of retail prices, therefore, this index will not be a good guide to movements in its own cost of living. We know, for instance, that the lower the income and the larger the family, the higher the proportion of family income which tends to be spent on food. Consequently, if the prices of foodstuffs rise appreciably more, or less, than most other prices used in the index, this means that the cost of living of those with low incomes is also likely to be rising more, or less, than the "average". Special price index numbers based on different expenditure patterns have, for example, been calculated for pensioner households. The index for single pensioners, for instance, rose by 44 per cent between 1962 and 1970, compared with a 40 per cent rise in the index of retail prices.

It is also worth pointing out at this stage another reason why the measure of average living standards may be misleading. This is because in a country which has been undergoing a period of fairly steadily rising prices, like Britain in recent years, different groups of persons tend to be more or less well placed to secure rising money incomes than others. This is really a question of flexibility and speed of adjustment. The more rapidly any set of incomes can be increased the better off those concerned will be relative to others. It is dangerous to generalize on this matter, and some trends in the shares of different income groups have already been noted earlier in this chapter. But it may be said that persons whose incomes are fixed in money terms, such as those on fixed pensions, have tended to lose relatively to those who have been well organized to secure increases without delay. For this reason, the government announced in 1971 its intention to adjust basic pensions automatically to changes in the price level every two years.

Individual Circumstances and Poverty in Britain

There is one final qualification which must be made to the general discussion of the standard of living. This concerns the particular circumstances of individuals. For it would not be reasonable to say that an income of say £1,000 a year will provide the same standard of living for Mr. Green and Mr. Black, for Mr. Green may be a single young man with no dependants to look after, while Mr. Black may be a married man with five children and a widowed mother-in-law, all of whom he has to support. It would, of course, be quite impossible to go into details of the different circumstances of individuals here. One aspect of this matter which is of relevance, however, is the extent to which people in Britain are still living in what might be called poverty. In order to provide useful information on this subject, it is necessary to set first some minimum living standard, and then count the number of persons below it. There is no unambiguous definition of such a poverty line. But if the level fixed by the government as a national minimum for the purpose of making discretionary social security payments (supplementary benefit, formerly national assistance) is taken as a guideline, then a recent estimate suggests that something of the order of 4 to 9 per cent of the population (5 million or so persons) were living in poverty in Britain in the 1960s. Rather less surprising, perhaps, is the estimate that over a third of such people were pensioners and another third were children. We cannot take the question of the causes of poverty further in this book, but it is worth pointing out that a considerable number of those entitled to supplementary benefit (and to national assistance before it) have not in fact been claiming it.

INTERNATIONAL LIVING STANDARDS

We found it useful when we were discussing population to keep our perspectives right by comparing this country with the rest of the world, and it is no less desirable to do so when dealing with living standards. The main reason why one is more hesitant about making such comparisons is that the statistical basis for them is much more inadequate.

It has already been pointed out that the national income figures for a single country should not be regarded as being of a tremendously high order of accuracy, though they are good enough for a great many purposes. When we try to compare national income statistics for different countries, however, the scope for possible error is greatly magnified. There are many reasons for this which cannot be discussed in detail here. To some extent they arise from differences in the efficiency of national government departments which prepare the estimates, but they are also due to differences in the quality of countries' output and in coverage. The last of these requires a word of explanation. The national income of a country normally includes only those goods and services the output and value of which can be reasonably well estimated and which, in turn, usually means those that are bought and sold. In subsistence economies in poorer parts of the world, for instance, families tend to be much more self-sufficient and to meet a smaller proportion of their needs by trading outside the family. In such circumstances national income estimates are inclined to understate the standard of living.

Moreover, there is no really reliable way of converting income statistics prepared in national currencies, pounds, dollars, francs, rupees, dinars, kyats, pesos, etc., into a common unit for comparative purposes. Official exchange rates do not, unfortunately, fill the bill completely for various technical reasons. Only more or less satisfactory compromises allow the job to be attempted at all.

With these reservations in mind we can approach Fig. 8.11, which sets out estimates of the average income per head of the population for selected countries in the world, in 1968, in terms of pounds sterling. It is at once clear that differences are so large, with countries at the top of the scale enjoying a real income per head twenty or thirty times that of those at the bottom, that it seems inconceivable they are simply due to statistical errors.

It would be tedious to comment on the relative position of all the individual countries in the diagram, but it is worth drawing attention to the foremost position of the United States and our own place, considerably behind North America, but still among the leading countries in the world. More generally, we can obtain quite a useful summary of the pattern of international living standards by considering countries as belonging to one of two groups—the "developed" economies of North America, Western Europe, Australia, New Zealand and Japan; and the so-called "developing" economies in Asia, Africa and Latin America. Although this excludes a number of countries, mainly in the Communist blocs, it contains the majority of the world's population and enables us to draw certain extremely significant conclusions—in particular that something of the order of two-thirds of the world's population enjoy not much more than 10 per cent of world income, while the developed countries with less than a tenth of total population have over a third of total income. The differences in income per head arise, of course, partly from these differences in population size. Indeed, the main reason why the diagram in Fig. 8.11 is shaped like a

pyramid is because there are relatively few countries with high income
per head, and a very large number with very low incomes.

Note incidentally, but importantly, that this problem of international
disparities in incomes is likely to remain with us for a long time. Even
if income per head rises faster in the developing than in the advanced

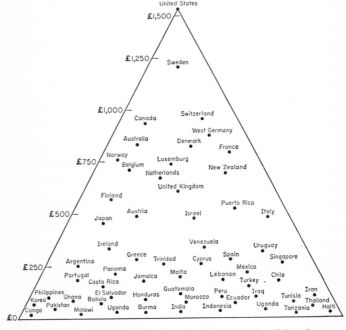

Fig. 8.11. **Average Income per Head of Population, Selected
Countries, 1968**

Estimates in Terms of Pounds Sterling

countries, the *absolute* differences in real income per head may still
increase because of the very large gap that exists at the moment.
(Doubling a £100 income raises it to £200. A 50 per cent increase in an
income of £1,000 produces one of £1,500. The absolute difference
between £1,500 and £200 is greater than that between £1,000 and £100.
Moreover, many developing nations are currently experiencing declining
death rates and rising birth rates which increase their populations, in

uch the same way as we noted earlier occurred in Britain from the
d of the eighteenth century. This can exaggerate their problem, and
rovides illuminating background to the attempts by governments in
any low income countries to keep birth rates in check.

Bringing all the advanced countries together in a single group, as we
ve done, conceals, of course, differences between them. It prevents
e comparison of recent growth in the British economy, discussed
rlier in the chapter, with that of other western countries. Such
mparisons for the period since about 1950 tend to show this country
not having had a very high rate of economic growth in most years
lative to that of a number of others. In the so-called "league tables,"
herein countries are sometimes roughly ranked according to the
tes at which their incomes have risen, the United Kingdom has
nerally appeared well behind several important European nations—
tably West Germany, France and Italy (which together with the
nelux countries formed the Common Market—*see below*, Chapter 10),
ough much closer to others, such as the United States. Calculations
this nature should be treated with some reserve. There are many
asons behind the rank ordering during a relative short period of time,
d it would certainly not be legitimate to conclude that it is necessarily
sirable for us to emulate any other country's performance. However,
eir experience may very well be relevant to the formation of British
onomic policy, and it is undeniable that the experience of countries
th more rapid rates of economic growth has to some extent affected
e objectives at which we have tried to aim.

A final cautionary word is in order regarding the meaning of the
ernational comparisons of income per head of the population used
ove, lest the approximations be considered identical with what one
s in mind when using the term standard of living. For one thing, the
cumstances of individual countries may be completely different.
me, which are less favourably placed, may have to make bigger
orts to surmount natural obstacles in order to achieve identical
ing standards to others. In cold climates, for instance, a lot of
oduction is needed simply to keep people as warm as they are
turally in places where temperatures are higher. On the other hand,
ne countries possess places and treasures of great natural beauty
ich require little or no effort for their enjoyment. It should be
nembered, too, that people in some countries work for longer hours
an in others. National income statistics record only output of goods
d services, though leisure also undoubtedly affects living standards.
oreover, the calculation of average income per head of the population
ores differences in income among people within countries. One

cannot assume that everybody in a low income country, such
India, has a smaller real income than everybody in a rich one like t
United States, for it is simply not true.

Finally, we must beware of imagining that the term real income p
head is in any way synonymous with "happiness." Any attempt
measure the latter is quite beyond the bounds of economics, even
pleasure is not itself inherently unmeasurable. Who can say, f
instance, whether the crudest home-made mud marbles give a pers
in one part of the world more or less pleasure than someone else
another part gets from a costly model railway? Indeed, there a
those who believe that differences in the entire way of life of peopl
who live in so-called "primitive" and "civilized" societies are so gre
that national income comparisons between them are close to bei
meaningless. It is perhaps appropriate to end this section by putti
their viewpoint.

WEALTH

When we were considering the accounts of joint-stock companies
Chapter 3, attention was drawn to the fact that the record of incor
and expenditure for any year, in the Profit and Loss Account, was
much better guide to the financial condition of a company if it w
studied in conjunction with the Balance Sheet statement of assets,
stock of wealth, which the company owned. The same thing is equa
true for a person. When we think of someone as being rich or po
we rarely restrict ourselves to a consideration of the income which
currently earns but include, in addition, some idea of the amount
property, or capital, which he has somehow or other accumulated
the past. For it is a combination of these two—income and wealth
which makes a man rich.

THE NATIONAL CAPITAL

The identical argument applies also to a nation. It was pointed out
the beginning of this chapter that Britain has been devoting about
fifth of the national income in recent years to the renewal and accum
lation of capital, and that this helps to promote economic growth. No
estimates of the national wealth are significantly less reliable th
many other economic statistics, but calculations made by the Centr
Statistical Office suggest that the tangible fixed assets of the communi
were probably worth something of the order of £150,000 million
1970, or, perhaps, four times the national income itself. The natior
wealth, it is true, is something more than simply the tangible asse
of the community. A good part of the expenditure on educatic

for instance, should really be counted as part of the total, since it undoubtedly helps to raise productivity in the economy in a very similar way to expenditure, which results, say, in the production of a new machine. Without education it is inconceivable to think of ideas for improving the efficiency and design of existing machinery. But such intangible national assets are very difficult to evaluate and they are ignored in Fig. 8.12, which shows the major categories of the nation's

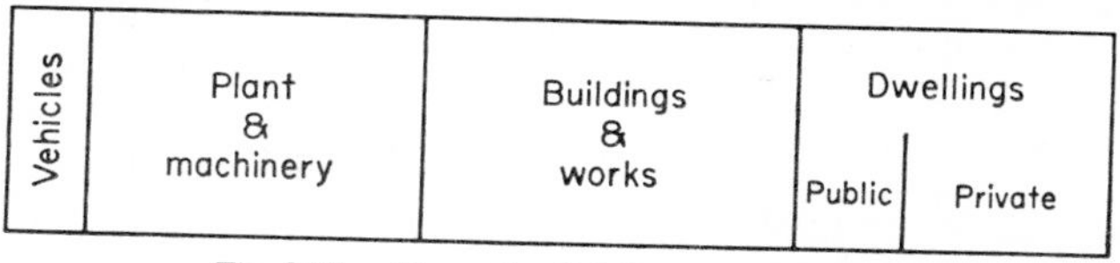

Vehicles	Plant & machinery	Buildings & works	Dwellings	
			Public	Private

Fig. 8.12. **Gross Capital Stock, U.K., 1970**

capital stock. It will be noticed that dwellings account for nearly a third of the total. These, it is true, are not capital goods of the kind which we have previously discussed. But, because they are long-lasting they help to provide enjoyment of high living standards in the future, and for this reason are really part of the nation's capital resources.

PERSONAL PROPERTY

When we turn from a consideration of the wealth of the nation to the personal ownership of property we must introduce an important distinction. For a man's wealth may take one of two principal forms—

1. It may, like the national wealth, take the form of real pieces of property, such as houses, machinery or other business assets. The only point to be made here is that it is dangerous to assume that the apparent holder of such property is, in fact, its owner. Thus, it is common to find a person living in a house which is legally his, and yet the "owner" may only have been able to buy it at all by borrowing the money from some other person or institution. Until he has repaid the loan in full we cannot truly count the whole of the value of the house as the occupier's property.

2. The second form which property may take consists not of tangible assets, but of paper tokens, which may, however, be just as valuable. A paper token may have value for the simple reason that it is the document giving legal ownership to a certain tangible asset. In our previous example of a house, the document giving *title* or legal owner-ship to it is called a deed, and would be held by the money-lender as

security for his loan until it had been fully repaid. Similar paper claim
to wealth are the share certificates given to those who have put mone
into joint-stock companies. For the value of all the share capital of
business is closely related to the value of the assets of that business
which in the last resort it represents.

It is necessary to point out, however, that some property, consistin
only of paper claims, is of value in spite of the fact that the document
do not directly represent any real assets at all. Cash, in the form of
notes or coin or deposits in a bank, is generally acceptable as a mean
of payment for goods and services and provides a good example of
this. The National Debt is another very important one. This, it wi
be recalled, is the total outstanding government debt to the public
much of it arising from borrowing to pay for past wars, and althoug
the guns and equipment, etc., for which it was used may have lon
since disappeared, the paper claims on the government (governmen
securities) continue to have some value as long as the governmen
guarantees to repay the loan eventually, or at least to continue to pa
a fixed rate of interest each year to individual holders.

The individual person derives two distinct benefits from the owne
ship of property. In the first place, he has a reserve of capital whic
can always be used to maintain his standard of living. Even if he
unemployed he can allow his bank balance to run down, sell some of
his houses, land or any of his shares or debentures, while he may b
earning nothing at all. The second benefit which accrues to a perso
owning property shows us that this last possibility is not, in fact, likel
to occur. For the possession of most property, other than cash and rea
property in personal use, involves as a rule the receipt of some incom
as a direct result. This is obvious in the case of a landlord who lets h
house or farm in return for rent, but it is also true of other propert
such as shares in joint-stock companies and holdings of governmen
securities, as we have seen earlier. And even a deposit in the Nation.
Savings Bank earns interest at $3\frac{1}{2}$ per cent per year. It is true that th
small amount of property owned by the vast majority of people ca
hardly count as an important addition to their incomes. For instanc
£100 in the Savings Bank earns about a penny a day. For the real
wealthy, on the other hand, income from property can and does becom
of far more significance.

THE DISTRIBUTION OF PERSONAL PROPERTY

A census of property has never been taken in modern Britain, but th
value of all personal wealth is probably of the order of £100 millio

or about three times the annual total of personal incomes. Fig. 8.13 is based on a statistically derived estimate of the distribution of personal wealth. It shows a degree of inequality which is significantly greater than that of income distribution; and it must be added that the manner in which the estimates were made almost certainly understates the

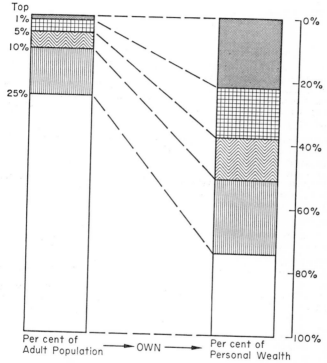

Fig. 8.13. **The Ownership of Personal Wealth, Great Britain, 1969**

degree of concentration of wealth in the hands of the rich. Even ignoring this last point, the diagram shows that, whereas three-quarters of the population own only about a quarter of total wealth, nearly 40 per cent is concentrated in the hands of the top 5 per cent of wealth holders, including the richest 20,000 people in the country, who own over 20 per cent of all personal property.

This concentration of wealth in relatively few hands has been a regular feature of our society for a long time, and the institution of inheritance helps to maintain it. Over the past half-century some reduction in the degree of inequality is thought to have taken place, partly as a result of the operation of death duties (*see above*), but this has failed to alter the general picture, which remains one of relatively few persons with a great deal of property and the majority who have very little.

EXERCISES

(For key to symbols indicating sources, *see* p. 14.)

1. How much did the national income increase last year (*a*) in money terms; (*b*) in real terms? Calculate the changes which took place in the real national product for each of the last five years compared with the previous year. How does the average compare with the post-war trend mentioned in the chapter. (Use figures for Gross Domestic Product—G.N.P. less overseas income—if others are not available.) (*M.D.S., E.T.* or *A.S.*)

2. For each of the main industry groups in Britain last year, find out:
   (*a*) Average weekly earnings of manual workers;
   (*b*) Numbers employed;
   (*c*) Numbers unemployed.
Calculate the rate (per cent) unemployment for each group, and list them in two rank orders according to (i) average earnings and (ii) unemployment rates. Compare your results. (*M.D.S.* or *A.S.*)

3. Draw a graph to show the division of the national income between consumption and investment for the last five years. Compare your results with Fig. 8.1. (*M.D.S.* or *A.S.*)

4. For the latest year for which you can find statistics, look up—
   (*a*) The percentage change in average weekly wage-rates over the previous year.
   (*b*) The percentage change in average weekly earnings of manual workers over the previous year. Note the difference, and repeat the exercise for average *hourly* wage-rates and average *hourly* earnings. (*E.T., M.D.S.* or *A.S.*)

5. Prepare a table showing the distribution of personal wealth in Britain. Use the following ranges of net wealth and show for each the number of individuals in each class and the total wealth.

under £1,000	£10,001 to £25,000
£1,001 to £5,000	£25,001 to £100,000
£5,001 to £10,000	Over £100,000

Calculate the percentage of the total number of individuals and the total amount of wealth in each size class. (*A.S.*)

6. Compile a table for a recent month and for the same month a year ago showing average weekly wage rates of all manual workers, and compare this with the changes in prices over the same period—
   (*a*) of all items in the retail price index,
   (*b*) of foodstuffs,
   (*c*) of housing.   (*M.D.S.*)

7. Prepare a graph on the lines of Fig. 8.5 showing the distribution of incomes, by number of incomes of different sizes, before and after tax for the latest year available. Calculate also the proportions of total income of all persons accounted for by the different groups. (*A.S.*)

8. Make a list of the six most important goods on which (*a*) Customs and (*b*) Excise duties are payable, and find the proportion which each contributed to total revenue in the most recent year for which you have figures. (*W.A.*)

9. Find out the size of each of the main items of central government expenditure in a recent year and ten years ago. Calculate the percentage of the totals for each item and pick out any significant changes which may have taken place. (*A.S.* or *W.A.*)

10. Prepare a table showing the amount spent on the various kinds of National Insurance benefits as a proportion of the total for the last financial year for which statistics are available. (*W.A.* or *A.S.*)

11. The current Rate for your local authority area is given as so much in the pound. Find this and also the rateable value of the house in which you live, and calculate the rate bill for the year. How is this sum distributed among the various expenditure items?

12. Calculate how much direct tax each of the following persons has to pay in the current year—

1. A single man earning £1,000.
2. A married man, with two children, earning £1,250.
3. A married man, with no children, earning £8,500.
4. A single woman earning £750 in a job and £100 dividends on shares. (*W.A.*)

13. Try to find out how your weekly family income is distributed among the main groups of items of expenditure used in the index of retail prices. Assemble the information for the whole class and compare your own family's pattern of expenditure with the average and with that shown in Fig. 8.10. Do you think such differences as you may find are because your family income is higher or lower than the others?

CHAPTER 9

Finance

ALMOST every economic activity involves money. For, although th
production and distribution of goods and services could in theory b
carried on without it, money is in fact an indispensable part of th
equipment of an advanced economy.

The Functions of Money

The best way to understand the significance of money is to imagine wha
life would be like without it. In our complex society, things would b
completely unmanageable. Production could in principle still continue
but problems would abound. How, for example, would the busines
man pay for his raw materials and for his labour? The farmer migh
conceivably obtain machinery in exchange for his farm produce, an
offer to engage his labour on the same terms. But he would nevertheles
be very unlikely to find individuals who would agree to be paid in food
stuffs and foodstuffs alone. Everyone would prefer payment in term
of money, part of which they could use to buy food and part to purchas
other things that they wanted. Most manufacturing businesses woul
be even worse off. Who would go to work in a coal mine to cart a loa
of coal home every pay day, or to an iron foundry to be paid so man
girders per year? Clearly, apart from their bulkiness, unless one coul
buy food and clothing for lumps of coal or girders in the market, coa
miners and steel-workers would starve and would, therefore, rathe
stay at home and cultivate their own garden plots for nourishmen
while their wives spun and wove crude woollen garments to cloth
them. We should, in other words, be back in a primitive society wher
there was no specialization and where the standard of living wa
accordingly low. The difficulties involved in such a society wher
exchange took place only directly between commodities are real enoug
to need no exaggeration, and they could be overcome only by th
introduction of a means of payment which was generally acceptable t
everyone, and through the medium of which any commodity could b
exchanged for any other. Money is just such a means of paymen
although, in the past, man has employed a variety of other things fo

the same purpose, from seashells to cattle, and during the war cigarettes often served in prisoner-of-war camps, where real money was not available. The one essential feature of all these means of payment was that anyone would accept them in payment of wages or debts, since in doing so he knew that he could use them to purchase anything that he happened to want. Thus all that money really is, is a means of payment which is generally acceptable, and it is its existence which makes possible the complex economic life of present-day Britain. It avoids the need for anyone who has something to sell having to hunt around for someone else who will offer him in exchange just what he happens to want. He can sell his commodity for money to anyone who will buy it, and can use money to buy anything he needs. It enables the business man to employ labour whether the article he produces is one that his workers want or not. It enables him to make a reasonable assessment of how his business is paying at any particular time, and it is also a much more convenient way in which he can store his wealth than the accumulation of large stocks of physical commodities.

Forms of Money

Although in modern times we no longer employ any of the primitive forms of money, there are still more different types in use than we might perhaps at first imagine. A good way of illustrating this is to consider the various ways in which we might pay for what we buy.

1. COINS

If the sum involved is a small one, the most likely way of making payment is with coins. In Britain we have, in current circulation, three "silver" and three "copper" coins, though the metals used are no longer pure silver and copper, but alloys of copper and nickel, and bronze. These coins are manufactured or "minted" by a government department known as the Royal Mint, which is the only authority allowed to do so. Government control is also exercised over the acceptance of coins in payment of debts and, in order to protect creditors from having to accept large quantities of them, it is laid down that "copper" coins are *legal tender* up to 20 pence, and silver (other than the 50p piece) up to £5. This means that, if for example you try to buy a 25p box of chocolates and offer 13 twopenny pieces in settlement, the shopkeeper is legally entitled to demand payment in some other form, though of course if he is short of small change he may be very pleased to have them.

2. NOTES

For larger debts it is much more common to pay in notes. Bank-notes, or paper money as it is sometimes called, have an interesting origin. In England in the seventeenth century the most general form of money was the gold coin. Rather than keep a large quantity of gold at home, people quite naturally used to take them for safe keeping to the local goldsmiths, who were the first bankers. In return for the gold the goldsmith issued a receipt, on which it was stated that he promised to pay on demand to the holder of the receipt the amount of gold mentioned. Following upon this, the custom grew for individuals to accept these receipts or notes in payment for debts, since with the signature of a reputable goldsmith, and later a banker, on them they were in fact "as good as gold." Today, bank-notes are one of the principal forms of currency, though it is no longer open to any banker or goldsmith to issue them. In England and Wales this right is now exclusively reserved for the Bank of England. Bank-notes, however, still retain their original form, and if you look at a £1 note you will find printed there still a statement which no longer has any real meaning (since gold is no longer obtainable on demand in exchange for notes), but which is signed by the Chief Cashier on behalf of the Bank of England and reads "I Promise to pay the Bearer on Demand the sum of One Pound." The notes in general use at present are for one pound, five pounds and ten pounds. About £4,000 million of notes are in circulation, some ten times the amount of outstanding coin.

3. BANK DEPOSITS

By far the most important means of settling debts today does not involve the handling of notes or coin at all, but is carried out with the assistance of the banks and usually involves the drawing of cheques. The origin of the cheque is not dissimilar from that of a bank-note. After depositing his gold in a local bank or with a goldsmith, it became common for a person to write a letter to his banker instructing him to pay a sum of money to a person he would name. He would then give the letter, not to his banker, but to the person to whom he owed money, and the latter would dispatch it to his own banker who would arrange to collect the cash and hold it for him. Quite soon, this form of settling debts became so important that it was unnecessary to write a special letter every time one wanted to make a payment, as the banks themselves began to print letter forms which were known as cheques, and which only needed the insertion of the amount, the date, the name of the payee and the signature of the person making the payment. Today the banks issue books containing such cheques to their customers, although there are other means of transferring money in bank accounts.

The advantages of making payments through the banks are simplicity and safety, especially when the sum involved is large. All business firms use the banks, as well as many private individuals for personal purposes, and the great importance of bank deposits in comparison with the volume of notes and coin in circulation is shown in Fig. 9.1 below.

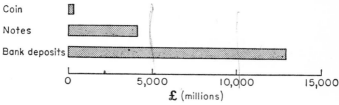

Fig. 9.1.   **Money Supply, U.K., March, 1971**

4. OTHER MEANS OF PAYMENT

Payments can be effected in a variety of other ways. The Post Office opened a National Giro in 1968, to provide machinery for the transfer of money through most post offices in the country. Settlement may also be made using credit cards, I.O.U.s, Promissory Notes, etc., though in such cases it is effectively only temporary, as far as the payer is concerned.

THE BANKING SYSTEM

The importance of banks has already been mentioned in connexion with the use of cheques. This is, however, only one aspect of their business, and we must examine them in some more detail. This may most easily be done under two headings—

1. The Commercial Banks.
2. The Bank of England.

1. The Commercial Banks

For the past hundred years or so the principal type of banking institution for the conduct of everyday business has been the commercial bank, formed on the lines of a joint-stock company. This has not always been the case. Previously, the joint-stock form of organization had been prohibited to banks, leaving the business in the hands of a multitude of small private partnership concerns and the Bank of

England, which was founded by Royal Charter. It took a year of financial crisis, in 1825, to show up the weak points of the system and bring about an alteration in the law.

Bank mergers in the nineteenth century and during the First World War brought the numbers down to a situation where five large banks

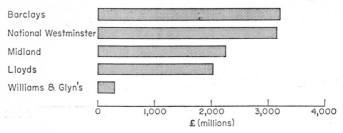

Fig. 9.2.   **Gross Deposits of the London Clearing Banks,**
17 March, 1971

dominated the scene until the end of the 1960s. Then a new spate of merger activity took place, between the Westminster, National Provincial and District Banks to form the National Westminster from January 1970 and between Barclays and Martins (a more extensive merger proposal between Barclays, Lloyds and Martins was opposed by the Monopolies Commission). As can be seen from Fig. 9.2 the "Big Four" control virtually all the deposits of these banks which make use of the facilities of the London Clearing House (*see* next paragraph). The other banks shown in the diagram are, in fact, subsidiaries of Scottish banks, of which there are three, with total deposits worth about 10 per cent of those of the London Clearing Banks.

THE BANKERS' CLEARING SYSTEM

Every time someone draws a cheque in favour of another person it is necessary somehow or other to transfer the amount of money involved. If the two people both happen to have accounts at the same bank, then it is a very simple matter. All that happens is that the bank makes entries in the accounts of the two people concerned, debiting the one and crediting the other. If, on the other hand, they have accounts at different banks, clearly this will not be possible. The most straight-forward solution is for the bank of the person making the payment to hand over to the other bank the sum of money in question. This is what did, in fact, happen in the distant past. Very soon, however, the bank clerks who used to be sent around the City of London collecting these moneys realized that a lot of work would be saved if they could all meet each day and go carefully through the different payments that were due. For it very often happened that a bank clerk was collecting from another bank, while his counterpart was round at his office collecting a similar payment. Obviously, if the amount involved was exactly the same in the two cases, then there was really no need for either of them to be collecting at all. But even if the amounts were not equal, then the smaller could be offset against the larger, and the clerk from the latter bank could collect the difference, still cutting the work in half. The essential requirement for the successful working of this system of offsetting claims against one another and leaving only residual amounts to be collected, now known as "clearing," was simply that the clerks should all meet together for a "grand sort out." In the early days in the eighteenth century the clerks took this upon themselves and began to meet regularly at a local inn, but today there exists a large official Bankers' Clearing House in the City of London, to which most of the big banks belong. Here all the cheques presented for payment every day are sorted and the differences calculated; these are then transferred in cash or by cheque between the various member banks.

THE BUSINESS OF BANKING

Bankers are in business to make a profit. For a commercial bank is essentially a borrowing and lending institution; that is, it borrows money as cheaply as it can from one set of people and lends it to others at a higher rate. But how, one is tempted to ask, is it possible for the bank to lend other people's money, which it is supposed to be holding in safe custody? What happens if the people who have money in the bank come along and demand payment, and the banks are unable to give them their money? The answer to these questions revolves around a fact which the earliest goldsmith-bankers did not take very long to notice, namely that it is very rare for all their customers to come along to demand money *at the same time*. Consequently, all the banker has to do is to keep a reserve immediately available to cover the proportion of his customers whom he thinks might possibly demand payment at one time. Moreover, he can keep this cash reserve at a minimum by relying also on a second line of defence by holding some financial assets which earn only a small rate of interest but which are, so to speak, "near money" in the sense of being speedily and easily exchangeable for cash. So protected, the banker can make loans to other persons and institutions at a rate of interest which allows him to make a profit. The best proportions of cash and *liquid assets*—as money and near money assets are called—to deposits were evolved as a result of experience. Traditionally a ratio of cash to total liabilities (deposits) of 8 per cent has been observed by the banks. We shall examine their liquid asset holdings in a moment. But it is relevant to know that the proportions in which the banks divide their assets is not nowadays something over which they have complete freedom. They are subject to control over this and certain other matters by the Bank of England, in ways which will also be discussed later.

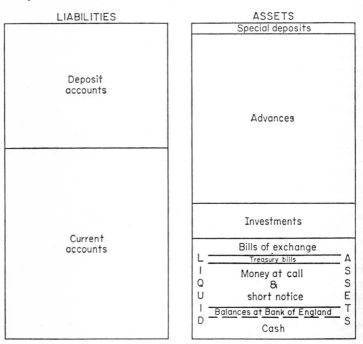

Fig. 9.3. **Assets and Liabilities at 17 March, 1971**

Fig. 9.3 shows the two sides of the banks' business. On the left-hand stand their deposits. These constitute the total of their liabilities—credit standing in the accounts of their customers, some of which may be demanded at any time. It also constitutes the resources which the bank has available to lend to other people (that is, all but about 8 per cent of it), and the distribution of its lending is shown in the right-hand side of the chart.

DEPOSITS

Bank deposits may be kept in either of two different kinds of accounts—

1. *Current Accounts.* Money kept in one of these accounts is withdrawable on demand and without notice, merely by presenting a cheque. It generally does not earn any interest and, in fact, the customer will probably be called upon to pay a small bank charge to cover the office work involved in keeping his account.

2. *Deposit Accounts.* Most businesses do not need to keep all their money on current account where it earns no interest and, accordingly, place some of it in a deposit account. Here it earns interest, but is not legally withdrawable without seven days' notice although, in practice, the banks seldom object if customers make transfers of reasonable amounts from deposit to current account for immediate payment. In all, something like two-fifths of all bank deposits are held in deposit accounts and three-fifths in current accounts.

ASSETS

When looking at the assets held by the banks it is most useful to list them according to the degree of liquidity which each possesses. At the same time we may take note of the fact that certain assets have come to be considered relatively liquid as a group. These include cash itself and what we have referred to earlier as "near money," which is held as a quick reserve, because it can be turned into cash with great speed.

Liquid Assets

1. *Cash.* As previously mentioned, the banks have for many years been in the habit of keeping a ratio of 8 per cent of cash to total deposits. Of this about two-thirds is held as notes and coin in the banks' safes. The remainder is held in a special account at the Bank of England, which performs the function, among others, of acting as a bankers' bank. Credit balances at the Bank of England are, therefore, virtually as good as cash in the till to the clearing banks.

2. *Money at Call and Short Notice.* This constitutes money lent by the banks on the understanding that it is repayable at the banks' demand or at short notice. It is lent at relatively low rates of interest to financial firms and institutions in the City, who use it to finance their everyday business (*see, e.g., below,* p. 239).

3. *Bills Discounted.* These are bills of exchange and Treasury bills. They represent loans made for short periods to a trader or to the Government. The principle according to which these assets operate

may be approached by considering the conditions under which a bill of exchange might be drawn up in the first place.

Suppose there is a trader in one country, who sells some goods to a purchaser in another; and that the latter does not receive them for some considerable time after they have left the seller's premises. The purchaser may not want, or be able, to pay for the goods until they arrive; but the seller may, at the same time, not wish to have to wait so long for payment. A solution is for the seller to draw up a bill of exchange, which he sends to the debtor for signature. The debtor writes "accepted" across the bill, signifying that he has agreed to make the payment, and returns it to the drawer. As bills are usually drawn to be paid at a specified date in the future (three months is not uncommon), the seller does not receive his payment immediately. He can, however, sell the bill through his bank to one of the specialized financial institutions who look after this sort of transaction, and receive cash immediately, even though the purchaser of the goods (who is the acceptor of the bill) has not yet paid over the money. The sale of the bill by the trader is known as "discounting" and the amount he has to pay depends on the discount rate. Thus, if a seller discounts a bill worth, for example, £100 in three months' time, and the discount rate is 6 per cent per annum, he will have to forgo a quarter of £6, and will get only £98·50 when he discounts the bill. Bills of exchange were in common use, especially in international trade, before the First World War, but they are much less frequently seen today. The banks still hold a substantial number of bills, however, although a considerable number are of a special type known as *Treasury bills*. These are similar to ordinary trade bills in that they are promises to pay a certain sum of money at a future date, but the promissor in the case of a Treasury bill is the government, which issues a number of them every week in order to finance current expenditure.

Other Assets

The other assets that the banks hold are generally less liquid than those mentioned above in the sense that they may be less easily or certainly converted into cash in a hurry. However, they tend to be more profitable, and to earn more interest for the banks.

1. *Investments.* A portion of the banks' resources takes the form of a portfolio of certain securities, mainly issued by the British government. As explained in the previous chapter, these securities form part of the National Debt, which has provided governments past and present with funds for large-scale expenditure. As a general rule these securities ar

garded by the government as a way of raising long-term finance.
hey are therefore redeemable, if at all, a good many years after they
ere issued. Since the State has, however, been selling new securities
 raise additional funds for a very long time, there are virtually always
 me which are due to be repaid within a year or even less. Hence the
 quidity of the securities held by the banks can only be known if the
 act holdings of each security are also known (with, of course, their
 aturity dates). The banks do not publish these details, but merely state
 e proportion if their holdings of such securities have less than five years
 run to maturity. The proportion tends to be around 60 per cent.

Advances. A major part of the banks' lending activities consists of
 aking advances to their customers. Roughly half of the resources
 the commercial banks is used in this way, and it is here that the local
 anch manager assumes a key role. It is to him that a business or
 rson in need of a loan goes, and it is often left to him to decide
 ether it shall be granted. Business men wanting cash to help in the
 pansion of their operations, for example, must make their proposi-
 ns appear sound ones. Sometimes, too, the banks require some
 curity or "collateral" such as share certificates, and they have a
 stinct preference for loans of relatively short duration, such as those
 de to finance seasonal fluctuations in trade. In any event, out-
 nding loans are reviewed annually. Straightforward personal loans
 fixed sums are made, but advances are more commonly on an
 verdraft" basis. Under this system permission is merely given to the
 stomer to draw cheques up to a certain stipulated amount. This
 ocedure is very convenient, especially for borrowers whose needs
 liable to fluctuate. It avoids borrowing a larger sum than is really
 cessary and it tends to be cheaper, since interest is payable only on
 amount overdrawn and not on the limit of the overdraft.

The rate of interest charged by the banks on advances is subject to
 nsiderable variation from time to time, and is partly affected by the
 k attached to the loan under consideration. Advances are, however,
 most profitable of the operations that banks undertake. The dis-
 bution among the main types of borrowers is shown in Fig. 9.4.
 vances to customers are, in general, illiquid assets, in that it would
 impossible to call some of them in at short notice. At the same time
 umber of advances are being repaid at any particular time.

Special Deposits. There is one other financial asset of a non-liquid
 d which the banks may hold and which must be mentioned—
 cial Deposits. These consist of balances which are placed in a
 cial account at the Bank of England and which differ from the

normal cash balances held there in that they are "frozen" and canno[t]
be withdrawn for use. Special deposits may be called for from time t[o]
time by the Bank of England as part of the mechanism by which tha[t]
Bank may try to control their lending activities, and they were intr[o]-
duced for the first time in 1960. A call for special deposits, for exampl[e]

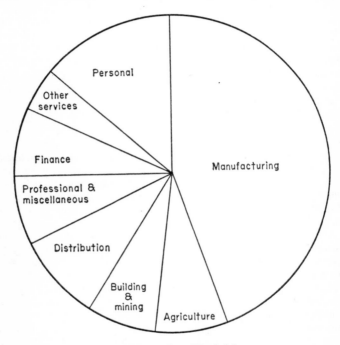

Fig. 9.4. **Distribution of Bank Advances**
Proportion of loans by London Clearing Banks outstanding at
17 March, 1971

seeks to reduce the banks' holdings of liquid assets by freezing some [of]
their cash and influencing their willingness to make loans. A release [of]
special deposits, on the other hand, is designed for the opposite effect[.]

It is important to notice that all the ways in which the bank emplo[ys]
its resources (with the exception of holding cash itself) involve t[he]
sacrifice of ready money for some asset which will bring in a larg[er]
sum at a future date. As a general principle, it may be said that t[he]

longer the wait and the greater the risk, the more profitable the loan is likely to be. To sacrifice all for the chance of big profits, however, would soon lead to the collapse of the bank, and it is the maintenance of a nice balance between profitability and ready cash which is the whole art of banking.

It should be recalled, too, that the banks are nowadays subject to some control from the Bank of England as to the disposition of their assets. In the last few years this has meant effectively that the banks have ensured that the ratio of what have been so far called their liquid assets to total deposits should not fall below 28 per cent. In May 1971, the Bank of England put forward proposals for certain changes in the manner by which control might be exercised over the banks in the future. A particularly relevant aspect of these changes was the introduction of a new notion, called the *Reserve Asset Ratio*. The document setting out the proposals referred to assets that would qualify as reserve assets. They are

Credit balances at the Bank of England (other than special deposits);
Money at call with the London Money Market (*see below*, p. 239);
Treasury bills;
A proportion of commercial bills of exchange;
British government securities with a year or less to run to maturity.

On inspection, the list of reserve assets resembles closely the assets previously classed as liquid assets. However, cash in the form of notes and coin in the banks' safes is not classed as reserve assets, but regarded as a "stock-in-trade" to meet the needs of the banks' customers. It should be noted, too, that only a proportion of bills of exchange, other than Treasury bills, qualify as reserve assets, though "long-term" government securities with a year or less to run to maturity are, not unreasonably, included. It will, of course, be necessary to wait some time before trying to assess the effectiveness of the changes.

The Bank of England

The history of the Bank of England goes back to 1694, when it was founded by Royal Charter. Originally a private concern owned by its shareholders, its great importance led to its nationalization in 1946, when the shares were taken over by the government. A few relics of its earlier ordinary banking business remain, but today the Bank is on an entirely different footing from the commercial banks, over which it exercises a profound influence. The Bank of England controls the issue of currency, and acts as banker to both the government and the

commercial banks. It also plays a key role in the government's mone
tary policy, and its activities may be discussed under the headings o
the two main departments into which it was divided by the Bank
Charter Act of 1844.

1. THE ISSUE DEPARTMENT

The monopoly of the note issue in England and Wales which th
Bank of England now enjoys is traceable to the 1844 Act, though th
process of taking over the issuing rights of other banks was a gradua
business. This means that, apart from a few banks in Scotland an
Northern Ireland which still retain their old privileges, the Bank c
England is the only institution which is allowed by law to print an
issue bank-notes. The work of this department of the Bank is illustrate
by the weekly return of its activities which it must publish, the chie
items of which are as follows—

BANK OF ENGLAND

Issue Department, 17 March, 1971
(£ million)

Notes in circulation	3,672	Government securities	3,412
Notes in Banking Dept.	28	Other assets	288

At one time the amount of notes which the Bank was allowed t
issue was very closely related to the value of the gold which it held i
its vaults. Today only a minute fraction is covered by gold but the no
issue is not completely unlimited. The remainder, which is known a
the "fiduciary issue" (from the Latin *fiducia* meaning "trust"),
covered by government securities of unimpeachable standing. Th
amount of the fiduciary issue is subject to considerable variation fro
time to time by governmental decree, in accordance with the public
need for cash. It is traditionally raised, for example, at Christmas tim
when the demand for money increases. On 17 March, 1971, it stoo
at £3,700 million. Of this amount, some £3,672 million was in gener
circulation, leaving £28 million in the Bank which could at any tim
be released without an increase in the fiduciary issue being made.

2. THE BANKING DEPARTMENT

The more important as well as the more interesting of the Bank
England's activities concern the Banking Department. Here it is th
the Bank functions as the government's bank and the bankers' ban

The similarity between Fig. 9.5, which shows the operations of the Banking Department, and Fig. 9.3 is more apparent than real. For although the Bank of England, like the joint-stock banks, is concerned with the lending and borrowing of money, it is not primarily in business to make a profit but to put into effect the monetary policy of the

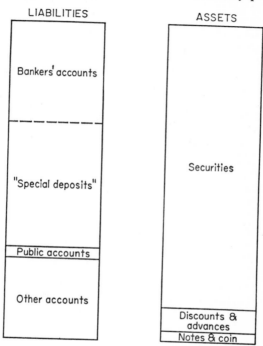

Fig. 9.5. **Bank of England**
Banking Department, Liabilities and Assets, 17 March, 1971

government. A closer inspection, too, reveals that the similarity is almost entirely confined to major headings, while the individual types of deposits and the distribution of assets differ substantially.

LIABILITIES

There are three main groups of accounts which constitute the liabilities of the Bank of England—Bankers' Accounts, Public Accounts, and others.

1. *The Bankers' Accounts.* The largest group of deposits are those belonging to the commercial banks. These are used to settle accounts between banks as, for example, after each day's clearing operations. This is what is meant by saying that the Bank of England is the bankers' bank, for as each of them adds to or draws upon its deposits, so its account goes up or down. Balances held to the credit of the commercial banks, other than the "special deposits" referred to earlier which are not available for drawing on, are the most liquid assets of the banks after the notes and coin that they hold themselves. Such balances form part of their reserve assets, which the Bank have suggested that they keep at about $12\frac{1}{2}$ per cent of total deposits. Consequently, any change in the size of the banks' credit balances at the Bank of England will, other things being equal, affect the level of their Reserve Assets—a rise may lead them to be freer, a fall to cut back on advances to their customers. This is most important, since the Bank of England is, in fact, able to some extent to control the size of the commercial bankers' accounts by dealing in securities (*see below*).

2. *The Public Accounts.* The second, much smaller, group of deposits of great importance arises from the Bank's function as the government's banker. These are called the Public Accounts, and it is under this title that the government banks its money. Thus the Public Accounts reflect the current state of the government's finances. When taxes are flowing in quickly, then the Public Accounts tend to go up, while when the government is spending faster than receipts from all its various sources are coming in, then they go down.

3. *Other Accounts.* The third group of deposits covers the small amount of ordinary banking business in which the Bank of England still indulges. The Bank's private customers in the main comprise a number of financial firms in the City and some foreign banks who like to keep an account in London.

ASSETS

The other side of the Bank's activities shows a marked difference from the search for profitable lending of the commercial banks. There are three principal groups of assets—

1. *Cash.* The notes and coins in the Banking Department are in no way a safety reserve to fall back upon as are the commercial banks' cash holdings, for the Bank of England can always have a few more notes printed if it is short of cash. It is, rather, merely the carry-over of the note issue from the Issue Department, and is available for release at any time that it is required.

2. *Securities.* Of outstanding importance among the assets of the Bank of England are the various kinds of government securities, including Treasury bills. The Bank may buy or sell these in the open market as part of a policy of trying to influence the lending activities of the joint-stock banks. When it sells Treasury bills, for instance, these may be bought by the commercial banks (or their customers) and paid for out of the balances standing to the credit of the commercial banks at the Bank of England. Such balances are, as stated earlier, regarded as highly liquid and as part of the reserve assets which they hold against total deposits. Provided that there has been no compensating movement at the same time in another component of the banks' reserve assets, a change will affect their disposition to make loans. In this case, the sale of Treasury bills by the Bank of England tends to cause a reduction in the bank's reserves and discourages them from making advances to customers. Conversely, when the Bank of England buys securities in the open market, they are paid for by the Bank and this has the effect of putting up the total of the commercial banks' cash balances. This tends to give the latter greater freedom for lending. The buying and selling of securities in this manner by the Bank of England are known technically as *open market operations.*

3. *Discounts and Advances.* Relatively insignificant by size, but none the less important, are the discounts and advances of the Bank of England. The advances are made to its private customers in the normal course of business, but the discounts are of special significance. For, although the Bank does not, as a general rule, discount bills of exchange and Treasury bills, it is nevertheless always willing to do so. Firms who do discount bills are aware that the Bank is continually available as a "lender of last resort," although they are not very keen to go to the Bank for this facility, as it is normally expensive. They may, however, be forced to do so if the commercial banks recall some of the short loans on which they are operating. The rate at which the Bank of England is prepared to discount Treasury and other fine bills is known as *Bank Rate,* and it can be changed by a formal announcement, which is usually, though not always, made on a Thursday morning. Bank Rate is generally well above the current market rate of interest, so that the Bank's business in discounting bills is very limited and only temporary.

MONETARY POLICY

The term monetary policy is given to action taken by the government attempting to control the balance of the economy through the monetary mechanism. The Bank of England plays an important part

in this because of its close relationship with the commercial banks and
in particular, of the influence which it can exert on the latters' lending
activities. When the economy seems to need expansion the banks may
be encouraged to increase the advances they make to customers, and
when the opposite pressure is required, their lending may be dis
couraged. The means by which influence can be brought to bear upon
the commercial banks are involved, but attention has already been
drawn to the ways in which the amount of the banks' reserve assets
can be influenced by the call or release of special deposits, and by open
market operations. It has also been explained how the Bank of
England sets bank rate, and it should be added that pressure can also
be exerted, in either direction, on other interest rates. A rise in interest
rates means higher costs of borrowing, and tends also to be regarded
as a signal for tighter bank lending. The converse may also apply.

It may be added that the Bank frequently uses several of its "weapons"
at the same time. It is, moreover, in a unique position for simply
persuading the commercial banks to change their policies in some way
or other. Its influence is indeed so strong that even hints dropped by the
Bank are unlikely to be ignored. Written requests, for instance, to trim
advances, which have sometimes been made, have had great force.

In May 1971, as we remarked earlier, the Bank of England made
what was generally regarded as an important announcement on the
mechanism of monetary policy. One change which has already been
discussed was the introduction of the notion of the reserve asset
ratio, which the Bank suggested might be appropriately set at $12\frac{1}{2}$ per
cent (*see above*, p. 233). It is too early to assess the full significance of
the Bank's statement, but it would certainly appear likely that attention
will in future be shifted from the old liquid asset ratio and be con
centrated on the value of those assets which qualify to be treated as
reserve assets (credit balances at the Bank of England, money at call
with the London Money Market, Treasury bills, a proportion of
commercial bills, and British government securities with a year or less
to run to maturity). The announcement of May 1971 also suggested
that future emphasis will probably be more on changes in interest rates
and calls and releases of special deposits than previously. One means
of control—the imposition of maximum ceilings on bank advances—is
certainly to be dropped. It should be recognized, however, that the
effectiveness of each of the techniques that the Bank can adopt is
dependent upon a complex of circumstances, including the entire
structure of the commercial banks' assets and the general state of the
economy prevailing at the time. Generalizations on this subject can be
most misleading, but it may be sufficient to recall that the government

has also adopted fiscal and other weapons of economic policy in pursuit of its goal of stabilization (*see above*, pp. 203–4).

The Money Market

The prime importance of the banking system stems from the fact that bank deposits are widely used to pay for transactions in the economy, and in this connexion, as we have seen, the banks function as lending organizations. But there are other financial institutions which channel borrowing and supply credit to those who are prepared to pay for it, and which make their living from the margin between the rates of interest they charge and receive. They differ from the banks in that individually they are often smaller in size but also, more significantly, in that each type of institution tends to specialize in a particular class of financial business, borrowing and lending either on short-, or long-term, and supplying credit, e.g. to agriculture, industry, house purchasers, hire-purchase consumers or the government.

Each section of the financial market is to a certain extent unique, but it is common to make a distinction between institutions which are largely concerned with longer-term lending and those concentrating on shorter-term finance. The latter group are referred to as the Money Market and involve two principal types of financial house whose business concerns bills of exchange and short-term lending—Discount Houses and Accepting Houses.

1. THE DISCOUNT HOUSES

As their name implies, these are the firms which do most of the actual discounting of bills of exchange and Treasury bills. The latter have for some years been the major source of bills in the market. A number are offered for sale each week by the Treasury and, although some variation is only to be expected as the Government's need for finance is never quite the same in two successive weeks, the value of a weekly issue in recent years has been of the order of £200 million.

There are now eleven discount houses in the London Money Market. When they discount a bill either for the government or for a private trader they must, of course, supply them with cash and to do this they borrow money largely from the commercial and other banks. This is, in fact, none other than the Money at Call which, we observed above, the banks lend at quite low rates of interest; and the discount houses are able to make a profit by charging a rate for discounting slightly above the rate which they have to pay for this accommodation. Although the bills which they discount usually become due for payment only after anything from two to six months, and the money which they borrow is repayable at shorter notice, the discount houses are not left short of funds, since it generally happens that when one bank is calling in its loans, another is offering more to the discount market. Even if this is not the case, the discount houses can always turn to the Bank of England as the lender of last resort. As they may have to borrow here at bank rate, which is normally well above the market rate, they will probably show a loss on these transactions, which they naturally try to avoid. The frequency with which the discount houses are forced "into the Bank" depends upon the general financial state of the country and the monetary policy of the government.

The discount houses hold on to a considerable number of the bills which they discount until maturity, but they are also in the habit of rediscounting some with the banks which, as we have seen, like to keep a proportion of their assets in this form. In fairly recent times they have also become quite important dealers in other government securities as these approach maturity.

2. ACCEPTING HOUSES

The willingness of the discount houses to discount bills of exchange depends, quite naturally, on their estimate of the risk that when any particular bill is presented for payment it may not be met. Consequently unless they have some pretty reliable information about the credit-worthiness of the acceptor of the bill, they will in all probability refuse to discount it at any price. For the British exporter in the nineteenth century, selling perhaps to a small firm in South America, this could have been a serious matter, had it not been for the existence of the Accepting Houses. These financial institutions, sometimes called "merchant bankers," include famous names like Rothschild, Baring, Hambros and Lazard, which appear in history books, occasionally even influencing the fate of governments. The accepting houses grew up to fill this need. By establishing agents in the major trading centres of the world, they were able to check on the financial standing of most firms of traders. They were therefore willing, in return for a commission, to guarantee that an appropriate bill would be paid on maturity, which they signified by adding their name to the original acceptor's, or by accepting the bill in his place. The British exporter would have no trouble discounting such a bill in the market, for, thus guaranteed, the discount houses know that, if need be, the Bank of England would always advance them money (*rediscount* the bill) on the strength of such "eligible paper."

Today, sixteen merchant banks belong to the Accepting Houses Committee and still perform this traditional function, though British and overseas deposit banks now also offer a similar service, and the British government operates the Export Credits Guarantee Department (E.C.G.D.) which provides assurance against risk of default by importers in a wide range of cases in return for a payment of a premium (*see below*, p. 252). The merchant banks have, at the same time, spread their activities to compensate for the declining function of accepting bills. They indulge in a certain amount of ordinary deposit banking business, and they make a speciality of offering an investment advisory service. Finally, they are often employed in the capacity of issuing houses, which, as we shall now see, are concerned with the raising of new capital for companies in the market.

OTHER FINANCIAL INSTITUTIONS

The money market, just discussed, provides a considerable amount of finance for merchants and for the temporary needs of the government but it supplies relatively little directly for the main body of industry in the country. And it has been emphasized, too, that the banks, while not completely eschewing medium- and long-term loans, have a distinct liking for those of shorter duration.

Apart from years of depressed economic activity the productive capacity and capital assets of the country are nearly always growing. As stated in the last chapter, something close to a fifth of the national income has been used for new and replacement capital in recent years in the public and private sectors of the economy. The finance for this development is provided ultimately out of the savings of persons, companies and the State. The relative importance of two of these sources has changed significantly during the last decade. The exception has been that of personal savings which, having risen remarkably from the 1950s, settled at a level of providing roughly a quarter of total savings throughout most of the 1960s. (This represents about 8 per cent of post-tax personal income.)

Company savings are the undistributed profits of corporations after tax. Their share in total savings fell steadily during the decade ending 1970, from about a half at the beginning to less than a third at the end of the period. At the same time, there has, of course, been a parallel upward movement in savings by the public sector (surpluses of current receipts over current expenditures by the central and local government plus the undistributed profits of nationalized industries), which accounted for nearly half of total savings in 1970.

Profits ploughed back into the business have generally received some tax advantages over those paid out to shareholders in the years since the Second World War, though this policy is no longer in favour as was pointed out above (*see* Chapter 8, p. 198). Expansion through the ploughing back of profits has its limits, in any case, particularly when the desired scale is large compared with annual profit rates, and it is naturally not at all available as a source of capital for completely new firms.

It is hardly necessary to point out that the channels through which funds pass, from the actual savers to the final spenders, are decidedly complex. They are, however, of considerable importance and it is necessary to examine in some detail the institutional framework for the supply of capital for industry and other long-term finance.

New Capital Issues

A major source of funds from outside the firm comes as a result of the issue of capital by offering shares on sale to outsiders. In recent years £500 or £600 million has been raised annually in this way, though the amount varies greatly from year to year with the general state of the economy. There are three main methods which may be employed—a public issue, an offer for sale, or a placing.

(i) *The Public Issue.* The most straightforward is the direct offer of shares on sale to the public. Most firms contemplating this normally prefer to obtain the co-operation of a specialist financial institution, such as the merchant bankers who undertake this work in addition to their other activities, and there are also a number of Issuing Houses which make it a wholetime function.

After the preliminary decisions about the size of the issue and the various dividend, interest and voting rights which the new shares or debentures will carry have been taken, an advertisement must be placed in the Press in a special form known as a Prospectus, containing details of the capital structure and voting rights, the financial record of the company and other particulars. A closing date for applications for shares is announced, after which the shares are allotted. If applications are in excess of the total shares advertised, some scaling-down of individuals' requests will have to be adopted. Such an issue is, of course, a definite success but there is always the risk that the result will not be so good and that, even after all applicants have been allotted shares, some will still remain unsold. This risk can be avoided by having the issue *underwritten.* This is usually done in return for a commission by the issuing house concerned, and consists merely of a guarantee to purchase for itself any shares which are left over at the end. The issuing house generally spreads this risk by getting it sub-underwritten, and nearly every house has its own list of business firms and institutions which are prepared to take up a small proportion of any issue of shares. Public issues are an attractive method of raising capital for a company but they are a costly one, involving fees, under-writing commissions, advertisements, duties, and accounting and legal charges, and for small firms they are disproportionately, and as a rule prohibitively, high. A cheaper method in general use, open only to existing companies, is to send circulars to its own shareholders offering them new shares in proportion to their current holdings in exchange for cash. Such "rights" issues may be made on favourable terms.

(ii) *Offer for Sale.* An alternative to the public issue of shares, which avoids some of the expense of the latter, is the offer for sale. The procedure has much in common with an issue by prospectus, but in this case the company sells its shares directly to the issuing house, which then disposes of them to the public.

(iii) *Placing.* Finally, especially if the issue is a small one, the company may choose not to offer the shares on sale to the public at all. Instead it tries to find a number of investors who agree privately to buy blocks of shares. This again is generally undertaken through either an issuing house or some other financial institution with suitable contacts, such as an investment or insurance company or a firm of stockbrokers. As there is less need to underwrite placings, the cost is accordingly kept down, though the commission payable tends to be higher.

The foregoing discussion of the issue of shares to the public should not be taken as implying any necessity for shares to be held directly by individual persons. Of course individuals do hold such shares, and we discussed the distribution of share ownership earlier, in Chapter 3. But our interest here is rather in the intermediary financial institutions, the existence of which provides a channel for savings of all kinds, and makes finance available for business enterprises.

Insurance Companies

The first of these institutions which we may consider are the insurance companies, which have exceedingly large financial resources at their disposal. The business of an insurance company is to take over from individuals or firms specific risks in which they are involved in return for a relatively small payment, known as a *premium*. They are able to do this because, although something may be completely uncertain for an individual, it is not so for a company which specializes in risks of a particular type. Thus a businessman can, naturally, have no idea whether his factory will have a serious fire next year, nor can any motorist know whether he will meet with an accident on the roads.

But an insurance company dealing with thousands of these risks is in an entirely different position. For the law of averages works very well with large numbers.

On the basis of claims experience and detailed statistical analysis, insurers are able to assess the risk; the essential principle of insurance being the pooling of risks and their proper classification into groups. For example, the rate of premium to insure fried fishmongers' premises against fire is much higher than that to insure those of wet fishmongers who do no frying. Likewise, in motor insurance, vehicles are classified and the claims experience under many thousands of motor policies enables insurers to fix adequate premiums to cover the cost of meeting claims and expenses and, if they are fortunate, a margin of profit. For example, the premium to insure family cars used for social and domestic purposes is very different from that to insure high-speed sports cars owned by youthful drivers.

It should be noted that some insurance business is not conducted by companies but by Lloyd's underwriters (*see below*).

TYPES OF INSURANCE

The principal types of insurance are as follows—

Marine Insurance. This mainly concerns the insurance of ships and their cargoes against maritime perils. Many of the world's shipping fleets are insured in London by insurance companies, but some of this business is conducted through the financial institution known as "Lloyd's" (so-called after Edward Lloyd's coffee house in Tower Street in the City of London, where business has been conducted since the seventeenth century). Lloyd's today is an organization with two kinds of members—underwriters and brokers. The underwriters do not deal direct with the public; all business is placed by brokers who operate on commission. The existence of a large number of underwriters greatly helps in the insurance of really big risks. Large modern luxury liners worth many millions of pounds are insured over the whole market. For while a single company or underwriter would be understandably reluctant to stand an entire risk of, say, £10 million, such a sum can be spread among a large number of insurers each of whom would only be liable for a proportion of the total in the event of a loss.

Fire Insurance. Buildings and their contents, from small country cottages to modern industrial blocks, are insured against material loss or damage by fire and kindred perils. Profits insurance is also transacted to cover loss of profits and the cost of alternative temporary accommodation during rebuilding occasioned by fire.

In recent years, too, fire departments have undertaken insurance of special (otherwise termed extra, or additional) perils such as riots, tempests, floods, burst pipes, and earthquakes.

Accident Insurance. The most recent branch of insurance is termed accident, and it embraces all types of cover not dealt with in the marine, fire and life departments (see below). The main classes of accident business include cover for motor vehicle insurance. In addition, there are several other major and minor categories dealt with under the heading of accident insurance from employers' liability for accidents to their employees at work, to damage to plate-glass windows. Engineering and aviation insurance are technically accident insurance, but on account of their volume and specialization they are dealt with separately.

Life Assurance. The fourth and most important single category, however, is life assurance. This differs from the other main types in one important respect. For, although one can take out a life assurance policy in the same way as a fire or accident policy, there is no doubt in the former case that one will in fact die, whereas there is doubt as to whether there will or will not be a fire. Hence the very name is slightly different—life *as*surance and fire *in*surance.

The risk in life assurance, then, is not whether one will die, but *when* that unfortunate event will take place. Here again the assurance company is in a position to know much better than the individual what the chances are of his living to any particular age, since roughly the same proportion of people in each age group die every year. A person wishing to take out a policy of life assurance will have to pay a premium based upon the average expectation of life of everyone in his age group. If he lives longer than the average he (or his family) will not benefit as much as if he died very young, but he will probably be too pleased about that to worry. The annual premium that he pays will usually be a constant one, in that it will not increase as he grows older, but naturally will be higher the older he is when the policy is first taken out. There are two broad alternatives between which he will have to choose.

1. *Whole-life Policy.* This is the most straightforward and cheapest type. A given annual premium results in a capital payment on his death, whenever that takes place. Personally he gains nothing but, if he has dependants, he knows that they will be provided for when he dies. If, for instance, he starts to insure when he is thirty, an annual premium of £25 will bring his heirs a sum of about £2,000 on his death.

2. *Endowment Assurance*. This gives the individual a more lively interest in the policy, since it matures either on his death or upon his reaching a certain stipulated age. The premium is rather higher than for a whole-life policy but, against that, it enables the person to provide not only for his dependants but also for his own old age. Endowment assurance policies are consequently a popular and convenient way of assuring an income in later life.

Life assurance business is divisible into *ordinary* and *industrial*: the ordinary policies with annual premium payments, which are also popular with businesses as a means of financing small pension schemes and the industrial assurance policies where the premiums are collected largely at weekly or monthly intervals, by house-to-house collectors. The latter are mainly small working-class assurances and have been declining in relative importance in recent years, though premiums from industrial business still account for nearly a fifth of the total from all life policies.

It is also generally possible for a person to choose between a policy offering a benefit fixed in advance, and one with a lower limit but with the chance of earning additional bonuses related to the company's profits. The tendency for the general price level to rise in Britain and favourable conditions in recent years have made these "with profits" policies particularly attractive and popular.

Mention should also be made of *Annuities*. These are really in quite a different category and hardly rank as assurance at all. They offer an individual, in return for a lump sum, a fixed annual payment for the rest of his life. A man aged sixty-five, for instance, can secure a continuous income of about £1 per week for every £400 put down, no matter if he lives to be a hundred and twenty. It is not uncommon for someone to take out an endowment assurance during his working life and purchase an annuity with the capital sum which he receives on its maturity, which is calculated to coincide with his retirement.

THE FUNDS OF THE INSURANCE COMPANIES

The importance of life assurance companies and, to a smaller extent, of those engaged in other insurance business in collecting savings and making them available as capital for industry is very great; for, as might be expected, the companies manage to make their profit by lending their accumulated funds in such a way as to earn more than they have to pay out. The total funds at the disposal of insurance companies of all types in 1970 was approximately £15,000 million, figure which might well be compared with the total assets of the commercial banks, though their turnover is much slower. Of course these are also accumulated funds. The amount made available each year is much smaller, but in recent years has been running at well over £500 million. Again, not all funds find their way into industry. Those of the life companies, comprising the bulk of the total, are in the best position to do so, and the distribution of their assets is shown in Fig. 9.6. Government securities which used to be the largest single type of asset, are seen to account still for about a quarter of the total, but holdings of shares and debentures in joint-stock companies now

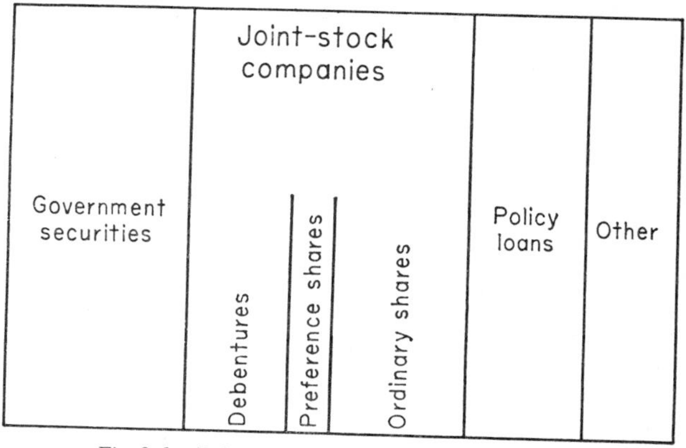

Fig. 9.6. **British Life Assurance Companies, 1969**
Total Assets

comprise about two-fifths of all assets. The proportion of funds used to purchase ordinary shares at 20 per cent is particularly significant.

PENSION FUNDS

It has already been mentioned that some businesses operate pension schemes which are administered through life assurance companies. A growing volume of pension schemes in the private and State sectors of the economy, however, are self-administered. A company may, for instance, choose to make provision for pensions for its employees by setting up a separate pensions fund of its own, to which it allocates a part of its income and on which it earns interest by buying securities. The accumulated pension (or "superannuation") funds now amount to over £7,000 million and have been increasing at the rate of some £600 or £700 million per year. Much of the total is used, as are the funds of the life assurance companies, to purchase shares in joint-stock companies, and a proportion of these have been ordinary shares.

Building Societies

The total resources of the building societies available for investment in 1970 were approximately £10,000 million, somewhat more than those of the pension funds. Building societies, however, are less important

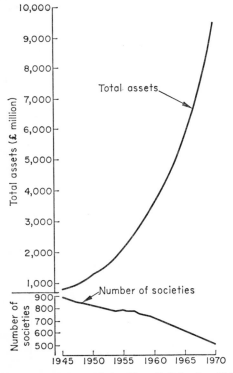

Fig. 9.7. **Building Societies, Great Britain, since 1945**
Total Assets and Number of Societies

in the general capital market as their lending is largely restricted to house purchase loans.

The societies have a history going back to the eighteenth century, when many were founded locally by small groups of people to finance the building of their own houses. Today there are about 500 of them, as shown in Fig. 9.7, though the number has been on the decrease for some time as the smaller ones have been absorbed by the rapidly expanding big societies. About half of the business is in the hands of half a dozen of the largest companies, of which the Halifax and the Abbey National are easily the most important.

The prime function of building societies is not the building of houses but the lending of money to borrowers for house purchase, and over 80 per cent of their funds is used in this way. The method of borrowing money from a building society is known as obtaining a *mortgage*. An individual desirous of buying or building a house obtains a loan for a period of years by surrendering to the society the title deed of the house and by paying interest on the sum involved at a rate varying with conditions in the market. For suitable house property in first-class condition the societies are, in normal times, prepared to lend about 90 per cent of the value of the house, so that the borrower has only the balance to find immediately from his own resources and can pay off the mortgage over a period, generally fifteen or twenty years or even longer.

The building societies obtain the money which they lend to house purchasers by borrowing in their turn at a lower rate of interest, and in this they are greatly assisted by a legal concession which makes them liable to income-tax at a reduced rate. Money is lent to them either on deposit or in return for shares in the society. Shares earn a slightly higher rate of interest than deposits and represent about 90 per cent of the total. They are, however, quite different from the shares of joint-stock companies. The distinction between building society shares and deposits is much closer to that between deposit account and current account deposits in the clearing banks. Withdrawal of funds in the form of shares formally requires a month's notice but shareholders, like those with deposit accounts at the commercial banks, can normally expect to make withdrawals much more quickly. Indeed as people have come to regard their holdings as quite liquid assets, the building societies as institutions have come to be considered as possessing some of the characteristics previously associated with banks alone.

A noticeable feature of the flow of funds into building societies is associated with the fact that their interest rates often tend to lag behind those in other parts of the market. Consequently, when interest rates are rising generally, the societies tend to experience a distinct shortage of funds and it becomes more difficult for would-be borrowers to obtain mortgages, and vice versa. The ease or difficulty of getting a mortgage, moreover, is a very important factor affecting the price of houses.

There are over three million borrowers on the books of the building societies at present. The average mortgage was around £3,000 in 1970, but is increasing as house prices rise. The societies are important

9A

collectors of small savings, but some house purchase is, also financed by assurance companies and local authorities.

Savings Banks

More conventional as channels for the small saver are the facilities provided by the National and Trustee Savings Banks, including here National Savings Certificates, Premium Bonds and other securities similarly offered by the government through the National Savings movement. Savings held in one or other of these forms earn a fixed rate of interest, all or part of which is, in most cases, exempt from

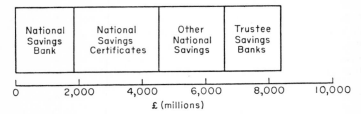

Fig. 9.8.   **National Savings, U.K., January, 1965**
Total Sums Invested

income tax; or in the case of Premium Bonds, the right to participate in a monthly lottery with money prizes, and they are quite easily withdrawn. The holding of any one individual is limited, but there are more than twenty million active National Savings Bank Accounts, and nearly ten million in the Trustee Savings Banks. The total volume of these savings stands at about £8,500 million, though the net additional sum coming forward each year, is, of course, much less. It has varied quite a lot from year to year, but during the second half of the 1960s in fact there was virtually no net increase in the total remaining invested, as other channels for savings became more attractive. The main components of National Savings are shown in Fig. 9.8.

Investment Trusts

Rather different from insurance companies and building societies are investment trusts. These are companies registered in the normal way, issuing share capital (including debentures) of their own, but not being actively engaged in running any separate business. Their function is, rather, to purchase and hold shares in other companies. The attractions that they offer to investors are full-time expert management of their holdings and an indirect participation in a much larger number of different companies than might otherwise be possible. There are about three hundred such trusts operating in Britain, and the total value of their holdings is of the order of £5,000 million.

Similar, at least superficially, to the investment trust is the *unit trust*, which became a popular medium for small savers in the 1950s and 60s. Purchasers of the "units" offered for sale, however, do not acquire shares in a joint-stock company, but receive certificates which entitle them to participate in the earnings of the trust, which are received as a result of its shareholdings in other companies. There are, therefore, no unit trust holders receiving a fixed rate of interest, as there are debenture holders in investment trusts, and the consequent absence of any "gearing" (refer to p. 45 *above*) is an important distinguishing feature of unit trusts. Small savers have been particularly attracted to unit trusts, as the units are usually sold in small denominations (£1 or less is common) and they can be bought and sold with a minimum of formality. The value of the assets of the two hundred or so unit trusts in Britain in 1970 was approaching £1,500 million.

Hire-Purchase Finance Houses

The provision of funds for hire-purchase and credit sales comes from several sources, including banks and retailers. There are also well over a thousand specialized finance houses, or "industrial bankers" as they are sometimes called, operating in Britain, though rather more than a dozen of them, such as the United Dominions Trust, are of outstanding importance. As we saw in Chapter 6 (p. 155), the total outstanding balance of instalment credit in 1970 was approaching £1,500 million, and well over half of this was owed to the finance companies. The main business of these companies is to provide capital to finance credit trade, mainly in consumer goods, especially cars, but some is certainly used by smaller firms to buy plant and machinery. The rates of interest charged on hire-purchase loans tend, as a rule, to be notably higher than on bank overdrafts. Like all financial intermediaries, the companies borrow in order to lend, and they obtain finance from depositors, the banks and discount houses, and shareholders. Deposits are generally subject to withdrawal after fixed terms of three or six months.

Specialist Finance Corporations

There have always been certain types of business which have experienced particular difficulty in securing supplies of capital through normal channels, and a number of financial institutions have been created expressly in order to meet their needs. Chief among those not adequately catered for have been the smaller firms, for whom the cost of a public issue of shares is usually prohibitive. The first signs of an improvement in their position began in the 1930s, when a few companies were established with the object of providing capital for small firms. The Charterhouse Industrial Development Company, and Credit for Industry Ltd., both set up in 1934, are two of the most important. Their scope was, however, limited, and a welcome addition in 1945 was the Industrial and Commercial Finance Corporation (I.C.F.C.), which had, for example, about £130 million lent to some 2,000 companies in 1970.

There are too many other highly specialized finance companies to list here. But finance for agriculture is available from the Agricultural Mortgage Corporation on the security of land or buildings, and insurance cover for exports from the Export Credits Guarantee Department of the Department of Trade and Industry. A sister-organization to I.C.F.C.—the Finance Corporation for Industry (F.C.I.)—which was established at the same time in order to assist the development of major industries has, however, proved a less important addition to the capital market than the Industrial Reorganization Corporation (I.R.C.) which operated from 1966 to 1971 (*see above*, pp. 88–90).

The Non-Banking Financial Institutions and the Commercial Banks

The way in which the operation of monetary policy involves the Bank of England in influencing the lending activities of the commercial banks was explained earlier in the chapter. It is now necessary to add that the existence of the non-banking financial institutions just described may be relevant to the effectiveness of this influence, because of the substitutability that exists between them and the banks. True this is limited but a would-be borrower, whose request for a loan is turned down by his bank, can always try an insurance company or other non-banking financial institution, depending upon the purpose of the loan. The relevance of the growth of these institutions in recent years to the manner of exercising monetary policy is controversial. The government has in the past used measures involving the terms of repayment of hire purchase debt as a tool of controlling non-banking credit directly, but these were abandoned in 1971. Indeed, there is no more controversial area involving major issues of economic policy than the whole question of the efficiency of monetary policy itself for controlling the level of activity in the economy. We cannot take up this matter here.

THE STOCK EXCHANGE

The Stock Exchange is really nothing more than a market place—though of a very specialized kind—where the shares of joint-stock

companies are bought and sold. The development of the business of
buying and selling shares, which as we saw earlier was closely associated
with the growth of limited liability, was greatly dependent upon the
presence of a market place where dealings in shares could take place.
For a prospective investor with capital to lend is far more likely to
invest in a company if he knows that he can always sell the shares
quickly should he suddenly need to lay his hands on some money, or
should he prefer to transfer his capital to some other company whose
prospects he now fancies.

This is not to say that the Stock Exchange has no longer a history
than that of limited liability. Business in shares had been transacted
for many years before the early stockbrokers began to meet regularly,
as did so many other financiers, in a convenient coffee house—in this
case Jonathan's, in Exchange Alley—in the eighteenth century. But
the Stock Exchange first began to resemble its present-day structure,
with a formal constitution and on its present site, about the year 1800.

Members of the Stock Exchange

The Stock Exchange is not an open market where the general public is
free to buy and sell, but in its organization rather resembles a society
or club open only to its own members, and managed by a Council
elected by them. Eligibility for membership does not require the possession of any professional qualification, but is more a matter of putting
up the necessary entrance fee and satisfying the Council of one's suit-
ability. The present membership of the Stock Exchange is of the order
of 3,500. The majority do not operate on their own but join one of the
established firms already in existence which, since the regulations
stipulate unlimited liability, are nearly all partnerships.

The Working of the Stock Exchange

Stock Exchange firms are of two distinct kinds, known as "jobbers"
and "brokers." The stockbrokers are the only members who are
allowed to deal with the general public, while stockjobbers are similar
to the wholesalers of the distributive trade, and do their business with
the brokers. Thus an investor wishing, let us imagine, to buy 1,000
shares of the Dublecrore Shoe Co. Ltd., gets in touch with his broker
and tells him of his intentions. The broker then goes on to the Stock
Exchange in search of jobbers who deal in the shares of this particular
company. Since jobbers tend to specialize in a few groups of companies
and to have their "stands" in certain parts of the "house," this is not
difficult. Approaching the jobbers in turn, he asks them the price of

the shares without saying whether he wishes to buy or to sell them for his client. The jobber then quotes him a two-way price, such as 75p–80p which, being interpreted, means that he, the jobber, is prepared to buy shares at 75p or to sell them at 80p. The difference between the two prices is the jobber's "turn" or profit, and this is the way that he makes his living. Having asked the prices from several jobbers, the broker returns to the one who offered to sell at the lowest price and, if the quotation has not risen in the meantime, reveals that he wishes to buy 1,000 shares, and the deal is then noted by both parties.

Types of Investors

The prices of securities on the Stock Exchange are liable to fluctuate daily with changes in reports of the profitability of particular companies and with the general state of optimism or pessimism in the market. For investors who intend to hold on to their shares for a number of years in order to receive an income from the dividends which the company pays, these fluctuations are not of great significance. There is, however, another class of investors who buy shares without intending to keep them for very long, but to make a profit by buying at a lower price than that at which they sell. Thus a person who anticipates that a particular company's shares will shortly rise in price buys them in the hope of selling later at a profit. He is known as a "bull." His opposite, the "bear," is the person who believes that there will be a fall in price and therefore sells, hoping that before he is called upon to deliver the shares he will be able to buy them for less than the price at which he sells. A third Stock Exchange "animal," known as a "stag," applies for new issues of securities intending to sell them as soon as dealing begins, hoping, of course, for a rise in price. It should be remembered, however, that by no means all investors are persons. The financial institutions which we have just discussed have become of outstanding importance in view of the substantial funds of which they dispose.

Settlement of accounts takes place every fortnight; each successful bull or bear will then receive from his broker a sum equal to the difference between the price at which he bought and that at which he sold his shares. If the change in price hoped for has not materialized, the investor may wish to postpone settlement. In the case of an unsuccessful bull this may be done by payment of a rate of interest known as a "contango." If the supply of shares is very short, however, the unsuccessful bear will be called upon to pay "backwardation." It is also possible to deal in "future" securities, as in commodity markets (*see above* p. 142), by purchasing an *option* to "put" or "call" shares at a date in the future—usually three months.

Types of Securities

The Stock Exchange deals in stocks and shares. There is no more than a superficial difference between these two names that a company can give to the capital that it issues, except that shares are always in fixed units of nominal value, such as £1 or 25p, while stock can be bought or sold in odd amounts, such as £101·55. The types of securities dealt in have been mentioned already at various places in this book but may be worth repeating here. Altogether there are nearly ten thousand classes of shares with a market value of well over £100,000 million, dealings in which are published daily in the Official List. These include ordinary shares (commonly called "equities"), preference shares, and debentures or loan stock; but it is usual to consider further divisions based upon the type of business activities involved. The most important general group of shares is known as "industrials," but there are many specific groups such as textiles, shipping, oil, mines, breweries, insurance, motors, etc. The shares of the largest and best known of these are called "blue chips" and are considered sound because there is always an active market in them. There are also shares in investment trusts, whose assets, it will be remembered, consist of shareholdings in a number of other companies. A final class is government securities, those of the British government being referred to as "gilt-edged" because they have the unquestioned backing of the State behind them.

Business in New Capital Issues

The principal function of the Stock Exchange is to deal in existing securities but it also plays a part in new capital issues. This can happen in two ways. In the first place, stockbrokers sometimes undertake the duties of an issuing house, particularly when a private placing is contemplated and they have sufficient contacts, through their customers and elsewhere, to dispose of the shares. Even when the issue is not made through a firm of stockbrokers, the Stock Exchange comes into the picture since any issue has a much greater chance of success if permission is obtained from the Council for the future shares to be dealt in. Actually the Council decision is never taken until the prospectus has been issued, but the law almost always requires the return of money to applicants should this permission not, in fact, be granted. This is only proper in view of the importance to the shareholder of the existence of a market where he may sell his shares. Furthermore the prospective investor may well feel less uncertain about the integrity of a firm whose credentials, he knows, must satisfy the Stock Exchange before permission to deal is granted.

EXERCISES

(For key to symbols indicating sources, *see* p. 14.)

1. Prepare a table showing (i) the total currency (notes and coin) in circulation
(ii) the total of clearing bank deposits; (iii) the Gross National Product for the las
ten years. Calculate the ratio of (i) plus (ii) to (iii). What trends do you observe
(*A.S.*) [Try to find figures for a year before 1950 (*K.S.*). Was the ratio very different
then?]

2. Obtain a copy of the latest balance sheet of any large commercial bank
Group the assets into the main categories given in the chapter, and calculate th
percentage of each group in the total. Compare results with Fig. 9.3.

3. Using a recent weekly return of the Bank of England, prepare a chart on
the lines of Fig. 9.6, showing the size of the various deposits and assets in th
Banking Department. (*B.E.*, *F.S.*, *F.T.* or *T.*)

4. Imagine that you want to borrow money in the London Money Market i
the following cases—

    (i) To discount 3-month Treasury bills to the value of £10,000 issued today
    (ii) To discount a 6-month commercial bill for £100 issued three months ago
    (iii) To discount with the Bank of England a 3-month commercial bill for £30
       issued today.
    (iv) To borrow £10,000 for twenty-four hours.

How much would you have to pay in interest at current market rates in each case
(*B.E.*, *F.S.*, *T.* or *F.T.*)

5. Draw a graph showing the trends of total advances and total deposits of th
London Clearing Banks—

    (i) For the past 10 years. (*A.S.* and *K.S.*)
    (ii) For the past 12 months. (*E.T.*, *B.E.*, *F.S.* or *M.D.S.*)

6. For the latest year for which statistics are available, calculate the proportion
of the total of new capital issues for the U.K., accounted for by the followin
industrial groups—

Chemicals and allied industries	Other manufacturing industries
Engineering, shipbuilding and	Public utilities, transport and
electrical goods	communication
Food, drink and tobacco	Distributive trades

                                           (*A.S.*, *B.E.* or *F.S.*

7. Prepare a historical graph showing the total assets and total holding
of ordinary stocks and shares of life assurance companies in the U.K. over th
past five years. Calculate the proportion of total assets held in this form each year
(*A.S.* or *F.S.*)

8. Make a list of all building societies whose assets exceed—

    (i) £100 million,
    (ii) £25 million,

and then calculate the percentage (*a*) of total assets, (*b*) of the total number o
societies, represented by (i) and (ii). (*W.A.*)

9. Prepare a chart showing the net receipts (total receipts minus total payment
for the following classes of national savings for the past ten years—

National Savings Bank	Trustee Savings Banks
National Savings Certificates	All National Savings (*A.S.*)
Premium Bonds	

10. Imagine that you have £10,000 to invest, £1,000 in each of the following groups of securities—

British government stock	Oil companies
Foreign government stock	Retail shops and stores
Textile companies	Vehicle manufacturers
Mining companies	Breweries
Steel and engineering companies	Miscellaneous industrials

Select one class of shares of a company in each group, and calculate how much profit or loss you would show if you bought the shares today and sold them in three weeks' time. Would you have done better to sell today and buy in three weeks' time? (Disregard stamp duties, stockbrokers' commissions, contangos, etc.) (*E., F.T.* or *T.*)

11. Construct a table with columns showing the level of total savings made in each of the last five years by (*a*) persons, (*b*) companies and (*c*) the public sector. Calculate—

(i) the percentage each of these classes bears to the level of total savings in each year,

(ii) the percentage of the total national income saved by all three categories together in each year.

(*A.S.* Refer to the table "National Income—Combined Capital Account" or *F.S.* Refer to the table "Financial Accounts, Net acquisition of financial assets".)

12. Prepare a graph showing the trends in the following interest rates over the last five years. (i) the average yield on industrial ordinary shares; (ii) the average yield on long dated British government securities; (iii) Bank Rate. Are the movements associated in any way? (*A.S., B.E.* or *F.S.*)

CHAPTER 10

International Trade

REFERENCE has been made many times in earlier chapters to the part that specialization plays in the promotion of economic efficiency inside Britain. Individuals specialize in different occupations, firms in various branches of production, and regions tend to concentrate on one or more particular industries. Nations, however, differ from each other in certain fundamental respects more than regions. These differences are largely political in origin. The most important arise, first, from the fact that factors of production are on the whole able to move more freely within countries than between them, and, secondly, from the existence of separate currencies that nearly all nations possess. There are additional matters, like variations in taxation, economic and social policies and in general ways of life, but they may be regarded as lying behind the two differences noted, and adding to their strength.

Specialization and International Trade

Nevertheless, it is only a very small step from regional specialization to the specialization which takes place between different countries. For nations, like individuals and regions, usually find that they are best suited to certain lines of production rather than to others, and international trade exists to effect the exchange of the products of one nation against those of another.

Some of this interchange of goods takes place because most nations are incapable of satisfying their needs for every product. In the main, this is due either to the uneven dispersion of minerals over the world, or to the existence of different climates in different areas. Thus, for example, Canada is very rich in nickel deposits, Spain and Italy in mercury and South Africa in gold, while we in Britain have virtually none of any of these metals. Again, climatic differences are responsible for the inability to produce certain agricultural crops. Britain with her temperate climate virtually cannot grow such tropical and sub-tropical products as coffee, tea, cotton, rubber or cocoa. The only way in which we can obtain any of these or other agricultural and mineral products which are not produced here is by importing them from abroad in exchange for goods which we, in turn, produce for export.

Apart from the complete inability to produce certain goods, a major part of international specialization and consequent trade springs up because nations find that, although they can produce many different types of goods, they are nevertheless very much better at producing some of them than others. These differences tend to be reflected in relative prices and it becomes profitable, therefore, to concentrate on the production of those goods for which a country is best suited, producing more than is actually needed for home consumption and exporting the surplus to other countries, importing in exchange goods for which other nations are in a more advantageous position. International differences in the size of the labour force and in its particular skills, in the amount and fertility of the land, and in the quantity of capital equipment that has been accumulated over past years, are the principal factors which make such specialization profitable. They explain why, for example, although we in Britain can and do produce meat, we find that it pays us to buy some of our requirements from other countries like Argentina and New Zealand, where land is more plentiful, and to export instead manufactured goods, which our fairly ample labour supply and accumulated equipment and skill enable us to do relatively more efficiently.

The Pattern of World Trade

It will help us to appreciate the special significance of Britain's foreign trade if we start from a broader basis, taking the world as our canvas. It is important to realize, for instance, which are the major world trading nations. Fig. 10.1 sets out details of the value of the total imports and exports of the twelve leading countries, which together are responsible for approximately two-thirds of all the international trade carried on. Between these leaders, however, it is immediately apparent that there are great differences. The scene is dominated by the United States, which exports and imports nearly a sixth of the world total. Germany is her nearest rival, and the gap has been narrowing in recent years. The United Kingdom, Japan and France are all of roughly equal importance behind them. This situation presents a very different picture as far as the U.K. is concerned from that of earlier years, for this country has been undergoing a period of long-term decline in her importance in world trade. Before 1960, the U.K. was in second place as world exporter and importer, and earlier, at the turn of the present century, our share in world trade was approximately one-third.

But the size of a country's exports or imports can be very misleading as a guide to the significance of foreign trade to that nation. A very large country can have an extensive foreign trade which is nevertheless disproportionately small in comparison with that of a much less important nation. The relationship between the value of imports and the total national income, which is shown for a number of countries

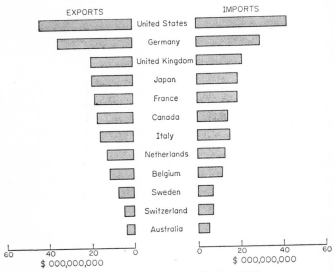

Fig. 10.1.   **Major Trading Nations, 1970**
Values of Exports and Imports (in $ U.S.)

in Fig. 10.2, is one indicator of the wide differences which exist. Thus the U.S.A., which is the world's leading importing country, depends much less on imports than the majority of others, and only about 5 per cent of her total income is spent on imported goods; while a relatively small country like Denmark spends over one-third. Belgium is even more dependent on imports than Denmark; the Netherlands spends more than half of its income on imported goods, and we in this country spend something between a quarter and one-fifth. Thus, although a decline of, say, 50 per cent in foreign trade in the United States would make a fair hole in the total volume of world trade, it would make comparatively little difference to the United States itself.

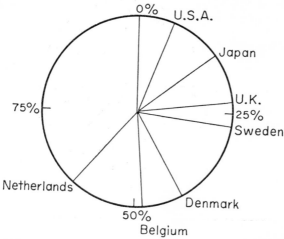

Fig. 10.2. **The Relationship between Imports and National Income, Selected Countries, 1969**

Imports as a Percentage of National Income

(The percentages are measured separately for each country from the "12 o'clock" origin.)

n the other hand, the complete cessation of imports by Denmark ould have not much more than a 1 per cent effect on world trade as whole, but it would very gravely disrupt the Danish economy.

he Trade of the United Kingdom

lthough we can obtain a rough guide to the importance of foreign ade to any country by comparing the value of its imports with its tal income, the only thorough way of assessing this is to consider in etail the actual goods which it imports and exports, and the various untries with which it trades. We shall, accordingly, proceed to exam- e the commodity structure and regional distribution of the trade of e United Kingdom.

)MMODITY TRADE

1e principal goods which Britain imports and exports may first be scussed with reference to Fig. 10.3.

Imports. The outstanding feature of Britain's position in the world onomy has long been characterized by her great dependence upon

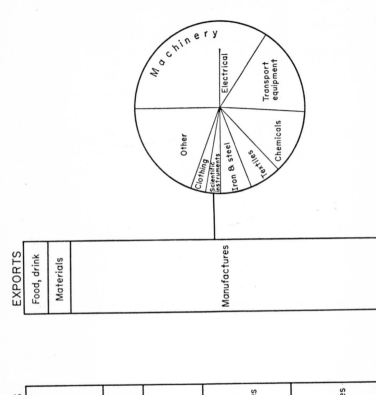

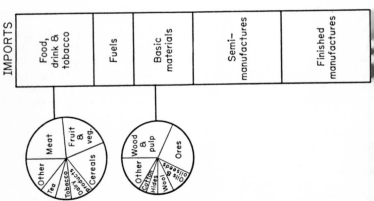

foreign sources of supply for essential raw materials and foodstuffs. It is, however, no longer true to think of this country as purchasing only primary products. The importance of these items in the import bill has diminished substantially as substitute synthetics have been developed, production has swung away from raw material consuming industries such as textiles, and domestic food production has remained reasonably high. Nevertheless, foodstuffs, fuel and basic materials still account for about half of total imports.

Among foodstuffs, meat of most kinds is the chief item, closely followed by fruit and vegetables, cereals, especially wheat, dairy produce (like butter and cheese), tobacco and tea. Other important foodstuffs imported include sugar (although some is produced in Britain), beverages, especially wine, and fish.

The fuel imports are almost entirely petroleum, over three-quarters of which by value arrive in its crude state. Petroleum is, in fact, the most valuable single category of imports. In addition to being a fuel, it also provides the basic material for many industrial and chemical products (*see above*, Ch. 5, pp. 124–6). The other important basic materials are wood and pulp, especially from the huge coniferous forests of Northern Europe and North America, and wool, the raw material of the Yorkshire textile industry. Among the metal ores, iron to supplement the domestic deposits for the steel industry predominates, but smaller quantities of many others, from antimony to zinc, are also imported. Other primary products brought from overseas include oil and oilseeds, hides and skins, cotton for the Lancashire spinning and weaving trades, and rubber, used in motor-car tyres and many other products.

The category of semi-manufactures includes the non-ferrous metals, copper, aluminium, zinc, lead, etc., that are not technically raw materials, since to save shipping space they are not generally imported in the form of ores, but are first processed to remove the valuable metal which is brought into the country in the form of bars and ingots. The chief other semi-manufactures are paper, board, wood products and precious stones. The dividing line between semi- and finished manufactures is not, perhaps, easy to draw, but the latter category has been growing more rapidly than any other class during the course of the decade ending in 1970, at which date they accounted for about 25 per cent of total imports—roughly double their share in 1960. Three-quarters of the finished manufactures are capital goods, especially machinery; the most important consumer goods being clothing and cars.

Exports. The contrast between the pattern of British imports, with the emphasis still on food and materials, and British exports is very

striking, if a little less so than a decade or more ago. For these product
are conspicuous only by their insignificance in our export trade. I
view of the volume and range of our food imports it is perhaps surpris
ing that we export any food at all. Nearly all the foodstuffs are in ver
small quantities, however, though there is one item of importance–
Scotch whisky—for which there is a great foreign demand. Th
category of materials includes fuels and lubricants. The only product
worthy of mention are petroleum, wool and other textile fibre
Exports of coal are no longer at all significant. As we saw in Chapter :
this is part of a long-term decline. The rate of coal exports has bee

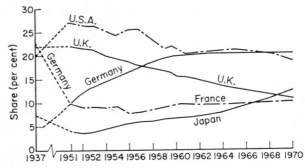

Fig. 10.4.   **Percentage Shares in World Trade in Manufactures,
1937 and 1951–70**

less than 5 million tons per annum in recent years, compared with
pre-war average of 50 millions.

Manufactured goods, on the other hand, are the solid backbone
British exports. It is no longer true that we are the major manufacturi
country in the world, and our share in world exports of manufactur
has fallen to under 11 per cent, taking fourth place after German
U.S.A. and Japan (*see* Fig. 10.4). But it is nevertheless still the case th
the United Kingdom lives largely by selling manufactured products
the world market, and these account for nearly 90 per cent of Briti
exports.

Our knowledge of the structure of British industry is quite a goo
guide to the particular types of manufactured goods on which v
concentrate, and it should be realized that the pattern in 1970 is ve
different from that which existed in the early years of the prese
century. Textiles, for example, which in 1913 accounted for abo

50 per cent of total British exports of manufactures, had dwindled in importance to about 5 per cent, and had been overtaken by chemicals and several other products. Pride of place is now taken by machinery, which, with transport equipment (mainly vehicles and chassis), brings in about half of the total receipts from manufactured exports, while chemicals, textiles and iron and steel bring in another quarter.

GEOGRAPHICAL DISTRIBUTION OF UNITED KINGDOM TRADE

The commodity composition of British imports and exports is only one aspect of our overseas trade. It is also important to know something about where those commodities come from and go to—our leading suppliers and largest overseas markets. This is shown in diagrammatic form in Figs. 10.5 and 10.6 where, for convenience, the countries of the world have been divided into four groups—Europe, the Sterling Area, America and the Rest of the World.

1. *Europe.* The countries of Europe have been our most rapidly growing trading partners in recent years. They accounted for more than 40 per cent of our imports and exports in 1970. Almost half our European trade is with the countries of the Common Market (*see below*, pp. 281–4). Germany is our major market and supplier of imports (mainly manufactured goods of various kinds). She is followed by the Netherlands, which sends mainly dairy produce, bacon, fruit and vegetables and other foodstuffs. France (manufactures, wines and spirits), Italy (fruit and vegetables and manufactures, especially textiles and cars), and Belgium and Luxemburg (mainly manufactures) complete the Common Market list of countries in 1970.

About a third of our European trade is with the countries of the European Free Trade Association (E.F.T.A.), formed in 1960 with the United Kingdom as a member. Sweden is our most important E.F.T.A. partner, supplying us especially with iron ore, timber, wood-pulp and manufactures thereof. Denmark is another large market and supplier bacon and dairy produce), and so are Norway, Finland and Switzerland as can be seen in Figs. 10.5 and 10.6.

Trade with Eastern Europe can also be seen to be on a relatively small scale, though it has been growing at much the same rate as that of the rest of Europe in recent years. The U.S.S.R. itself is easily the most important country in the group, sending us (cereals, wood and pulp, machinery, etc.) more, however, on balance than we send to her. One other European country which does not belong to any of these groupings, but which is particularly worthy of mention is Spain supplier especially of fruit, vegetables and wine).

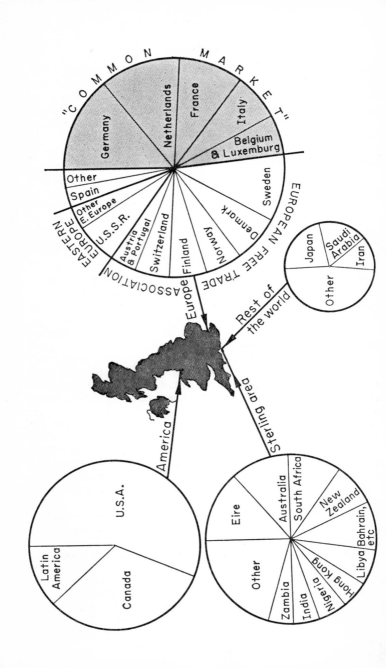

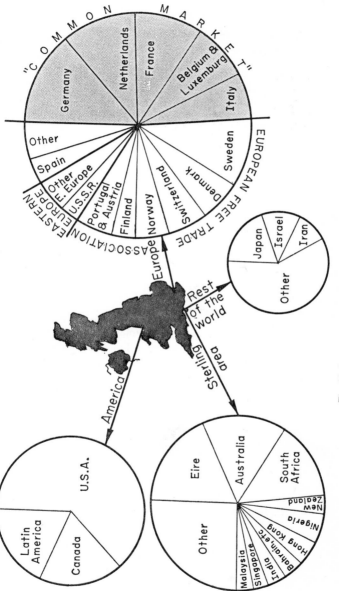

Fig. 10.6. U.K. Exports by Destination, 1970

It should be emphasized that these trading patterns relate to the years leading up to 1970, when the U.K. was not a member of the Common Market. The negotiations between the existing and new candidate members of the Common Market, which ended in 1971, are likely to see some major regroupings, and very possibly, changes in the structure of intra-European trade.

2. *The Sterling Area*. The second major grouping of countries are those in what is known as the Sterling Area. This arrangement finds its origin in the early 1930s at the time of world economic depression when many countries which conducted most of their trade with Britain or in sterling agreed to observe certain financial restriction which will be discussed below, but which helped to prevent world trade declining still further in the 1930s. All the countries of the Commonwealth, except Canada, are members of the sterling area, as are a number of others including South Africa, Eire, and several countries in the middle east.

The Sterling Area as a whole accounted for not much more than a quarter of British foreign trade in 1970. Though still, therefore, substantial, there has been a significant and quite long-term decline in the relative importance of this group. About half of our trade with the Sterling Area is with the developed countries, Eire, Australia, South Africa and New Zealand. As world trade expanded since the Second World War, that of Britain with the Sterling Area lagged well behind and especially so with regard to these developed members. The major countries which imported and exported to and from the U.K. in 1970 were Eire (livestock, especially beef cattle, meat, dairy produce and beer); Australia (cereals, meat, fruit, dairy produce, sugar, aluminium and wool); South Africa (fruit and vegetables, metals, ores and diamonds); New Zealand (dairy produce, meat, especially lamb, and wool). Other important Sterling Area suppliers and markets are the oil-producing countries in the middle east (Bahrain, Kuwait, Qatar etc.), Hong Kong (miscellaneous manufactures, especially clothing and toys), Nigeria (vegetable oils and tin), India (vegetable oils, textiles and hides and skins), Zambia (copper), Malaysia and Singapore (rubber), Kenya (tea and coffee) and Jamaica (sugar and fruit).

Again it should be emphasized that the picture given is that of trade in 1970. In so far as new trading arrangements may be made in the 1970s between the U.K. and countries in Europe, as mentioned in the previous section, this may very likely mean that the decline in the relative importance of Sterling Area trade to Britain will continue and perhaps even be accelerated.

3. *America.* Trade with the countries of the American continent is not now very much less important to the U.K. than that with the Sterling Area. It is, of course, dominated by the United States, which engages more than 10 per cent of both our import and export trade, and has been our largest single trading partner for more than a decade. The principal goods which the United States sends to Britain are, as might be expected, manufactures, but that country is also one of the most richly endowed in the world with natural resources, and exports to Britain some of these, especially cereals, tobacco, paper, pulp and several non-ferrous metals. Though a long way behind the U.S.A., Canada happens, nevertheless, to be the second largest supplier of imports to the U.K. of any country in the world, the value of her trade being at least twice the size of that of any Sterling Area country, and only approached at all in magnitude by Germany. Canada exports many products to us, but particularly wheat, wood and pulp, paper, and several of the base metals including copper, nickel and aluminium with which she is richly endowed. Both Canada and the United States are more important as suppliers than as markets for the United Kingdom. The same is true also of the group of Latin American countries, though each is of relatively small importance. Brazil (iron ore, coffee and other foodstuffs), Chile (copper) and Argentina (beef and wool) are the three leading Latin American suppliers in the U.K. market.

4. *The Rest of the World.* Trade with one or other countries in the three groups already discussed accounts for over 90 per cent of the total for the United Kingdom. None of these countries is of outstanding importance. Japan leads the field, but it should be emphasized that this country, though one of the leading world international traders (*see* Fig. 10.1, p. 260), does remarkably little business with us (sending a range of miscellaneous manufactures, chemicals, tinned salmon and other food). Iran and Saudi Arabia, with their mineral oil, are worth a special mention, but the only other country of any significance, and that mainly as a market, is Israel (exporting mainly citrus fruits).

INVISIBLE TRADE

1970 was not a typical year for U.K. foreign trade. Rather it was an exceptionally favourable one. Our imports and exports were almost exactly in balance. This is an extremely rare occurrence. Much more commonly the value of U.K. imports exceeds that of U.K. exports. In order to explain how this can come about it is first necessary to point out that there is no reason, in principle, why the value of exports and imports should be exactly equal in any particular year. As long as other countries are prepared to make loans (or even gifts) to us, we can always have an import surplus. And if we are making loans and gifts on balance to foreigners, we can expect to have an export surplus.

Having said this it must next be admitted that international trade is not confined to the exchange of physical commodities but that there are, in addition, other types of transaction involving payments to, or receipts from, foreigners for "invisible" services rendered. These invisible imports and exports are important for the United Kingdom and the principal categories are set out in Fig. 10.7.

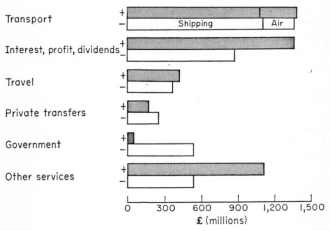

Fig. 10.7.   Invisible Trade, U.K., 1970

On the top lines are the invisible exports. These result in receipts for services rendered to foreigners in exactly the same way as do exports of physical goods. The lower lines show payments made for invisible imports. Transport is a large item and covers, in the main, freight charges for shipping imports and exports. This used, traditionally, to be a net credit to the United Kingdom. The decline in our merchant fleet relative to those of other countries, mentioned earlier, is largely responsible for the present small deficit, though this is approximately offset by a favourable balance earned by the civil air services. Foreign travel payments and receipts cover spending by tourists and travelling businessmen. They have shown relatively small net credits in the last few years, largely reflecting a surge of popularity among foreigners for holidays in Britain. The item called private transfers consists mainly of personal transactions, involving the transfer of assets by migrants and gifts. They fluctuate from year to year, but are usually a net outflow for this country. The major source of drain among invisibles is government expenditure, the bulk of which is military, but includes also diplomatic expenses and grants made to developing countries in the form of aid.

Two categories of invisible transactions traditionally show substantial net credit balances for the United Kingdom. Interest, profit and dividends received by British residents exceed the payments in respect of the same items to foreigners, reflecting the accumulation of assets abroad over a period extending back into the nineteenth century. The second main source of invisible receipts consists of the category described as "other services." This contains several highly significant items, about which precise information is not available, but it includes the earnings of the "City of London" in respect of banking, insurance and other financial services, and of royalties.

When all the invisible credits and debits are added up, the result is the balance of invisible transactions, and it is usually favourable to the United Kingdom. When the balance of visible and invisible transactions are taken together, we refer to the result as the *Current Balance*, or the Balance on Current Account (though some texts use the term the balance of total trade).

Current Balance

Trends in the current balance since 1952 are shown in Fig. 10.8. Before then, it may be noted, the early post-war years had been very serious ones for this country, when large deficits on visible trade were incurred while we were beginning the task of recapturing lost export markets. In those early years, too, even the balance of invisible transactions was unfavourable, reflecting among other things the wartime damage to the British merchant-shipping fleet, the continuance of heavy Government expenditure on armies of occupation, the sale of British-owned interest-earning assets in foreign countries and the debts incurred to foreigners during the hostilities. Concentrated efforts produced a reduction of the deficit, but re-armament and the Korean war in 1951 caused a big increase in the value of imports and deferred return to more normal peacetime conditions.

The main features of the period since then can be appreciated by studying the chart. It shows, in the first place, a consistently favourable balance of invisible transactions, offsetting, in most years, an adverse balance of visible trade.

More striking is the pronounced instability of the visible trade

balance. This is not more than a graphic description of the fair
regular alternation of ups and downs in the balance of trade whic
have distinguished the post-war period. To some extent the cris
years have been associated with the building up of stocks of ra
materials and other goods. But they have often also reflected bas
movements in the economic position of the country and in governme

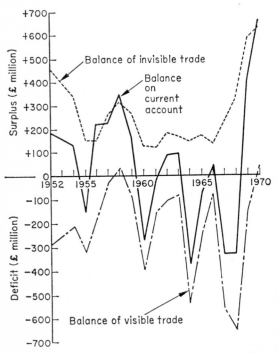

Fig. 10.8. **Balance on Current Account, U.K., 1952–70**

policy. In particular, when the economy has been booming a
incomes rising fast, imports were at the same time increasing relativ
rapidly. And the same periods have, to some extent, probably be
ones of relatively rising British prices, when our exports were rat
less competitive in world markets. The years of improvement,
contrast, have tended to be associated with lower levels of econo
activity.

THE TERMS OF TRADE

The trade balance is influenced not only by the relative prices of competing exporters, but also by the relative costs of imports compared with the value of exports. Movements in the latter, in fact, played a significant part in the deficits of the early post-war years as well as in the later recovery. For if the prices of imports go up while those of exports fall, or even remain constant, it is necessary to export a larger quantity of goods in order to pay for the same amount of imports. This is exactly what was happening between 1938 and 1951, and is clearly brought out by reference to the United Kingdom's "terms of trade" (Fig. 10.9), which shows the relation between import prices and

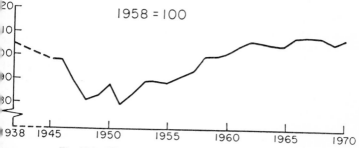

Fig. 10.9. Terms of Trade, U.K., 1938 and **1945–70**
Quantity of Imports Obtainable for a Fixed Quantity of Exports
(An upward movement corresponds to an improvement
in the U.K.'s terms of trade.)

port prices. More precisely, the terms of trade are defined as the ices of exports divided by the prices of imports. Thus, if, from one ar to another, the prices of imports rise more than the prices of ports, the fraction represented by the terms of trade will fall in lue and become less favourable in the country in question. The rp downward movement of the terms of trade of the U.K. until 51, revealed in the chart, emphasizes the further problem which faced s country, as the prices of the goods which we needed to import, ecially foodstuffs and raw materials in short supply after the war, e in price more rapidly than did those of the mainly manufactured ds that we export. Later, the improvement in the terms of trade 1952–53, when the prices of our imports fell while those of exports

remained roughly constant, considerably eased the situation. Sin
then the terms of trade have moved slowly but fairly steadily in favo
of the United Kingdom in most years.

The Balance of Payments

The current balance is, as we now know, the difference between
total payments and the total receipts for goods and services made o
a certain period of time between the residents of one country and th
of the rest of the world. It is, however, only one aspect of the financ
relations between a country and foreigners. Payments are made a
received for other purposes than the purchase of goods and servic
We in fact already met a most important example of another type
transaction—foreign loans—when we were discussing the way in wh
a country might maintain an import surplus.

The full *Balance of Payments* contains details of *all* transactic
between the residents of a country and foreigners. Those transactic
which are not put into the Current Account belong in what is called
Capital Account (sometimes called the Investment and Financ
Account). Indeed, it may be a useful starting point here to think of
latter as being an account of the way in which a current deficit can
financed. For the balance of payments is an accounting concept wh
must, of necessity, balance, as we shall see.

For example, if the current account is in exact balance, then
total of all payments to foreigners for goods and services equals
sum of all receipts from them. There is no need for any entries in
capital account at all (though, of course, there may be some for
lending and borrowing going on, there need be no *net* lending).
however, there is a current account deficit, then this must be matc
either by net borrowing from foreigners, or by running down of
gold, foreign currencies or holdings of other international assets,
as reserves. Conversely, if there is a current account surplus of exp
over imports, this must be matched by an equal and opposite net
of lending to foreigners, or by a rise in the foreign currency reserve

Alternatively we can think of all the currency flows togeth
payments and receipts for goods and services and all lending
borrowing. If we add all these together, we end up with a *net* surplu
deficit currency flow, and this must be matched or balanced b
equal and opposite change in the reserve asset position. This wa
looking at the balance of payments may now be illustrated by inspe
the table which sets out the transactions for the United Kingdon
the average of the years 1968–70. (The average of three years is t
because the items included tend to fluctuate so much from one yea

another that it is hard to find a single year which can be considered reasonably "typical".)

Turning first to the Current Account, we find that the U.K. had a favourable current balance of £250 million. From the first line in the Capital Account, however, we see that there was a net outflow of capital of £50 million (represented by lending by U.K. residents to foreigners of £50 million more than borrowing from them). We might, therefore, expect that there would be an improvement in our reserve asset position of £200 million (£250 million minus £50 million). This is, in fact, exactly what did occur, though we can see that this improvement took two slightly different forms—£180 million of it was represented by a repayment of debts incurred in some earlier years when the balance of payments had been less favourable to us; and £20 million did take the form of an increase in our gold and foreign currency reserves.

UNITED KINGDOM BALANCE OF PAYMENTS
1968–70 annual average
£ million

I. CURRENT ACCOUNT

Visible Imports	.	.	.	7,330	Visible Exports	.	.	7,070
Invisible Imports	.	.	.	3,610	Invisible Exports	.	.	4,120
Total Payments for Goods and Services	.	.	.	10,940	Total Receipts for Goods and Services	.	.	11,190
Current Balance	.	.	.	250				
				11,190				11,190

II. CAPITAL ACCOUNT

Foreign Lending by U.K. (net).	50		
Inflow of Gold and Reserves .	20		
Repayment of Intergovernmental Loans	180	Balance on Capital Account .	250
	250		250

Our next step should now be to add a commentary on the trends in our own foreign lending and borrowing, which have been taking place. In particular, we should like to know how much long-term investing by U.K. residents in the rest of the world has been occurring, not to mention the equally important extent of the reverse flows of long-term investment by foreigners in Britain. Knowledge of these matters would tell us not only something about the extent of foreign ownership of industry, but also (a) in the longer term, how much the U.K. may hope to gain or lose on balance from interest, profits and dividends from new foreign lending, (b) how much short-term lending and borrowing has also been taking place, which, if suddenly reversed, might cause a major financial crisis.

In the nineteenth century, the United Kingdom was the traditional and largest single supplier of foreign capital to the rest of the world, and today she still continues to make long-term foreign investments on a considerable scale. The flow of capital is, however, no longer one-way, and investments by foreigners (particularly from the U.S.A.) are also being made in Britain. Indeed we have seen a reflection of this in the Current Account of the Balance of Payments, as payments, as well as receipts, of interest, profits and dividends.

Foreign investment can take one of two forms—*direct* investment in overseas subsidiaries of home-owned companies; and *portfolio* investment, involving merely the purchase of foreign securities or of shares in foreign-owned companies. These kinds of transactions appear in the capital account of the balance of payments, but it is exceedingly difficult to know, especially with portfolio investment, which are really long term. Once a person, or a company, has bought shares in a foreign company, it may hold on to them indefinitely, perhaps acquiring a controlling interest and taking over the running of the company business. On the other hand shares may just as easily be sold the week after they were bought. So, although some clearly short-term capital movements (such as the purchase of a 3-month bill of exchange) can be identified, it is much harder to be sure how much potentially long-term investment is truly so. The difficulty has apparently been increasing in recent years, and the official balance of payments now fails to split the capital flows into long and short term, except for official long-term capital outflow, consisting substantially of aid to developing countries (generally kept close to the United Nations' target of 1 per cent of the national income).

This does not mean, of course, that we are completely ignorant of the volume of long-term lending and borrowing that has been taking place. It is estimated that outflows and inflows have been running fairly parallel, at a rate of roughly £600 million per annum each in the late 1960s; and that the value of overseas investment in British industry by 1970 was of the order of £7,000 million. British-owned foreign assets, on the other hand, were estimated to be worth about double that sum—one reason no doubt for the net credit in our favour of interest, profit and dividends, which we noted in Fig. 10.7 on page 270.

GOVERNMENT INTERVENTION

Much of the foregoing has been written in terms of Britain and other countries doing this and that, whereas this is really only a shorthand way of saying that it is individual persons, firms and traders in a country who actually do the importing and exporting. The government has only entered the picture in respect of its direct spending and lending, but in fact the government can play a much more important role than this.

Countries suffering balance of payments pressures, for instance, do not, and, indeed, cannot carry on indefinitely borrowing and using up their reserves, and the government may well consider alternative courses of action to improve the situation. It is true that the general level of activity in the country may eventually fall and bring with it the relief of falling imports. The government may, indeed, even choose this way out and actively encourage it. But they may also consider alternative policies, controlling payments and receipts for international transactions, or, alternatively, hoping for an improvement as a result of letting the value of its currency fall. We shall now examine the measures which have been taken to this end and, since so many involve the restriction of trade, the international co-operation which has grown up for trade expansion.

Trade Restrictions

Some of the obstacles to trade are natural ones, like the cost of transport, which, particularly with bulky items, may well explain why trade is not carried on. Many, however, are artificial and designed by man specifically to discourage international transactions to obtain relief from balance of payments pressures or to encourage the development of domestic production by offering a degree of protection from foreign competition, for political, strategic or, in some cases, economic reasons.

1. TARIFFS

Among the best-known of these restrictions are import duties, or tariffs. These consist of taxes placed by the government on the import of certain commodities, often calculated as a percentage of the value of the good in question. They are, therefore, able to serve two purposes:

(a) of raising revenue for the State, and (b), of raising the prices of imported goods, leading generally to a reduction in the quantity imported and, where applicable, to a privileged position for the domestic producers of the particular commodity taxed.

The British tariff, as we saw in Chapter 8, accounts for a substantial proportion of total government revenue. The great bulk of this revenue, however, comes from a mere handful of items, and import duties on the vast majority of commodities are aimed rather at the restriction of imports, either to protect particular industries, or to reduce the value of imports to a level nearer to that of the country's exports.

During the second part of the nineteenth century and the first decade or two of the twentieth, Great Britain eschewed import duties almost entirely. A departure from this policy of "free trade" came in 1915 in the middle of the First World War, when the so-called "McKenna" duties of $33\frac{1}{3}$ per cent on the value of imports were imposed. These taxes on imports fell principally on a relatively small number of luxury goods, such as motor cars, and were designed largely to reduce imports and so save shipping space for wartime essentials. The duties were nevertheless, retained after the end of hostilities and, in 1921, were supplemented by a second list, known as the "Key Industry" duties. These were originally planned to last five years but, like the McKenna duties, they were continually renewed. They were prompted by the desire to protect certain key industries (mainly precision instruments, optical glass, wireless valves and synthetic organic chemicals) from foreign competition by imposing a tax on them, originally of $33\frac{1}{3}$ per cent, now varying between 10 and 50 per cent.

These two sets of duties were, it should be stressed, of relatively minor significance, and the great majority of British imports in the 1920s were still admitted duty-free. It was not until the world economic depression at the end of the decade had brought about a great decline in British exports that a major departure from the free-trade principle of the nineteenth century took place. The immediate cause of the Import Duties Act of 1932 is to be found in the very unfavourable balance of trade in the previous year. The need to improve the situation by reducing the amount of imports found its expression in the imposition of a general tariff of 10 per cent on all imported goods with certain stipulated exceptions (principally foodstuffs and raw materials) known as the "free list." The same Act established an Import Duties Advisory Committee with power to recommend changes in the rates of duty on particular items although, since 1939, this function has been placed directly into the hands of government departments.

Substantial reductions in rates of duty on goods entering the United

Kingdom have been made since 1932 in agreement with other countries. Special interest attaches to those affecting countries of the Commonwealth and in Europe, which are discussed below.

2. IMPORT QUOTAS

A second obstacle to the free flow of international trade consists of the direct quantitative restriction of imports. This is usually achieved by the issuing of licences for which intending importers must apply to the government. It is a very much more certain way of bringing about a reduction in imports than the mere imposition of a tariff, though it brings in no revenue to the government. For this reason import quotas were widely adopted in the immediate post-war years, when the balance of trade was most unfavourable, and they were then, accordingly, much more important than the tariff in restricting imports. Since that time a considerable easing of quantitative import restrictions has taken place, particularly so far as those affecting the countries of Western Europe are concerned. Such liberalization was initiated by the Organization for European Economic Co-operation set up at the time of the "Marshall Plan", which offered U.S. aid to European countries shortly after World War II. The removal of the few remaining restrictions continues, however, to be an objective of policy of the existing international organizations.

3. EXPORT CONTROLS

There are two quite different kinds of export controls, those restricting and those encouraging exports. Neither is of very great importance in Britain. There are, however, a few items for which a licence is required before export, but these are mainly of strategic or military importance, or specialities like national art treasures.

Direct export subsidies are naturally unpopular with the countries with which one is competing, and international organizations to which the United Kingdom belongs have rules restricting their use. Indirect encouragement to exporters may, however, be given by granting exemption from certain internal taxes. Rather different are the more general services that the government provides. The Department of Trade and Industry, for instance, operates an export insurance scheme against risk of default, and maintains extensive information services for exporters. In addition, in 1964 the British National Export Council was formed to provide more systematic assistance.

4. EXCHANGE CONTROL

The controls discussed so far have mainly involved direct intervention in the country's visible trade. Exchange control, in contrast, is concerned specifically with restrictions on the purchase and sale of foreign currencies for any purposes. It is, therefore, the means by which the government can try to exert an influence on invisible transactions and on international flows of capital. In the United Kingdom, measures of exchange control were introduced at the outbreak of war in 1939, and were continued after the end of hostilities. Since then they have been progressively relaxed, though not to the same extent for residents and non-residents.

To understand the system of exchange control in Britain, it is necessary to emphasize that our overall trading position with the rest of the world consists of favourable balances with some countries and unfavourable balances with others. So long as the favourable balances are in currencies which may be converted into the currencies of countries with which there are deficits, trade can be conducted on a *multilateral* basis, as distinguished from *bilateral* trade where two countries maintain a separate and quite distinct trading relationship.

Currency convertibility, however, has been limited to some extent by exchange control regulations. During and shortly after the Second World War, for instance, the world experienced a severe dollar shortage due to the fact that the United States (and, to a lesser extent, Canada) was in the unique position of possessing the food, materials and other resources urgently needed for European reconstruction. Exchange controls on dollar transactions were used until the shortage ended.

At the present time sterling held by foreigners not resident in the Sterling Area (*see above*, p. 268) can be freely changed into other currencies. Sterling Area residents, on the other hand, while generally free to make transfers within the Area itself, are still restricted by exchange control regulations in respect of transactions with outsiders.

International Co-operation

Individual countries found it easy enough to impose restrictions on international trade during the depression of the 1930s. But many provoked retaliation, quickly destroying short-term advantages to one country, and it is not surprising that it has taken groups of nations acting together and by agreement to start lifting them. Broadly speaking, international co-operation has taken one of two forms; that which has been directed towards securing agreement between a large number of countries in fairly limited aims, and that which has sought a more ambitious programme among a relatively small group of nations.

1. REGIONAL

The two groups of countries with which the United Kingdom has been most involved in regional trading agreements are the Commonwealth and Western Europe.

(a) *Commonwealth Preference.* The desire to promote trade between the U.K. and the countries of the Empire has always been strong in Britain, and effect to this policy was given in 1919 when the import duties on McKenna goods were reduced by one-third if they came from Commonwealth countries. This preference given to Empire products was greatly increased after the appearance of the general tariff in the spring of 1932. In the summer of that year an important conference of Commonwealth countries had been held in Ottawa, as a result of which *Imperial Preferences* on goods entering the U.K., and vice versa, were extended. These agreements are now called *Commonwealth Preferences,* though they are also extended to certain non-Commonwealth countries, outstandingly the Republics of Ireland and of South Africa. It has been estimated that they originally covered over half of U.K.-Empire trade, and they were largely responsible for the substantial increase in that trade which followed in the 1930s. At the same time the advantage they offered in the form of reduction of U.K. import duties probably amounted, on average, to at least 10 per cent. By the 1960s, however, their significance had been notably diminished, and the direction of British trade had swung quite remarkably away from the Commonwealth, as we saw earlier in this chapter (*see* p. 268). In the 1970s, with probable U.K. membership of the Common Market (*see below*), such preferences as continue to exist will most likely become of minor significance.

(b) *Western European Unions.* Economic integration in Western Europe did not proceed far before the outbreak of the Second World War. The aftermath of war, however, and the need for reconstruction provided a stimulus for co-operation. American aid was instrumental in establishing the machinery of the Organization for European Economic Co-operation (O.E.E.C., now the Organization for Economic Co-operation and Development, O.E.C.D.), and assisting intra-European payments problems by adapting the existing Bank for International Settlements (originally set up in 1930 in connexion with German reparations payments after the First World War).

Then, in the 1950s, a major new grouping of countries was formed, the Common Market, followed a short while later by a second grouping, known as the European Free Trade Association.

The Common Market. The origins of the Common Market can be found in the attempts begun shortly after the end of the Second World War to form an economic union of Belgium, Luxemburg and the Netherlands in *Benelux*. These three countries, together with France, Germany and Italy, also made an agreement in 1952, known as the European Coal and Steel Community, to form a unified market for these products. The same six nations met again in 1955 at Messina, and decided to form a common market. Two years later they had signed the Treaty of Rome, establishing the European Economic Community (E.E.C.) and setting out a programme for the gradual elimination of tariffs between member countries and the substitution of a common external tariff to be applied by all members on goods coming from outside. The Community espoused also a number of other and wider aims, such as the free movement of persons, services and capital, co-ordination of economic and social policies with regard to matters like restrictive practices, agriculture and taxation, and the harmonization of social services.

The government of the United Kingdom was initially reluctant to join the Common Market for a variety of reasons, some political, such as the relinquishment of sovereignty, and some economic, such as the question of support for agriculture. Britain was also in a somewhat different position from the Six, because of the strength of her trading and other ties with the Commonwealth.

Instead of joining the Common Market, therefore, the U.K. made an agreement with Austria, Denmark, Norway, Portugal, Sweden and Switzerland, and these seven countries set up the *European Free Trade Association* (E.F.T.A.) in 1960, to which was subsequently added Finland. The aims of the E.F.T.A. were notably less wide than those of the E.E.C. In addition, although the E.F.T.A. countries agreed to abolish tariffs on each other's goods, they did not accept the need for a common external tariff on goods coming from outside the union. This procedure allowed the U.K. to maintain, therefore, some of its Commonwealth preferences.

In the years that followed, the six Common Market countries enjoyed a good deal more favourable economic conditions than those in the United Kingdom. Their rates of growth of national income per head of the population were significantly and consistently higher in the 1960s, and their balances of payments gave, in general, less cause for anxiety than ours. At the same time, Britain's trade with the Commonwealth, as we have seen earlier in this chapter, was in any case declining. The U.K. therefore decided twice in the 1960s to apply for membership, which she would probably accept if the terms of entry offered were satisfactory.

The first application was effectively turned down by the French, under the late President de Gaulle, in 1962. But a second application (made by a Labour government) led to the completion of negotiations (by a Conservative government) in 1971 which were regarded by the government and others as satisfactory, though they were not without their critics. If, as expected at the time of writing, the terms are approved by the British parliament, they will lead to several major changes in British economic life, some of which have been referred to earlier in this book (the different agricultural policy, pp. 104–5; the Value Added Tax, p. 200). Tariffs should be abolished between the U.K. and other members of the Community, and the Common External Tariff adopted, in five stages, ending in 1977. The Common External Tariff does not apply to countries which enjoy a special relationship with the E.E.C. Part of the terms negotiated by Britain were precisely for arrangements, especially for the transitional period, for some countries, such as New Zealand, which, because of the importance of the U.K. market to them, would otherwise be faced with major adjustments in order to reorient their economies to accommodate the new position.

The highly controversial and complex issue as to whether or not Britain should in fact join the Common Market on the terms offered has been widely debated. The supporters of entry believe that, on economic grounds, the larger market would give British industry advantages of large-scale economies; that the abolition of tariffs would make for better specialization between the U.K. and other members of the union, and for more effective competition against any tariff-protected domestic monopolies. In effect, they hope that the higher rates of growth achieved by the Six would become available to Britain.

The opponents of entry, on the other hand, see little further scope for economies of large-scale production in Britain resulting from membership of the Community. They are more concerned with worse specialization between the U.K. and the rest of the world than with better specialization within the Common Market; since the Common Agricultural Policy means that Britain must discriminate in her tariffs against low-cost food producers outside the Community, so that the housewife's food budget would certainly rise. Opponents of entry are also more worried about the formation of stronger international monopolistic combines, than they are hopeful of lower tariffs bringing more effective competition.

Several attempts to quantify some of the gains and losses likely to follow U.K. membership of the E.E.C. have been made, but they do not indicate any overwhelmingly clear case for or against entry. Moreover, there are of course many other aspects of this most complex issue, several of them political and inherently unquantifiable. At the time of writing, it seems highly likely, if not quite certain, that Britain will join. By the time that this book is in the shops it is completely certain that no one will know whether the decision taken was the right one.

2. GLOBAL

Outside the regional groupings already mentioned, there have of course been other movements towards some kind of economic integration in Eastern Europe, Latin and Central America, and elsewhere. The main international institutions with which the U.K. has, however, been otherwise involved are organized on a global rather than on a regional basis. They may best be considered under one of two headings. The first group are primarily concerned with financial arrangements for the settlement of international balances of payments; the second are more directly concerned with the promotion of trade itself. The origins of both stem largely from two important world conferences held in the mid-1940s.

1. *The Institutions of Bretton Woods.* The experience of the 'thirties, when international trade was at a very low ebb, prompted the calling, under the auspices of the United Nations, of a conference of forty-four nations at Bretton Woods in New Hampshire, U.S.A., in 1944. The principal object of this conference was to try to ensure that the expansion of international trade after the war should not be held up for the want of credit facilities. As a result two institutions were established.

(*a*) *The International Monetary Fund.* Attention has been drawn in this chapter to the way in which a country's balance of payments is liable to show very considerable fluctuations from year to year, and to the possibility of financial crises when sudden large-scale outflows of short-term capital occur. Such events were not uncommon in the 1930s, and they are by no means unknown in the post-war world.

Financial crises are easier to ride if a country has a substantial reserve of international liquid assets, which allow it a breathing space for the crisis to pass, or for the taking of appropriate remedies. In the absence of adequate reserves the country may well be forced into taking undesirable courses of action which may involve a reduction in the volume of trade, unemployment, etc., whose effects are likely, moreover, to spill over to other countries as well.

Gold has traditionally been the most universally accepted liquid asset for settling international payments. In addition, the major currencies, especially the pound and the U.S. dollar have enjoyed periods of international use for this purpose. The shortage of liquid assets for debtor countries in the 1930s however led the major world trading countries at Bretton Woods to propose the formation of the International Monetary Fund (I.M.F.) to alleviate the situation. The I.M.F. draws resources from quotas related to the size of member countries. These provide a second line of reserves that can be used by members in balance of payments difficulties, by direct loan and by the arrangement of "stand-by credits." These facilities have provided some relief, but the failure of the system to provide expansion of all international liquid assets at the rate at which the value of world trade was expanding led to general agreement that further provision of international reserves was essential. As a result new reserve assets, known as Special Drawing Rights (S.D.R.s), were introduced in 1970 to supplement those already in use.

One other feature of the work of the I.M.F. must be mentioned. The experience of the 1930s had led to one kind of practice which had what are widely regarded as most unfortunate consequences. This was what is called competitive exchange depreciation. For a country under balance of payments pressure, some temporary relief could be obtained by allowing the value of its currency to fall, effectively reducing the price of its exports to foreigners, and producing a temporary benefit until other countries retaliated. Membership of the I.M.F., therefore, has involved support for a policy of trying to maintain reasonable stability in the exchange rates between the currencies of the member countries, though it was always recognized that any country faced with a fundamental and lasting imbalance would have to be allowed to change the value of its currency. However, in fairly recent times official opinion in a number of leading countries has begun to move away from support of this policy to one of allowing more flexibility for devaluation and revaluation of currencies. There is therefore the possibility that the I.M.F. may consider revising its own formal attitude towards this matter.

(b) *The International Bank for Reconstruction and Development* (*I.B.R.D.*, and known, too, as the World Bank). The second of the institutions set up at Bretton Woods was also intended to make loans to individual countries which they might otherwise find difficult to secure. The difference in its function is that the loans of the Bank, unlike those of the Fund, are intended for much longer duration and are specifically designed to enable countries to undertake large-scale projects of economic reconstruction and development. The resources of the International Bank, as those of the Fund, were subscribed in the first place by the members of the institution in accordance with a schedule of quotas, but the Bank also has the power to raise additional capital and has, in fact, obtained most of its financial resources by borrowing in the capital markets of member countries—in New York and Western Europe—issuing its own securities (I.B.R.D. bonds) in the process. The loans which the Bank makes to various applicants have, in principle, to be tied to specific projects, and the bulk have been used for so-called "infrastructure" development, to provide the framework for economic growth where private investors are not usually so forthcoming, e.g. power and transportation. In this connexion the Bank has built up a number of advisory services, including expert field research teams to assist both it and borrowers to assess and improve particular development schemes. I.B.R.D.'s loans are intended to be made on normal commercial terms. The rate of interest charged is the same for all borrowers but varies from time to time with the rate the Bank itself has to pay on borrowed money. The World Bank has made loans totalling more than thirteen thousand million dollars between the start of its operations in 1947 and 1970; a substantial amount, though small in comparison with the total of aid from all sources. Many of its early loans were for the reconstruction of post-war Europe, but latterly it has been concentrating more on lending to the developing countries of Asia, Africa and Latin America.

The International Bank is obliged by its Charter to operate under certain conditions, one of which is that all its loans must be covered by Government guarantees from the borrowing countries. These are not always easy to obtain for private businesses, and an affiliated but independent organization, the International Finance Corporation (I.F.C.), was established in 1956 to help supply this particular set of needs, and its powers have since been extended to allow it to purchase ordinary shares in suitable private companies.

A second affiliate of the World Bank is the International Development Association (I.D.A.). This institution was established in 1960 to make so-called "soft" loans to less developed countries on generous terms. They have been for very similar schemes to those financed by the Bank itself, and the I.D.A. also only grants a credit to a government after satisfying itself of the economic soundness of a particular project, to which the loan is then tied. The main distinguishing feature is that no interest is charged to the borrower (though there is a $\frac{3}{4}$ per cent service charge) in order to help developing countries which are faced with special balance of payments problems. In view of the nature of its loans, the I.D.A. does not borrow on the world market, and its available funds are therefore limited to what it can raise from member governments.

2. *The Institutions of the Havana Charter.* If the meeting of the nations at Bretton Woods can be said to have been moderately successful, this was in no small measure due to the fact that it had fairly limited objectives. The second important post-war international conference, which sat for four months in Havana, Cuba, in 1947–48, set itself the much wider task of drawing up a code of conduct to govern all aspects of international trade. The document which was drafted, known as the *Havana Charter*, envisaged the formation of a new International Trade Organization to supervise international trade. But, largely since its chief sponsor, the United States, never set the draft Charter before its Congress for approval, it remains a dead letter.

One aspect of the Havana Charter which did, however, come into effect has been that concerning trade restrictions. The body concerned, known as G.A.T.T. (the General Agreement on Tariffs and Trade), was established in 1947 in Geneva, with the object of securing a general reduction in the tariff levels of the twenty-three countries signatory to the Agreement, in the event of the Charter not coming into force. A number of active meetings have been held, at which the contracting parties bargained with each other over the conference table, reducing and stabilizing the import duties on each other's goods on a reciprocal basis. A major so-called "Kennedy Round" of tariff negotiations was concluded in 1967, and the number of G.A.T.T. participants now exceeds seventy. A special chapter was added later to the Agreement designed to assist poorer developing countries whose trade is impeded by restrictions, but this particular economic problem has been taken up separately at special international conferences called under the auspices of the United Nations Organization (*see below* U.N.C.T.A.D.).

The United Nations Organization. No description of international co-operation on a global scale would be complete without mentioning the United Nations. For although that body is primarily political there are also important economic aspects to its work. Many of these are carried out under the auspices of the Economic and Social Council (E.C.O.S.O.C.), which operates various Commissions, including regional ones for Europe, Asia and the Far East, Latin America and Africa. There are also specialized United Nations agencies, among the best-known of which are F.A.O. (Food and Agriculture Organization), W.H.O. (World Health Organization) and I.L.O. (International Labour Organization), which like the I.M.F. and I.B.R.D. are associated with E.C.O.S.O.C. The functions of several of these bodies are advisory, including the calling of international conferences and the publication of reports and bulletins on economic affairs. One important series of United Nations conferences have been those held to discuss the specific economic problems of the developing nations. Two of the U.N.C.T.A.D.s (United Nations Conference on Trade and Development) have taken place in 1964 and 1968. The major issues have been the adequacy of aid, and the provision of preferential tariff treatment for the developing nations in the markets of industrial countries.

EXERCISES

(For key to symbols indicating sources, *see* p. 14.)

1. For the latest year available find out (i) the value of imports (in U.S. dollars), and (ii) the population, of the following countries—

Australia	South Africa
Belgium	Switzerland
Canada	United Kingdom
Germany	United States
India	

Calculate the value of imports per head of the population in each case. (*W.A.*)

2. Calculate the percentage increase in the value of total exports from each of the following countries since last year, and place them in rank order of growth—

Australia	Italy
Denmark	Japan
France	Sweden
Germany	United States
	(*W.A.*)

3. Calculate the percentage of the total value of United Kingdom imports accounted for by each of the following groups of commodities in the last year for which you have statistics—

Food, beverages and tobacco	Mineral fuels, lubricants, etc.
Crude materials	Manufactured goods

Compare your results with 1960. (*A.S., M.D.S.* or *W.A.*)

4. Calculate the percentage of the total value of United Kingdom exports of manufactured goods accounted for by the following items, in the last year for which statistics are available—

Chemicals	Iron and steel
Transport equipment	Textile yarns and fabrics
Electrical machinery	

(*A.S., M.D.S.* or *W.A.*)

5. Prepare a graph on the lines of Fig. 10.9 showing the quarterly movements in the U.K. Terms of Trade for the past three years. (*M.D.S.*)

6. Prepare two historical graphs for as many of the last five years as you can obtain statistics showing—

i (*a*) the value of U.K. imports, *and* (*b*) the volume of U.K. imports.

ii (*a*) The value of U.K. exports, *and* (*b*) the volume of U.K. exports.

Can you suggest any reason why the series may not have moved parallel to one another in either case? (Hint: Do exercise No. 5 first). (*M.D.S.* or *A.S.*)

7. Following Exercise 6, prepare another graph showing again the value of exports and imports of the U.K. for the same period *and* the Gross Domestic Product. Which series have moved in closest association? (*M.D.S.* or *A.S.*)

8. Make a list of the countries of origin of all things bought by your family this week which came from abroad. What proportion came from Commonwealth, and from Common Market countries?

9. Make up a table showing the total value of the official reserves (of gold, convertible currencies and Special Drawing Rights) held by the U.K. for each of the last five years. Use these figures to prepare a new column in the table showing the changes in reserves for each period. What proportion is the average level of reserves to the average value of imports? Is it the same in the first and in the last of your years? (*A.S.* or *M.D.S.*)

10. Prepare a table showing details of the balance of payments of the U.K. last year, including the following items, and compare your results with the table on p. 275—

Value of imports	Balance on current account
Value of exports	Balance of Investment and other capital
Balance of visible trade	flows
Balance of invisible trade	Changes in official reserves.

(*M.D.S.*, *F.S.* or *A.S.*)

Index

Where references are given in heavy type this indicates the main source.